Economic Development

CONSULTING EDITOR:
DONALD DEWEY
Columbia University

Alfred A. Knopf   NEW YORK

JOHN M. CULBERTSON
University of Wisconsin

Economic Development:
An Ecological Approach

To My Father

But if we accept the reasonings on which the dogma of Progress is based, must we not carry them to their full conclusion? In escaping from the illusion of finality, is it legitimate to exempt that dogma itself? Must not it, too, submit to its own negation of finality? Will not that process of change, for which Progress is the optimistic name, compel "Progress" too to fall from the commanding position in which it is now, with apparent security, enthroned? . . . A day will come, in the revolution of centuries, when a new idea will usurp its place as the directing idea of humanity. Another star, unnoticed now or invisible, will climb up the intellectual heaven, and human emotions will react to its influence, human plans respond to its guidance. It will be the criterion by which Progress and all other ideas will be judged. And it too will have its successor.

John Bagnell Bury, *The Idea of Progress*

Preface

This book began as an attempt to apply to the theory of
economic development a model of self-feeding processes
derived from my work in macroeconomic theory. My
intention was to illustrate how economic development can
be a self-contained process not dependent on foreign aid or
apocalyptic discontinuities. This material still seems to me
to have merit, and its attenuated remains are buried in
Chapter 6.

The book was broadened in its next stage of development
to include an application to the theory of economic
development of a number of other methodological
innovations of recent decades. At about this time, I found it
increasingly difficult to avoid admitting that the attempt to
explain economic development is a losing game, mainly for
the important reason that "economic development" is a
state of mind or a delusion. No revelation could be more
painful to one who has just written a book on the theory of
economic development.

In its final form, the book is a consideration of the
determinants of the standard of living that does not
presume the existence of a fixed path of progress known as
economic development. It also attempts a realistic and
naturalistic interpretation of the relation of population
growth and environmental destruction to the standard of
living, which theories of economic development do not and
cannot do.

To work out an ecological view of the economy, of man
and nature, which is the approach of this book, is a task
that perhaps will occupy economic thought for decades.
This will involve coming to think of changes in economic
systems and living standards within a naturalistic
framework, as an aspect of the continuing process of
interaction of systems of living things with one another
and with the inanimate elements of the earth. The
framework developed here provides one approach to this
task, as well as a framework for integrating the classical
and neoclassical economics with the recent literatures on
the population explosion, environmental destruction, and

the ecological approach or systems approach to man and nature.

The subject, however much we might wish it otherwise, has serious implications for the future of man and of earth. The theory developed here indicates that the pessimistic warnings that present-day civilization may come to an early end merit serious consideration. It also explains why the optimistic theories of economic development are believed, although they are false—or because they are false. I commend this argument to the consideration of those who care what happens to man's civilization, and who can contemplate that the truth may be other than we wish it to be.

I acknowledge with thanks research support from the Graduate School of the University of Wisconsin. I wish to express my appreciation especially to Robinson Hollister, as well as to Peter Lindert, Deborah Milenkovitch, and Hans Schmitt for comments on an earlier draft, and to Phillip Fawcett for thoughtful discussions. For secretarial help, I am much indebted to Mrs. Phyllis Nelson.

John M. Culbertson

MADISON, WISCONSIN
AUGUST 1970

Contents

Economic Development

CHAPTER **1 / Introduction**

The prospects of our civilization and our species are depicted very differently in two recent bodies of scholarly literature. The literature of "economic development" tells an optimistic story of progress, advancement, modernization, the conquest of backwardness, "development." This process is depicted as potentially automatic, and potentially universal if only its present beneficiaries will give enough foreign aid to help the rest of the world through "the take-off into sustained growth."

The recent literature of human ecology, emphasizing environmental destruction, population growth, and their implications, paints a picture equally extreme in its pessimism. It depicts the human species as headed not for unlimited progress but for the destruction of advanced civilization:

> *This is essentially the situation that confronts civilized man: he has thrown off the primitive customs that prevented population increase—so long ago that their former existence is today scarcely even credible—and he draws more and more for his livelihood on the united resources of the world, many of which are rapidly diminishing. The sequence now has reached the point where, if the increase is not controlled and halted within the next two or three generations, a crash seems certain; and even if some fragments of the human species were to survive, civilisation as we know it would almost certainly have been lost for good in the resulting chaos.*

3

*With the fossil fuels—coal and oil—largely gone, there might be no
"second chance."* [1]

This book explores the relation between these radically different stories of man's position and prospects. More specifically, it treats within a naturalistic, or ecological, or scientific
framework the topics covered in the modern theory of economic development. It offers a critical evaluation of the recent literature based on the concept of "economic development." The line of thought here developed leads to these
theses:

1. A scientific approach to the subject supports the pessimistic view that modern civilization faces a fall for want of
the control systems required to meet nature's terms for survival.

2. The existing academic literature on the theory of economic development is not based on a scientific or ecological
view of man. Rather, it derives from the myth of Judeo-
Christian culture that the universe revolves about man and
that the passage of time will raise him to an exalted position. In its secular version, this theory is the doctrine of
progress.

3. What is required to preserve civilization is the adoption
of societal control systems to limit population, preserve the
environment, and maintain or increase economic efficiency.
Such actions will not happen automatically with the passage of time but will require a radical departure from past
policies and from the predominant current view of man's
relation to nature.

THE SCIENTIFIC VIEW OF MAN AND NATURE

Man's relation to nature has been defined only recently. Darwin's formulation of the basic theory of natural selection is

[1] V. C. Wynne-Edwards, *Animal Dispersion in Relation to Social Behavior*
(Edinburgh: Oliver and Boyd, 1962), p. 402. See also Harrison Brown, *The
Challenge of Man's Future* (New York: Viking, 1954), pp. 222–223.

only a century old. Some important elements in the story have been discovered only within the past decade. These new pieces of knowledge involve the issues most in question in interpretation of man's present position: the role in natural selection of population control, environmental preservation, and the disciplining of individual behavior in the interest of group survival.

The scientific version of the story of life centers around the behavior of the species in relation to requirements set by the environment—by nature's rules. The story is one of continuing change and adaptation, to an indeterminate outcome. The usual pattern for groups and species is one of rise and fall. The expected outcome for each is ultimate extinction.

The classical economics of a century and a half ago reflected this logic. Its view of man was not one of inexorable and unending progress; rather, it fit the naturalistic pattern of rise and fall. An increase in economic efficiency temporarily would raise the standard of living, but this would increase population, which, given the limited endowment of nature, would lead to a reduction in living standards. Growth of population would bring the standard of living back to its lowest common denominator, that at which groups were willing and able to reproduce.

This story, expanded to deal with the lagging effects of industrial pollution and the exhaustion of resources, resembles the one we have just been hearing from natural scientists. The classical economists saw no way out. They did not believe that the human species—except within certain classes—could limit its numbers in order to preserve a high quality of life.

The mainstream of economic thought down to the present day remains consistent with this approach. It emphasizes the dependence of the standard of living on limited natural resources and on productive efficiency, and the dependence of efficiency on political and economic institutions that are not universal, nor readily attainable. The potential depressing effects of population growth on living standards is a traditional theme of economics, as is the finite endowments of natural resources. Thus the mainstream of economics is not inconsistent with a naturalistic view of man's prospects and his relation to nature. The inconsistency is, rather, between the mainstream of economics and other naturalistic approaches to man and nature, on the one hand, and, on the other hand, the approach based on the concept of "economic development."

THE THEORY OF ECONOMIC DEVELOPMENT

The accelerating revolt against the scientific view of man since the latter part of the nineteenth century carried the prevalent pattern of thought far away from this story. The theory of economic development that has predominated since the 1940s involves a basically different model of man and nature. Rather than the open-ended evolution of interaction, of rise and fall, it asserts unilinear evolution, single-track change: progress, advancement, the overcoming of backwardness, modernization, the realization of man's potential, "development."

Nature in this story does not severely limit man's future; it is his instrument, his birthright to be used to the full. Man's development requires the full development, the fullest exploitation, of the resources placed there for his use. Rather than leading to man's humiliation from his inability to discipline himself and to meet nature's demands, the process of economic development leads to man's self-realization, his exaltation.

This story gives little importance to nature. It reflects a humanistic or anthropocentric view of the universe and man's place in it. Progress becomes a free gift after a time, reflecting technological advance or man's natural betterment. The impediments to progress are depicted in humanistic terms: old-fashioned ideas of laissez faire and unwillingness to use man's new powers to the full, exploitation and class greed, lack of political reform or modernization. The rate at which success occurs depends on human virtues and vices; the overcoming of those human vices permits collection of man's dividend of progress.

Humanistic stories of man's inexorable progress and ultimate exaltation are by no means new. However, the influence of the prophets of progress[2] has varied over time, perhaps reaching a high-water mark in the 1950s and 1960s, when it was reflected in the modern theory of economic development. For the prophets of progress influenced not only everyday thought and the ideas of political leaders and policy makers, but also the academic theory of economic development. The vocabulary of the subject shows this influence: "Economic development," the "take-off into sustained economic growth," the role of foreign aid in helping nations achieve the take-off, the reliance on the concepts of "reform" and "modernization."

The obvious inconsistency of these two views of man's position and prospects, stemming basically from two interpretations of his relation to nature, calls for a critical reconsideration of the subject. As the predictions of the pessimists make clear, the stakes are very high. The approach taken here is to develop the naturalistic or ecological view of man and nature and then to use this as a framework for interpreting and evaluating the present-day theory of economic development.

LESSONS OF EXPERIENCE

The need for a fundamental rethinking of the theory of economic development is argued also by the outcome of the ambitious programs on its behalf undertaken in the decades since World War II. The 1960s did not justify "the revolution of rising expectations." Neither did they prove to be "the decade of development" that President Kennedy had envisioned. As Currie has stated, "In brief, the picture is one of floundering and uncertainty. There is a feeling on all sides that the magnitude of the effort since 1949, and particularly since 1961, should have led to greater results and that something must be

---

[2] As a reminder of the recurrence of these themes, this phrase is from *John Adams and the Prophets of Progress* by Zoltán Haraszti (New York: Grosset and Dunlap, 1964). Adams applies the skeptical or naturalistic view to the romantic view of progress as introduced to modern thought by Rousseau, Condorcet, and others. The terms of discussion have not been greatly altered since then.

inadequate in the various approaches, but at this point agreement ceases."[3]

As increases in economic output in much of the world have been largely offset by growth of population, the improvement in the quality of life of the mass of people has been disappointing. "One-half of humanity is hungering at this very moment. There is less food per person on the planet today than there was 30 years ago, in the midst of a worldwide depression."[4] The predictions of impending massive famine made by a number of responsible students cannot but be a matter of concern.[5] The fact that even the present unsatisfactory situation is not sustainable because it involves a rapid rate of environmental destruction only adds to our dismay. In view of the expectations engendered by the theory of economic development (which define, in a sense, its testable implications), surely something has gone wrong.

If one is sufficiently resolute in his adherence to the modern theory of economic development and its underlying premise that change is progress, he can try to explain away the bad news. The fact that many nations have not yet experienced a take-off into sustained economic growth simply means that foreign aid must be greater than it has been, because there is *some* amount of foreign aid that would provide enough capital to bring about a take-off.

According to this interpretation, the population problem will eventually take care of itself—this is a part of the automatic timetable of progress. When nations reach the stage where population growth must be limited, it automatically will slow down. The way to solve the population problem in poor societies is to bring about economic development, which, in time, will correct the population problem. Past events, in this view, disclose no error in the theory, but only the need

[3] Lauchlin Currie, *Accelerating Development: The Necessity and the Means* (New York: McGraw-Hill, 1966), p. 69.

[4] Robert S. McNamara, Address at University of Notre Dame, reprinted in *Christian Science Monitor,* May 3, 1969, p. 10.

[5] *Ibid.* See also William and Paul Paddock, *Famine—1975!* (Boston: Little, Brown, 1967), p. 8; Paul R. Ehrlich, *The Population Bomb* (New York: Ballantine Books, 1968), Chap. 2.

for greater efforts, for more of the same policies.

Although such a position is logically coherent, there is a growing uneasiness among those who have accepted this approach in the past. Perhaps the basic weakness in this interpretation is the (once this fact is pointed out) obviously humanistic nature of the story, its dependence on a universe in which nature is cut to man's measure. The implicit view that the universe has somehow been constructed so that man's population will prove to be automatically self-limiting demands in 1970 great credulity. The assertion that a parallel automatic mechanism exists to preserve the environment, in view of what man has done to it in the past, yet further strains one's will to believe. Perhaps the unrealism in this theory's depiction of man's relation to nature is becoming so flagrant that the theory cannot survive even another decade. The course of events motivates us to reconsider the subject from its foundations.

AGENDA

This book attempts to sketch a naturalistic approach to the topics of the present-day theory of economic development, to use this as a basis for evaluation of other approaches, and to indicate in broad terms the kinds of policy to which the naturalistic or ecological view of man and nature seems to point. Chapter 2 briefly characterizes the naturalistic or ecological approach to man and nature and contrasts it to the set of ideas underlying the present-day theory of economic development.

The theory of living standards used in this study is outlined in Chapter 3. The next three chapters deal with the three main components of this theory: the determinants of population and its relation to living standards, the relation of living standards to environmental preservation, and the determinants of increase in economic efficiency. Other major topics of the theory of economic development are then considered in Chapters 7 through 13. A critical discussion of the recent literature of the academic theory of economic development is given in Chapter 14. Some implications of the ideas developed in this book are considered in Chapter 15.

CHAPTER 2 / The Determinants of Living Standards: Alternative Approaches

What determines the standard of living or, in its economic aspects, the quality of life? That is the question under investigation. Quite inconsistent theories exist, which span the optimism-pessimism range and lead to diverse policy implications. The differences among these theories stem from differences in the terms of reference within which they have been developed. This chapter discusses some relevant tools and describes the foundations of alternative views of economic development.

CONCEPTS AND TOOLS

The usual focus of economics is the determination of the standard of living.[1] Carefully estimated data purporting to measure the standard of living have been available only in

[1] Adam Smith so defines his subject in the first two sentences of *An Inquiry into the Nature and Causes of the Wealth of Nations* (New York: Random House, 1937), p. lvii.

recent decades. These involve serious problems of conceptual-ization and measurement, leading to a possible bias in inter-preting economic change.

The usual measure of the standard of living is real gross national product (GNP) per capita. Gross national product refers to total goods and services produced by the economy, measured in current prices. To arrive at real GNP, this figure is deflated by an index of prices, yielding a measure of output defined in terms of dollars of constant purchasing power. Many nontrivial issues are involved in the definition and esti-mation of real GNP. There are three major issues: (1) produc-tive activity not oriented toward markets is omitted; (2) the side effects of productive activities and the changes in society that they entail are neglected; (3) an adequate unit in which to measure real output is not available.

With a few exceptions, GNP does not include any productive activity that does not lead to a sale in the market. There is a good enough technical reason for this exclusion; assignment of values to such services would be very difficult. In any case, year-to-year changes in such nonmarket productive activities in any given economy probably are not significant. But when the question is changes in the standard of living over a long period of time or comparison among different societies, the omission of nonmarket productive activities may be very im-portant. The Western economies have become increasingly market oriented over time. Thus use of GNP per capita to measure living standards in these economies over time over-states the degree of improvement. For example, GNP in-cludes the output of wives now working outside the home, but it does not include their earlier productive activities in the home.

Similarly, comparisons between the present-day United States and an economy less oriented toward the market exag-gerate the relative advantage of the United States. Gross na-tional product includes commercial entertainment but ex-cludes the informal entertainment and art that may confer deeper satisfactions. Informal means of preserving order through the social system are not a part of GNP, but any ac-tivity carried out by formal government—of whatever produc-tivity—is included in GNP at cost. It seems quite conceivable that a society, by departing from its earlier ways, becoming increasingly oriented toward market activities, and enlarging the role of formal government, could increase its gross national product while actually lowering living standards.

Side effects of changes in production methods and of industrialization are really a special case of the issue just discussed but merit special consideration. Some of these side effects may be favorable, such as the development of mental facilities from participation in complex and rationalized productive activities. But many are unfavorable: air pollution, water pollution, crime and disorganization associated with urbanization. These factors may be quantitatively important. The cost of overcoming the water pollution resulting from some abandoned coal mines is estimated to be greater than the value of the coal earlier removed from the mine. Some such side effects of modern productive activities occur only with a lag, as has DDT poisoning, and our knowledge does not permit them to be fully defined. When the lag is long enough that the burden falls on a later generation, there is an intertemporal problem of estimating living standards—one generation can increase its living standard at the expense of the next. Real GNP as it has been estimated and used as a measure of living standards in the past has taken virtually no account of these side effects. Thus it may have greatly overstated the improvement in the living standard of industrialized countries and the relative advantage of these countries over some that are less industrialized.

The final point runs in the opposite direction. Nominal products such as "an automobile," "an appendicitis operation," which are included in measures of output—or in the price indexes used to deflate measures of output—are not really constant over time. Improvement in technology and in the ability of people to buy industrial products has meant improvement in these products, which is not fully reflected in real GNP as presently measured. This error causes real GNP to understate both improvement in the major industrial nations and their degree of advantage over others.

How do these considerations balance out? Of course, we do not know. We could find out only by producing the true measure of real output per capita, first solving all the problems of conception and measurement to which we have referred. But it seems clear that real output per capita can be increased with a simultaneous lowering of living standards. Of the progress believed to have resulted from economic development, at least a part may reflect measurement error.

KNOWLEDGE, SCIENCE, AND THE THEORY OF POLICY

By "knowledge" within the framework of modern science we mean propositions characterizing natural laws, regularities of behavior, or causal relations. Knowledge is useful because it yields accurate predictions and estimates of the effects of actions. The choice among alternative actions depends on the consequences of each, which can be estimated only on the basis of knowledge. Thus rational or responsible policy requires knowledge.

Not all beliefs or propositions are, in this sense, "knowledge." Some do not accurately state the laws of nature and lead to false predictions of the outcome of actions. This must be the case, because many existing beliefs are inconsistent with one another and lead to different predictions of the outcomes of given actions.

The formulation of beliefs is governed by the natural laws of our universe, just as is everything else. Thus erroneous beliefs regarding man and nature, or false knowledge, do not come into being simply accidentally. Rather, they reflect belief-generation processes, which commonly involve a bias. One basic source of bias is the wish of man to believe a certain class of story because of the satisfaction he derives from believing it, such as the story that depicts man as rising to an exalted position. Moreover, particular kinds of beliefs may be supported by groups on which they confer some benefit in power, prestige, or financial gain. Thus the contest between competing beliefs ties into the general human contest for status, power, and gain.

Clearly, the definition and propagation of accurate models of natural law, or true knowledge, are not easy. Largely within the past few centuries, a small fraction of the tenure of civilized man, methods or procedures for distinguishing knowledge from erroneous beliefs regarding nature have been devised. In the area of natural science, these methods have been successful in defining models that produced effective predictions and in overcoming the bitter opposition of groups favoring other beliefs. On topics involving man, the scientific method has so far been less successful in defining theories that yield adequate predictions and in gaining acceptance even of the theories that do. A number of reasons have been suggested for this difference, but perhaps the one that is most relevant here is the greater susceptibility to bias of beliefs regarding man both because of man's preference for certain kinds of beliefs and because of the interests of power-wielding groups in maintaining certain beliefs.

The scientific method involves formulating beliefs in a manner sufficiently precise to yield implications that can be tested against the evidence of experience. When a belief or proposition is found inconsistent with some set of facts, a basis is provided for reformulating it in such a way as to make it consistent with all the relevant facts. Thus continuing testing and reformulation of the set of propositions that comprises knowledge enables it to be refined and improved. To fulfill its function, the scientific method must offer safeguards against the continued dominance of beliefs based on some kind of bias. It must modify existing beliefs in the direction of the true ones.

A useful concept is that of optimal—or best available—policies, which actual policies can try to approximate. The definition of optimal policies requires a set of preferences or a definition of the goals sought and requires knowledge or theory on the basis of which to estimate the consequences of alternative actions. Thus the choice of the optimal public policy can be viewed as involving (1) an unbiased definition of alternative policies meriting consideration, (2) unbiased estimates of the consequences of each policy on the basis of available knowledge, and (3) choice of that policy whose effects are most satisfactory as evaluated in relation to the set of goals.

Actual policies are made through procedures in which various men and organizations play different roles and exert different powers—as well as in many cases holding to erroneous beliefs regarding the effects of policies. Thus actual policies may reflect bias in the procedure by which they are formed and may not approximate optimal policies. Commonly they may reflect the particular interests and beliefs of groups exerting disproportionate influence over the policy choice. Moreover, the contest among groups over policy is a source of bias in beliefs, because each, in order to gain acceptance for its desired policies, tends to support beliefs that present these policies in a favorable light.

Because beliefs are generated in this manner, even beliefs that are very widely held may be erroneous. Surely this statement has been true in the past. That it may be true with reference to the theory of economic development is indicated by the inconsistency of this theory with the ecological view of man and nature.

MODELS OF CHANGE

Because the class of model or framework within which change is represented proves crucially to affect the interpretation of "economic development," it is useful at the outset to contrast two major kinds of model of change. Prominent in Western thought is the model of *unilinear evolution,* which "postulates that all societies pass through similar developmental stages."[2] This model is one of one-directional change. In Western thought such change is associated with the ideas of progress, advancement, or the realization of purpose.

This model of change is to be contrasted with that of *multilinear evolution* or *open evolution,* which can involve continuing processes that do not trace out a single one-directional path. The usual path can include cycles, processes of rise and fall. Different cases may involve different paths, rather than only different points on the same path.

The processes of change in life forms through natural selection are properly represented by a model of open evolution. It includes the rise and fall of species. Species and ecological systems may be stable for long periods. The modern story of earth and life ends with the extinction of earth and the life

---

[2] Julian H. Steward, *Theory of Culture Change* (Urbana: University of Illinois Press, 1955), p. 4. The discussion here draws on Steward's approach.

on it. The interpretations of natural selection that represent this story as progress—with man emerging as the end point of progress—transform it into one of unilinear evolution and thereby distort it.[3]

This distortion relates to another dichotomy of models, the *naturalistic* as opposed to the *humanistic* or *anthropocentric.* Naturalistic models or theories represent natural processes in an unbiased manner, or, in the current vernacular, "tell it like it is." The scientific method is designed to define naturalistic theories—though "scientists" do not always use the scientific method.

Humanistic models tell a story in human terms. They make the story attractive by giving it a happy ending or by showing man's condition as getting better and better. They make change appealing by depicting it not as a mechanistic process but as a reflection of goal or purpose, these again being associated with man and his exaltation.

This approach is also termed "anthropocentric." In some cases it explicitly depicts man as the center of nature—by defining man's elevation as the goal toward which natural processes are operating. In other cases it implicitly makes man the central element in the universe by defining natural processes in terms of man's interests and perceptions. The version of natural selection that depicts it as progress in giving rise to the perfected species, man, is thus anthropocentric. The naturalistic version of the story contemplates that man may fall, as have other species, and sees man as another player in the game, not as the purpose of the game. Evidence to support the anthropocentric approach, of course, is lacking. It reflects wishes, not facts.

The concept of anthropocentric versus naturalistic theories ties back to the concept of knowledge and its relation to effec-

---

[3] A recent approach of this genre is Julian Huxley's association of evolution with "progress" or "human destiny": ". . . all this does add up to something in the nature of a religion: perhaps one might call it Evolutionary Humanism. The word 'religion' is often used restrictively to mean belief in gods; but I am not using it in this sense . . . I am using it in a broader sense, to denote an over-all relation between man and his destiny, and one involving his deepest feelings, including his sense of what is sacred." Julian S. Huxley, *Evolution in Action* (New York: Signet Science Library, 1957), p. 132.

tive policy. If anthropocentric theories are biased—their content governed by man's wish to believe one kind of story rather than another—they will lead to a systematically false picture of the universe and to false estimates of the consequences of actions. Thus they will lead to policies that will not have the expected effects. The theories of economic development that have been conventional in recent decades appear to be theories of unilinear evolution and reflect a basically anthropocentric view of man and nature.

MAN, NATURE, AND ECONOMIC WELL-BEING: THE NATURALISTIC APPROACH

The method of science that views man as a part of the world of nature has produced a coherent story of change in the universe, in man, and in standards of living. The achievement of putting this story together is a recent one. The framework for explaining the origin and change in life, Darwin's theory of natural selection, is only a century old. Major modifications of this framework relating to population control and environmental preservation have been made only in the 1960s. New light on the origins and abundance of planets and the chemical processes involved in the origins of life emerged from the work of the late 1960s and from man's first trips into space. Thus the naturalistic story of man that now can be told is one that was not available to the makers of earlier theories about man.

THE BIRTH AND DEATH OF EARTH

The new theory explains, within the naturalistic laws of matter, not only what happens on earth but also the birth and death of earth, its sun, and their companions in space.[4] The stars themselves are not fixed but reflect a continuing cycle of change. Stars are born, age, and are extinguished, much

[4] A popular exposition is given in Robert Jastrow, *Red Giants and White Dwarfs* (New York: New American Library, 1969).

as are living organisms. The stars, however, do not proceed down a single-track path. Their course depends on the size of the mass of matter that condenses from the gas clouds of space. The local star, our own sun, has an expected life of about 10 billion years, about 6 billion left to go. Planets are satellites of the stars, not only locationally but also in their creation and life cycle.

For most of the history of thinking man, the earth was seen as the center of the universe. Until a few years ago it seemed possible that our earth was, at least, a rare thing, and that the planets of our solar system reflected some uncommon process of creation. The new information and thought of the late 1960s depict planets as rather common. A reasonable guess would be that in our galaxy alone there may be something like 100,000 earthlike planets.

THE STORY OF LIFE

Just as the formation, life cycle, and extinction of stars and planets are governed by the behavioral properties of the matter making up our universe, so are the formation and later behavior of living things. The story of life is an integral part of a larger story that includes the birth and death of stars. The process by which living things first were created on earth had long been a puzzle. Here also, the work of the 1960s has been illuminating.

It now appears that life evolved naturally through the formation of increasingly complex molecules. This process led eventually to the appearance of the amino acids and nucleotides that are the basic building blocks of living things. The formation of amino acids into proteins and of nucleotides into the nucleic acids and the crucially important DNA provided the structural elements and the control system that are the framework for the living creatures of earth.

The credibility of this story is buttressed by three recent achievements: (1) the discovery that all living organisms are built up from two kinds of molecules, amino acids and nucleotides; (2) the chemical synthesis in the laboratory of these molecules under conditions such as existed naturally on earth; and (3) the discovery of an object lying on the borderline between inanimate matter and life, the virus.[5]

How did complex forms of life evolve from the simple ones? This part of the story has been known for a century; it was Darwin's contribution. Once organisms develop the capacity to reproduce themselves and multiply, which exists at the level of the virus, any one of them has the potentiality, given enough time, to multiply to the point of using up the earth's total supply of the elements from which it is formed. The constraint of the limited size of the earth and the limited supply of elements from which to form organisms forces them into competition with one another. This competition leads to rationing of the creation and survival of living organisms.

But the rationing of survival and reproduction is not a random process. It reflects the performance characteristics of the organism in relation to the environment within which that organism competes against others, resulting in *selection* or differential survival and reproduction rates for organisms. This selection reflects the effectiveness of the organism's adaptation to its environment. The combination of "accidental" individual variation among members of a species plus continuous operation of selection can lead to continuing change in the species and the evolution of new species. If environments exist to which complex organisms adapt more efficiently than simple ones, the complex organisms eventually will evolve.

The diversity of the environment and the dependence of species survival on adaptive efficiency led to great specialization among living organisms. The complex tree of life developed—from bacteria and algae through corals and snails, to the fishes, air-breathing fishes and amphibians, reptiles, birds, and dinosaurs that were the lords of the earth for 100 million years. After the disappearance of the dinosaurs 70 million years ago (the reason for which is still a puzzle) came the era of the mammals, with their complex mechanisms for controlling their internal temperature. An animal similar to man appeared on the scene only 2 or 3 million years ago.

How does this story end? Ultimately, of course, with the

extinction of earth and the life on it, though at a time that is remote as we think of time. But can we predict the future position of any particular species, including man? Not in any simple way, for this evolution is open rather than unilinear. Species that do not meet nature's criteria for survival will disappear, as did the dinosaurs. Consequently, the abrupt disappearance of man is in no way inconsistent with this framework; neither is the disappearance of some subgroups or subspecies of man. In recent centuries, hunting-fishing man has proved ill-adapted to an environment largely shaped by civilized man. But as the dinosaur illustrates, lines of evolution that are highly successful for a time—even for a long period of time—may thereafter prove to be failures. Thus civilized man could prove to be an abortive experiment in evolution, hunting-fishing man surviving and replacing him.

But does not man's development of intelligence alter this story? Not in a basic sense. Development of the kind of verbal intelligence used by modern man can be viewed as an evolutionary experiment, a survival strategy based on a specialization of tissue, just as is the development of temperature-control mechanisms, vertebrae, or of external armor. Tree-living creatures needed arms and fingers, which then permitted them to use tools, which conferred survival value on the capability of developing better tools and remembering how to use them—and so man has gone on to more complex tools. This kind of intelligence made man highly effective in asserting his dominance over other creatures, from lions to bacteria, in conquering and exploiting his environment. But the survival of a species is threatened by the destruction of its habitat, by overdevelopment or excessive short-run success. Nature's criteria for survival on this score and the mechanisms of control by which species have met them are closely relevant to our subject.

SPECIES CONTROL, THE "STANDARD OF LIVING," AND SURVIVAL

Earlier interpretations of natural selection represented the production of very large numbers of offspring as the road to species survival. Largely within the past decade, the error in this interpretation and the far-reaching implications of the

required restatement of natural selection are under consideration.[6] The members of a species, after all, compete most
closely with one another. If their numbers are so great that
there is not enough food to go around, they may fall into a
weakened condition and be vulnerable to invasion. The survival value of the species would be enhanced by a limitation
of numbers sufficient to preserve the health and vigor of its
members. Such is the characteristic state of animals and, in
general, of primitive man. The existence of large numbers
of half-starved individuals is most characteristic of civilized
man.

Yet more crucially, the existence of excessive numbers
would destroy the food supply. Overgrazing destroys the
range; overpredation destroys the prey species.[7] Another
point that had been missed in earlier thought—as existing
species in fact *do not* destroy their habitat—was how sensitive
the food supply of many species is to excessive exploitation.
Surviving species that have passed nature's test for survival
characteristically do not overexploit their food supply. They
avoid this through mechanisms that limit their population, in
conjunction with feeding habits that preserve the food supply.
Again, this fact must have been true of primitive man. He
was not immune to the logic of natural selection; he was
created by it.

The mechanisms by which animals limit their numbers
and preserve their habitat vary greatly among species. Many
species have evolved remarkably complex systems for controlling their numbers, systems that heavily shape the life
patterns of the animals. Whatever its particular form, the
mechanism must (1) provide a means of taking a reading on
species density, (2) provide a rationing system that determines
which members are to survive or to reproduce in the event of
excessive numbers, and (3) provide mechanisms for getting
rid of or preventing excessive numbers, mechanisms that are
not themselves destructive of the species or its habitat.

What is involved here is group control over individuals on

[6] The major contribution is that of V. C. Wynne-Edwards, *Animal Dispersion
in Relation to Social Behavior* (Edinburgh: Oliver and Boyd, 1962).
[7] *Ibid.,* pp. 4–9.

behalf of group survival. The control systems were worked out through the trial and error of natural selection, through the advantage in survival of groups that had them over groups that did not. In animals, the control system is conveyed to the individual through genetic mechanisms and specific patterns of instinctive behavior. Man is from this point of view a great experiment, in lacking such specifically defined instinctive behavior patterns. In his case, group control over individuals appears to have been achieved in large part by means of culture. Cultural patterns producing an effective societal performance were selected for survival in the same way as efficacious instinctive control systems in animals. This survival strategy had a short-run payoff in making man dominant because of its flexibility and quick adaptability. But it involves an obvious long-run hazard of failure of the species from loss of societal control over individuals.

A striking aspect of the experience of modern man, and one closely relevant to our subject, is the rise and fall of advanced civilizations. In the past 5,000 years, a great many societies have risen in power, domain, and living standards, and then have declined and been extinguished. If there is a common theme to be found in the experience of civilized man, it is this pattern of rise and fall. The experience of modern industrial civilization is no exception to this pattern as yet, for its rise of two centuries is not exceptional.

Available knowledge does not provide a full explanation of the decline of earlier civilizations. However, the problem of societal control discussed here apparently played an essential role in the process. As earlier civilizations expanded, became urbanized, and incorporated foreign populations, they lost the system of cultural control that underlay their initial effectiveness. A common pattern of deterioration appears to have involved growth of population that led to a depressed living standard for the urban poor, deterioration of the environment, and loss of coherency of the society leading to growing internal conflict and ineffectiveness. The depiction of economic well-being by Adam Smith and later classical economists emphasized the dependence of the rise of a society on growing efficiency derived from efficacious institutions and described the subsequent decline in the standard of living as deriving from population growth in conjunction with the limitations of natural resources.

THE INTERPRETATION OF "ECONOMIC DEVELOPMENT"

Within this framework, the "economic development" of the West in the past two centuries is basically similar to the rising phase of earlier civilizations. As was true of them, its outcome will depend on the ability of the societies involved to meet the basic control problems of limiting population, preserving the environment, and preventing internal disorder and mutually destructive activities. This case differs from earlier civilizations in the state of technology achieved, the rapidity of the increase in technical achievements, its worldwide extensiveness, and the scope and intensity of the environmental destruction it has caused. None of these considerations overturns the basic logic that has governed earlier episodes. They do imply that the fall, if it comes, will be on a greater scale than before. It also may involve environmental deterioration on such a scale as to preclude development of another advanced civilization.

The most basic point is this: The naturalistic approach provides no basis for extrapolating indefinitely the events of the past two centuries or viewing them as steps toward a predetermined happy ending. In open evolution, no change can be indefinitely extrapolated into the future. Surviving species, and surviving societies, are those that again in each period meet the test of survival according to nature's rules. Earlier advanced civilizations reached a point at which they did not pass this test. To continue to pass it would seem to require the present-day civilization to achieve a kind of societal control over individuals that has not been achieved in the past and that is not presently being achieved by any advanced society.

FOUNDATIONS OF THE THEORY OF ECONOMIC DEVELOPMENT

The naturalistic model just discussed has never influenced or been understood by a large part of humanity. Moreover, parts of the story have been worked out only very recently or are only now in the process of formulation; they were not available to the thinkers of a decade or two ago who shaped the modern conception of "economic development." In any case, both policy and academic theory in this area seem to derive from another type of model, the origins of which we now outline.

MAN AND NATURE IN THE JUDEO-CHRISTIAN MODEL

Christianity inherited from Judaism the interpretation of human experience in terms of unilinear evolution, of single-track, nonrepetitive change in contrast to the cyclical notions of the Greeks. The concepts of Creation, the coming of the Messiah, and the ultimate exaltation of the Jews as the chosen people of God were incorporated into Christianity and thus into Western thought. Christianity added the second coming of Jesus and the millennium, the Judgment Day, and the uplifting of the favored to heaven.

In the Christian view, God had created the earth and the universe specifically for man. It was his to use, to exploit. This view contrasts with the earlier animistic religions that endowed natural objects with guardian spirits that men must fear if they disturbed nature. The animistic religions can be interpreted as cultural patterns derived through natural selection because of their function as a control mechanism in helping a society preserve its habitat. In most early religions nature is sacred or is protected by spirits, but in Christianity it is man's plaything, created especially for him by God.[8]

It followed from the Christian approach that man's success or failure depended not on meeting nature's criteria, because nature had no independent logic, but on following God's instructions as interpreted by religious leaders. These rules were derived from *human* considerations, *human* concep-

---

[8] This theme is emphasized in Lynn White, Jr., "The Historical Roots of Our Ecologic Crisis," *Science,* 155 (1967), 1203–1207; reprinted in Paul Shepard and Daniel McKinley (eds.), *The Subversive Science: Essays Toward an Ecology of Man* (Boston: Houghton Mifflin, 1969), pp. 341–351.

tions of vice and virtue. In contrast to the laws of primitive religions derived through natural selection, which commonly do seem to have played a controlling role in adapting man's behavior to nature's requirements, these man-centered rules seem to ignore natural law. This is an anthropocentric story of man's relation to nature.

As the growth of knowledge in natural science made the traditional form of Christian religion more difficult to accept, the basic story, whose psychological appeal had given Christianity its dominance, was translated into secular forms. A version similar to those of the present day is that of Condorcet. The pattern of unilinear evolution involves the growing perfection of man, epoch by epoch, until in the tenth epoch he arrives at an earthly state similar to the one earlier attributed to the afterlife and heaven.[9] The writings of William Godwin also epitomized the translation of the story from one of man's ultimate exaltation in heaven to his perfection and exaltation on earth.[10] The story retains its anthropocentric character, its depiction of man's exaltation as dependent solely on his human qualities and subject to no constraints of natural law. The theme of unilinear evolution leading inevitably to man's exaltation is the major theme of secularized versions of the Christian story. It is a story of progress.

Darwin's formulation of the theory of natural selection provided a new need and a new rationale for the doctrine of progress. By depriving man of other pretensions, the theory led to the assertion on his behalf of a new claim: "He now suffers a new degradation within the compass of his own planet. Evolution shearing him of his glory as a rational being specially created to be the lord of the earth, traces a humble pedigree for him. And this second degradation was the decisive fact which has established the reign of the idea of

[9] Marie J. A. Nicolas Caritat, Marquis de Condorcet, *Outlines of an Historical View of the Progress of the Human Mind* (London, 1795).

[10] William Godwin, *Enquiry Concerning Political Justice and Its Influence on Morals and Happiness* (Toronto: University of Toronto Press, 1946), first published in 1793. This school of thought reflected the earlier work of Jean Jacques Rousseau.

Progress."[11]   The version of the doctrine of progress that was most influential in the late nineteenth century was Herbert Spencer's corruption in which evolution is progress, leading to the perfection of man and the increase in his happiness.[12]

Using Hegel's pretentious justification of unilinear evolution in his doctrine of the dialectic, Marx provided a version of the story that was richly endowed with villains, attractive action roles, and the new epochal event of the revolution. But this story is basically the same, a drama couched in human terms with—despite its claims of scientific status—no place for man's need to meet nature's performance criteria or to adapt to natural law.[13]

The most prevalent framework for present-day thought about economic development, that of W. W. Rostow, derives explicitly from Marx.[14]   It is a framework of unilinear evolution and progress, wherein the take-off into sustained growth replaces the revolution, and automatic economic progress replaces the transition to idealized communism.   A happy substitution, perhaps, and a constructive one, but still a story of the same class.

Within this framework, the radical humanists of the 1960s appear to have taken a step further in asserting that technological progress and man's perfection have now reached the point of freeing him from even the traditional constraints. Marcuse represents technical progress as permitting a "change in the 'nature' of man" in reaching "a stage in which

---

[11] J. B. Bury, *The Idea of Progress* (New York: Dover Publications, 1955), p. 335.

[12] *Ibid.*, Chap. 19. That the doctrine of progress served as a psychological substitute for Christianity's promise of a future in heaven was recognized at the time.   Bury refers to "an eloquent discourse on the 'New Era,' in which the dominant note is 'the faith in human progress in lieu of celestial rewards of the separate soul.' "   The date was 1889.   *Ibid.*, p. 346.

[13] The origins of Marx's thought in Christianity, especially in the basic story of "paradise lost and paradise regained," are explored by Robert Tucker in *Philosophy and Myth in Karl Marx* (New York: Cambridge University Press, 1964).

[14] W. W. Rostow, *The Stages of Economic Growth: A Non-Communist Manifesto* (Cambridge, England: Cambridge University Press, 1960), especially Chaps. 1, 10.

reality no longer need be defined by the debilitating competition for social survival and advancement."[15]   In its emphasis on the self-realization of the individual and its de-emphasis of the demands not only of nature but of society, this approach perhaps reaches the limits of anthropocentrism.

Three major respects in which this framework differs from the naturalistic one merit emphasis:

1. It depicts man as not importantly subject to constraints defined by nature. In contrast, the naturalistic approach represents man as still governed by the game of natural selection, participating on the same terms as other forms of life.

2. In this approach, the factors determining man's success or failure—his obedience to God's laws, his following of moral rules, his pursuit of his self-realization—are defined in humanistic terms. The naturalistic approach, again, depicts the outcome as depending upon whether man meets nature's criteria rather than whether he conforms to conceptions derived from his own imagination.

3. The anthropocentric or humanistic approach emphasizes the happy ending, man's arrival at an exalted state being inevitable or nearly so. This story has little place for retrogression and failure. Within the naturalistic framework, man's ultimate disappearance is virtually inevitable, and on the basis of past experience an early fall of the present civilization is altogether likely.

THE THEORY OF ECONOMIC DEVELOPMENT

The major point of reference of this book is what is termed "the theory of economic development." This term is used to refer to the body of literature, epitomized by the contribution

[15] Herbert Marcuse, *An Essay on Liberation* (Boston: Beacon Press, 1969), p. 5. Other statements by members of this school are Abraham H. Maslow, *Toward a Psychology of Being,* 2nd ed. (Princeton, N.J.: D. Van Nostrand Company, 1968); Erich Fromm, *You Shall Be as Gods* (New York: Holt, Rinehart and Winston, 1966).

of Rostow, that has predominated during the 1950s and 1960s among economists and in policy discussions relating to the raising of living standards in nations with low living standards. This body of thought has the following characteristics.

First, its framework is one of unilinear evolution, emphasizing progress, the overcoming of backwardness, modernization, "development." The ubiquitousness of this set of concepts attests to the widespread influence of this approach.

Second, the conditions underlying or permitting such progress are conceived in certain conventionalized economic and political terms. The basic idea is that "backward" societies will accelerate their progress by bringing about certain features existing in "advanced" countries. Special emphasis is placed on investment, but other aspects of "modernization" are also discussed.

Finally, the approach does not emphasize natural constraints on living standards or progress. Its message is that the poor nations should progress by making themselves like the rich nations. To define the natural constraints that all societies must meet to maintain high living standards or to survive is beyond the scope of this approach. Thus population is treated within the framework of unilinear evolution, the assumption being that progress in other respects will naturally solve the population problem. Environmental destruction has been largely ignored by this approach.

A number of contributions to the theory of economic development are critically discussed in Chapter 14. The way these contributions fit into the structure of competing ideas under consideration needs characterization here.

DEVELOPMENT OF THE THEORY OF ECONOMIC DEVELOPMENT

The mainstream of economic thought up to the 1920s did not include any such theory of economic development. Neoclassical economics emphasized the dependence of economic efficiency on political and institutional arrangements that are not easily attained. It also pointed up the limited endowment of nature and the hazard of excessive population. The Malthusian League, founded in the 1870s, was active in establishing birth-control clinics in the United States in the 1920s. Another indication of the naturalistic approach to man was the eugenics movement, which concerned itself with the operation of selection and the quality of the human species.

Loyalty to this system of beliefs was severely tested by the catastrophe of World War I and the disorder and failures of reconstruction during the 1920s. The Great Depression submerged its adherents.

Symbolic of defections from this naturalistic framework of thought was the rejection of the Eugenics Society in 1932 by the eminent geneticist H. J. Muller, who attributed the depression to flaws in the capitalist system and concluded that this system was not an appropriate framework within which to apply eugenics. In 1933 Muller became Senior Geneticist at the Institute of Genetics of the Academy of Sciences of the U.S.S.R.[16] The eugenics movement and the Malthusian League were pushed aside. Neoclassical economics was submerged; intellectuals swung to Marxism or to the less radical Keynesianism.

The Keynesian model used the framework of unilinear evolution. In this approach, the maturing of capitalist societies led not specifically to the difficulties seen by Marx but to the problem of economic stagnation. In the moderate Keynesian position, stagnation could be dealt with by increasing the role of government in the economy. The policy problem was to overcome the opposition to this solution. The impediment to progress was classical economics and laissez faire. Rapid population growth in this view would help to stimulate investment and prevent economic stagnation.

The earlier beliefs were almost reversed. Limitation of population and establishment of economic rules favoring efficiency now were not the means of achieving high living standards; rather, they were the impediments to progress. The new story is a humanistic one. The contest pits the liberals against the backward-looking proponents of laissez faire. The natural constraints emphasized in earlier thought have dropped out of the picture.

This reformulation of ideas carried over to the economic

---

[16] Garrett Hardin, *Nature and Man's Fate* (New York: Holt, Rinehart and Winston, 1959), pp. 228–230.

models in which theory was expressed. The neoclassical emphasis on efficiency directed attention mainly to the rules of the economic game, which would encourage or discourage increased efficiency. The new economics emphasized aggregates—for example, aggregative ratios related to the problem of stagnation and the aging economy. The consumption function, or the dependence of consumption on income, was not a new idea. It was an idea that had little importance in the old framework, but was the centerpiece of the new theory.

The stagnation doctrine can be viewed as an application of the framework of unilinear evolution, leading to a theory emphasizing a few key relations among aggregative variables. It was natural to extend this approach to interpretation of economic growth using multiplier-accelerator models emphasizing two macroeconomic relations, the savings ratio and the capital-output ratio, as was done by Harrod and Domar.[17] It is consistent with this approach in less formal interpretations of economic growth to emphasize such aggregative variables, saving, investment, and the capital-output ratio.

The assembling of these intellectual building blocks into the theory of economic development seems to have depended heavily on the circumstances of the times—as had the stagnation doctrine. After World War II, when the fears of a postwar return of stagnation had been overcome, and following the reconstruction of Europe, a unique situation existed. The decolonialization of Asia and Africa left a large part of the world newly independent, organized into nations, and with low standards of living. Which way were these new nations to head? How were they to view their future, and what policies were they to adopt?

The communist nations had a formula to offer, the Marxist theory with its great appeal. What was the West to offer as an alternative, as its counterpart of the Marxist theory of development? That an alternative to the Marxian scenario should be assembled from the beliefs then prevailing in the West was both inevitable and constructive.

[17] R. F. Harrod, *Towards a Dynamic Economics* (New York: St. Martin's Press, 1948); Evsey D. Domar, "Capital Expansion, Rate of Growth and Employment," *Econometrica*, 14 (April 1946), 137–147.

The central theme of this theory is the achievement of progress through the means that, in the Western thought of that day, were believed to lead to progress. It was natural that the formula should include investment and modernization—to which the West attributed its own success and which it preeminently could provide to others—and the moderate government intervention or planning that was the preferred formula of Western thought.

Such a synthesis emerges naturally from the Western thought of the late 1940s and 1950s. Rostow's contribution can be viewed as one particular statement of an approach that was widely applied. His model was distinctive in its explicit derivation from the Marxian model and its explicit expression of unilinear evolution as involving a set of discrete stages.[18]

Doubtless because it was a synthesis of major themes in the thought of the times, Rostow's theory was the point of departure for most substantive theories of economic development during the 1960s. The theory of economic dualism, or of economies with an advanced or modern sector and a backward sector, seems interpretable as an extension of the Rostow framework to a situation in which one sector of the national economy has passed through the take-off whereas the other has not. The dualism theory appears to be an elaboration or a modification of this framework rather than a new and inconsistent theory. Similarly, the critical-minimum-effort thesis can be viewed as a subtheory elaborating certain of the conditions necessary to achieve take-off.[19]

It does not seem unreasonable to view the theory of economic development—this body of thought—as in part responsive to international political considerations. It was the West's answer to Marxism, designed to match Marxism in appeal. But evidence is now coming in that bears on this theory and the intellectual components from which it was built. Time and events have not dealt kindly either with Marxism or with this alternative to it.

---

[18] Rostow, *op. cit.;* "The Take-Off Into Self-Sustained Growth," *Economic Journal,* 66 (March 1956), 25–48.

[19] See Chap. 14.

THE THEORY OF ECONOMIC DEVELOPMENT IN RELATION TO THE MAINSTREAM OF ECONOMIC THEORY

The mainstream of economic theory was little affected by the theory of economic development, which existed, as it were, as a separate compartment of the discipline. Economics in general has accepted neither a model of unilinear evolution nor any proposition of inevitable progress. Microeconomic theory continues to emphasize the dependence of the standard of living on efficiency and on the availability of resources. Although economics may not have emphasized population as much as in earlier times, the potential depressing effect on living standards of excessive population was never extirpated from economics.

The theory of income and employment was dominated for a time by macromodels deriving from the stagnationist interpretation of the Great Depression, but an accelerating swing away from this view was occurring during the 1960s. In short, the theory of economic development is not consistent with the mainstream of economics. Much of economists' criticism of the Rostow theory and other aspects of the literature on economic development and foreign aid simply reflects the application to these subjects of the mainstream of economics.

CONCLUSIONS

The aberrations of thought caused by the depression of the 1930s are now some distance behind us. The experience with programs of economic development during the 1950s and 1960s has been illuminating, and disappointing to expectations and theories. The warnings of naturalists—powerfully reinforced by everyday experiences—may persuade more people that the natural environment is fragile, not an indestructible toy provided for man's use. They may even infer from this fact that man must be a part of nature rather than its purpose and goal. The past decade has brought important discoveries regarding the logic of ecological systems and man's relation to nature. And then there are the imminent problems of potential starvation and natural destruction that seem unlikely to be hidden by the best-chosen words. Given these considerations, it seems appropriate to restate the naturalistic approach to the determination of living standards and the economic aspects of the quality of life.

CHAPTER 3 / An Outline of the Theory

A national society can be viewed as an ecological system that interacts with other systems and is subject to continuing processes of adaptation and change. Its performance at any time can be explained only in terms of the past processes of change that have brought it to its present position. The state of economic well-being in a society thus is to be explained in terms of the processes of change to which it has been subject and the factors that, in turn, determine these processes. Aspects of the performance of the national society that particularly explain its standard of living are those affecting its population, the preservation of its natural environment, and its economic efficiency.

Before considering these aspects of societal performance, it is necessary to explore somewhat further the processes by which societies change and the factors that determine the direction of their change. Different societies have shown different rates of growth and of decline in population and in economic efficiency, and have developed and have destroyed their environments in various ways. The problem is to explain this differential behavior and the mechanisms governing it.

DETERMINANTS OF SOCIETAL
CHANGE AND PERFORMANCE

In the naturalistic interpretation of living things, selection operates continuously at all levels. Thus it applies also to man. Man is within nature's game, not above it. Selection operates as between man and other species, and man may fail and become extinct as they may. It also operates within the human species at several levels—among national societies, among groups within a national society, among individuals within such groups. If such is the case, the general framework within which to investigate the determinants of those changes in societal performance that affect living standards is the general framework of natural selection.

MULTILEVEL SELECTION: THE ECOLOGICAL SYSTEM

Natural selection tends to produce a complex system of interrelated forms of life, a web of life in the form of an ecological system. The outcome approximates the outcome of an optimizing process, tending toward the maximum biomass (amount of living organisms) sustainable, given the input of energy and the underlying materials. A high degree of specialization of species and complex interrelations among the species develop in most environments. The relations among species are not symmetrical. Some species are predators of others. Another asymmetry relates to the dominance of some elements in the ecological system, which define the environment to which others must adapt, as do the tall, deciduous trees that determine the amount of light reaching other plants in the forest. Man has played the role of a dominant in ecological systems.

Underlying a change in the ecological system is continuing competition and selection, to the effect that a species more efficiently filling an ecological niche will displace a less efficient one. Selection takes place, however, on at least three levels: among species, among the individuals within a species—which defines the change in the nature of the species—and among local groups of individuals. These local groups, as recent studies have shown, are the operating entities through which are performed crucially important functions, including population control. In a sense, it is their effectiveness that is decisive. The species survives only through survival of its local groups; the individual survives only as a member of a local group.[1]

What performance does nature require of a surviving species or local group? It must occupy its ecological niche so efficiently as to preempt its space and its place in the food chain, preventing invasion by other species. It must recover quickly in numbers and reclaim its territory and place in the ecological system after any temporary adversity. It must expand and claim new territory as the opportunity presents itself. It must not destroy its habitat or its food supply. Individuals and groups must avoid destructive competition with one another, and in many cases depend for survival on productive interaction with one another. Where the external environment to which the species adapts is changing, it must also change and preserve its efficient adaptation or risk replacement.

The gradual change in the physical structure and performance of a species through selection among individuals, as a result of the higher survival rates of the more efficient individuals, is straightforward. Closer to the present subject are the complex control systems that species must develop in order to achieve cooperative interaction, avoid mutually destructive activities among members of the species, and limit their numbers and preserve the habitat and the food supply.

The performance characteristics suited to species or group survival in the context of natural selection can be stated as follows.

(1) The group must have redundant capacity for reproduction in order to offset losses from adverse accidents and temporarily adverse environmental conditions and to expand the domain of the group whenever possible.

(2) But this redundant birth capacity must not operate continually or it would reduce all individuals to a weakened condition and lead to destruction of the habitat.

---

[1] See V. C. Wynne-Edwards, *Animal Dispersion in Relation to Social Behavior* (Edinburgh: Oliver and Boyd, 1962), pp. 18–21.

(3) Therefore, optimal performance involves some control mechanism that adjusts the birth rate or the death rate so as to preserve the numbers of the group in something like an optimal relation to available space and food supply. This adjustment requires a set of mechanisms that operate as a feedback-control system:

> *To build up and preserve a favourable balance between popula-tion-density and available resources, it would be necessary for the animals to evolve a control system in many respects analogous to the physiological systems that regulate the internal environment of the body and adjust it to meet changing needs. Such systems are said to be homeostatic or self-balancing. . . . Physiological homeostasis has in general been slowly perfected in the course of evolution, and it is thus the highest animals that tend to be most independent of environmental influences, as far as the inward machinery of the body is concerned. Population homeostasis, it may be inferred, would involve adaptations no less complex, and it might therefore be expected that these would similarly tend to reach the greatest efficiency and perfection in the highest groups.*[2]

A control system designed to adjust the birth rate or death rate to preserve something like optimal numbers requires the same classes of components as other feedback-control mechanisms, such as those for regulating temperature. As depicted in Figure 3.1, there must be a sensing mechanism to determine the existing population density and to compare this density with the standard or optimal density.

Beyond this point, however, the functional mechanisms of the population-control system become more complex than those of control systems of everyday experience. Rather than simply turning a furnace on or off, this control system (because of the discontinuous nature of births in most animals)

---

[2] *Ibid.,* p. 9. In a broad sense, these behavioral characteristics can be said to have survival value with reference to *all* systems operating in a changing environment. I made this point with reference to economic systems, in criticism of economists' presumption that globally stable systems have survival value, before I had become aware of the ideas systematized in the Wynne-Edwards theory. See my *Macroeconomic Theory and Stabilization Policy* (New York: McGraw-Hill, 1968), pp. 38–40.

must determine the number of births or deaths or emigrants required to bring the population to the desired level. The next complication is that, because the group or species consists of a number of discrete individuals, there must be mechanisms for selecting the particular individuals who are to be permitted to reproduce, excluded from reproduction, required to emigrate, or caused to die. Finally, there must be mechanisms sufficient to bring about the actions thus defined that do not themselves damage the performance of the group or species.

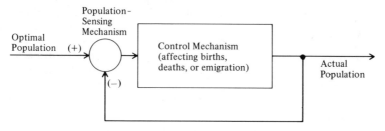

FIGURE 3.1 Population-Control System

The particular mechanisms that have evolved in animals to perform these particular functions as elements in the population-control system are diverse and in some cases very complex.[3] The sensing mechanism measures population density, giving a reading on existing numbers in relation to some defined geographical space, the territory or the breeding ground of the group. Thus the system is based on some form of territoriality—the assignment of the group, and in some cases of individuals within the group, to defined pieces of territory, either throughout the year or during the breeding season.

The males that are unable to establish a territory during the breeding season, the pairs that cannot procure a nest within the prescribed nesting area, the young that are pushed aside by their stronger brothers in competition for food within the nest, are excluded from breeding or from survival. In one

[3] Wynne-Edwards, *op. cit.*

form or another, the selection process is commonly related to a dominance hierarchy. This hierarchy is functional in selecting those individuals from within the group that will maintain a survival-related group inheritance.[4] Because it relates to control of the number of the group, such behavior is necessarily a group phenomenon, directed at group-related cues—in a broad sense, social rather than individual.

CONCEPTS RELATING TO SELECTION AND CONTROL

This concept of group control over the number of members in the group, through a feedback-control system, relates closely to some other concepts. A pioneering contribution was Cannon's theory of homeostatic systems, illustrated by the temperature-control systems of the bodies of mammals.[5] Wiener's development of the theory of systems of this class was termed "cybernetics."[6] Perhaps a further generalization of these concepts is the approach of systems analysis, or the systems approach.[7]

An interaction system involves a number of variables whose behavior is governed in part by feedback relations, by mutual dependencies within the system. Of particular interest are networks of feedback processes sufficiently complex that the implications for system behavior of a change in one element are not obvious but pose a substantial analytical problem.

These approaches emphasize that the performance of systems depends essentially on their interconnections, their feedback processes. It cannot be interpreted by dissecting them and looking at one piece at a time. Neither can it be dealt

---

[4] A brief characterization of the Wynne-Edwards theory in terms of its basic components of territoriality and dominance is given in Roger Brown, *Social Psychology* (New York: Free Press, 1965), pp. 6–22. See also Wynne-Edwards, *op. cit.,* pp. 12–22, 134 ff.

[5] Walter B. Cannon, *The Wisdom of the Body* (New York: Norton, 1932).

[6] See Norbert Wiener, *Cybernetics,* 2nd ed. (Cambridge, Mass.: M.I.T. Press, 1965); W. Ross Ashby, *An Introduction to Cybernetics* (New York: Wiley, 1963).

[7] A relevant discussion of the concept of *system* is given in Stafford Beer, *Decision and Control* (New York: Wiley, 1966), pp. 241–246. A collection of contributions to the systems approach is given in Walter Buckley (ed.), *Modern Systems Research for the Behavioral Scientist* (Chicago: Aldine, 1968).

with by defining equilibrium positions of the system, which is a common way for economists to simplify the interpretation of systems. Such attempts to simplify the interpretation of dynamic systems by abstracting from the interconnections that govern their behavioral properties will be misleading. Cybernetics also emphasizes the importance of control systems, their prevalence in surviving natural systems, and their creation by natural selection.

Recent years have seen rapid advances in the science of control, or control systems theory. Developed largely in connection with applications in electronics and communications, the theory is being applied to the problems of control of complex dynamic systems in other subject areas.[8] It explores the way certain kinds of mechanisms or feedback loops alter the performance characteristics of systems in which they are included.

Another conceptual framework for considering these topics is that of ecology.[9] This is a naturalistic approach, emphasizing the dependence of processes of change on interaction within and among complex systems, as governed by natural law. This book applies an ecological approach to the determination of the standard of living and the economic prospects of modern society.

Although the concept of homeostasis is only a few decades old and the concepts of cybernetics, control systems theory, and the systems approach are all very recent in their development, the basic ideas go back much further. Statements of the basic idea of cybernetics were given in the nineteenth century by the French physiologist Claude Bernard and the Scottish physicist Clerk Maxwell.[10] Malthus' earlier statement of the problem of population involved this concept, the

---

[8] A characterization is given in Olle I. Elgerd, *Control Systems Theory* (New York: McGraw-Hill, 1967), Chaps. 1–2.

[9] A selection of contributions is given in Paul Shepard and Daniel McKinley (eds.), *The Subversive Science: Essays Toward an Ecology of Man* (Boston: Houghton Mifflin, 1969). Another example is Harold and Margaret Sprout, *The Ecological Perspective on Human Affairs* (Princeton, N.J.: Princeton University Press, 1965).

[10] See Garrett Hardin, *Nature and Man's Fate* (New York: Holt, Rinehart and Winston, 1959), p. 52.

standard of living depending on whether population limitation through negative feedback came from the "preventive
checks" of birth limitation or, if these were not sufficiently
effective, by the "positive checks" of epidemic, pestilence,
plague, and famine.[11] Malthus' statement was a stimulus to
Darwin's formulation of the theory of natural selection.[12]

The ecological or cybernetic approach traces back to the
classical economists and the physiocrats. The Malthusian
view of population and the broader conception of the standard
of living as determined by a time process involving population, the environment, and the institutions governing economic efficiency were all effectively developed by Adam
Smith in *The Wealth of Nations* of 1776.[13]

GROUP-ORIENTED CONTROL OVER INDIVIDUAL BEHAVIOR

Selection among individuals on the basis of behavior relating to the external environment is straightforward. The gi-
raffes with the longer necks and legs find more food and leave
more progeny. In connection with the topics that most concern
us here, however, the operation of selection is not simple or
straightforward. As among individuals, to leave a large number of offspring has survival value and is conducive to favorable selection. But the group or species producing excessive
numbers destroys its habitat and does not survive—and the
individual cannot survive except as a member of a group and
a species. In this case, selection at the group and species level
dominates, and group success is to be achieved only through
control mechanisms of considerable complexity and subtlety.

The potential conflict of interest between the individual and
the group—or between the short-run interest of the individual
and his long-run interest—must be dealt with through mechanisms that involve a group-oriented system of selection.

---

[11] Thomas Robert Malthus, *Population: The First Essay* (Ann Arbor: University
of Michigan Press, 1959), p. 49.

[12] A review of other precursors of Darwin, including his grandfather, Erasmus
Darwin, is given in Cyril D. Darlington, *Darwin's Place in History* (Oxford:
Basil Blackwell, 1959).

[13] See also Hardin, *op. cit.,* p. 52, and pp. 257–264 of this text.

That is, the group must develop mechanisms that will result in negative selection of its individuals who do not respond to the group control system. Selection among groups on the basis of their ability to control their members leads to the development of such group-oriented control systems. The survival of groups and species depends on their ability to generate mechanisms that effectively control individuals so that the group can meet nature's requirements. To accomplish this goal, the group must work out rules leading to the intragroup selection of individuals who respond to the group's control system.

In animals the mechanisms preventing overpopulation, environmental destruction, and intragroup conflict are conveyed genetically. The patterns of instinctive behavior can be wonderfully complex. Not only food gathering and such feats of construction and division of labor as those performed by bees, but elaborate mating behavior, arrangements for territorial dispersion, and incredible feats of navigation in migration are all somehow conveyed genetically. The substance of what is conveyed is the fruit of earlier selection, of countless group trials in which success was rewarded by survival and failure was punished by extinction. The behavior conveyed is not only complex but can be conditional on systems of cues, including such time-sensitive patterns as imprinting.

Because natural selection produced the remarkably complex bodies of the animals with their internal control systems, it should not be surprising that natural selection can produce behavior patterns similarly wonderful, but it is not so customary to think of behavior—and especially social or group-oriented behavior—as the product of natural selection.

How does man fit into this story? He is an experiment with behavior patterns less specifically defined genetically; he is more capable of short-run variation of behavior. He had to meet the same performance criteria as other species; therefore, he could not have survived without control systems performing the same functions. These systems were provided more largely for man than they were for animals by conditioning or learning within the framework of intergenerational transmission of information through culture. Such a process involves a potential advantage of more rapid adaptation and

the use by local groups of different approaches to meet nature's criteria for survival. Some of these experiments will
work badly; groups will lose their culturally conveyed control
systems and destroy themselves. When the groups are small
and localized, such self-destruction by groups is no impediment to the survival of the species but is merely an aspect of
its adventurous strategy of survival that leads to rapid adaptability. When the experiment is successful to the point that
localization is lost and mankind becomes almost a single great
experiment, however, a single failure of man's systems of cultural control over individuals assumes a new importance.

Man's responsiveness to the requirements of nature thus
was achieved through group-oriented cultural systems and
through genetically conveyed mechanisms that tied in with
the cultural control systems—that made the individual responsive to the cultural control system. To achieve this response through natural selection required that groups with
effective systems of joint genetic and cultural control should
be favorably selected by nature and that these groups, in
achieving and maintaining their own effectiveness, should
provide for the negative intragroup selection of individuals
who did not fit in with this control system. Such actions as
the killing or exiling of deviant individuals presumably
played a role in this process.

The increase in man's efficiency in providing food and
transportation for himself led to replacement of small, localized groups by large and extensive societies. The genetically
conveyed emotional mechanisms that earlier had made man
responsive to his group now could tie him to a class, party,
religion, clique, or interest group, and thus could become the
basis for intergroup conflict and mutually destructive activities that would destroy the effectiveness of the society.

The loss of localism implied that the survival and influence
of groups did not depend on their preservation of a local piece
of territory, and therefore did not depend on their ability to
limit their numbers. On the contrary, whereas the long-run
success of the society as a whole depended on its preservation
of its environment, a group within the society might gain
power through rapid increase in its numbers. In such a case,
selection within the society operated to destroy the control

systems on which the survival of the whole society depended.

While the survival-related group was localized, leading to positive selection of groups that limited their population and preserved their habitat, the system of cultural control of individuals had a well-defined logic. When survival came to depend on larger political and then national groups—but with emotional attachments and a substantial part of control over individuals vested in nonlocalized subgroups—the logic was lost; man was running out of control and headed for a collision with nature's criteria for survival. This argument is one way of extending the theory of natural selection and group control to explain the rise and fall of advanced societies and the present position of man.

GROUP CONTROL OVER INDIVIDUALS IN MAN

Human behavior involves a response to the environment on the part of the individual; it reflects the "learning" of the individual about the consequences to him of different types of action. This idea can be conceptualized in various ways. One useful framework is Skinner's theory of behavior in terms of "operant conditioning."[14] The basic idea is that people learn from experience which actions have favorable outcomes and which have unfavorable outcomes and act as if they "prefer" the former. In Skinner's behavioristic approach, the "operant"—the action whose consequences are defined by the environment—is modified through conditioning, through experience in which some actions result in positive reinforcement and other actions do not, or result in negative reinforcement. Through repetitive experience, this process of operant conditioning increases the likelihood of the behavior receiving the positive reinforcement. Individual behavior thus becomes systematically responsive to the environment.

This theory requires no assertion of conscious planning or "rational behavior." Skinner's work was done largely with animals, the efficacy of operant conditioning being demonstrated through such achievements as teaching pigeons to play Ping-Pong. Yet the outcome is essentially the same one

[14] B. F. Skinner, *Science and Human Behavior* (New York: Macmillan, 1953).

that would result if the individuals were behaving rationally. By learning to play Ping-Pong, an activity to which pigeons have little natural inclination, when it "paid off" and by not doing so when it did not, the pigeons displayed the class of behavior sometimes attributed only to the "rational man" or "economic man."

The process of response of individuals to their environment can be conceptualized in various ways. Psychologists do not agree on details of the theory of behavior. The present argument requires only that people respond systematically to their environment, which is consistent with a wide variety of particular psychological theories.

Some of the mechanisms by which the group disciplines the behavior of its individuals are dealt with by sociology and social psychology. Recent work has viewed these mechanisms within an adaptation or evolutionary framework.[15] Social norms and goals, social roles, morality, conscience and guilt, dominance and dependency, myths and taboos—in the society that evolved through natural selection, all of these belonged to the survival-related system of societal control over the behavior of individuals.[16] They contributed to population control and environmental preservation. They also contributed to economic efficiency by providing a framework for division of functions and mutually rewarding relations among individuals and groups, and by suppressing conflict and destructive activities. On the other hand, for their own self-protection these mechanisms may be conservative, resistant to change, and thus may impede innovations that would increase economic efficiency.

These group mechanisms are the means of conveying the results of a social learning process, embodying the lessons of past experience and thus providing guidance to individual decisions. When it operates effectively, this process of joint or social learning increases the potentialities of human adaptation of behavior to the environment. It increases the body of experience relevant to the guidance of any given action,

[15] See John W. McDavid and Herbert Harari, *Social Psychology* (New York: Harper & Row, 1968), Unit II, especially Chap. 4.

[16] Bernard G. Campbell, *Human Evolution: An Introduction to Man's Adaptation* (Chicago: Aldine, 1966), pp. 313–324.

reducing the limitations otherwise deriving from the shortness of human life and memory.

The social learning process itself involves a structure, a system, that may differ from one society to another. Like computer programs for the iterative solution of complex problems, the social learning processes may have different structures and involve different performance characteristics. For example, the initial power system and structure of group interests may prevent a society from learning certain lessons that are essential to its survival. Increasing economic efficiency can be viewed as a problem like varying the rules of football in such a way as to bring about a desired adjustment in the resulting game.

The game analogy is usefully extended to another level: that of the metagame determining the rules of the economic game. This metagame is governed by the rules of the meeting in which football officials vote to change the rules of the game of football. Thus the rules of the lower-level game may be influenced by the rules of the higher-level game, which defines the relative power of different groups and thus affects the changes that are made. Consequently, if the laws of a nation affect individual behavior and thus the rate of change in economic efficiency, the laws of international economic dealings are relevant because of their influence over the external environment confronted by the nation, which influences its laws.

SELECTION IN THE LONG RUN AND THE SHORT RUN

Man's present position involves—within the framework of natural selection—a very short-run development, a single episode in a long story. The relation between the operation of selection during short and long periods of time is therefore of interest. The demise of earlier species and of high-flying human societies indicates that short-period success does not necessarily lead to long-run success.

Groups and species could win a short-run victory by adopting a strategy of expansionism—abandoning population restraint and becoming expansive and aggressive. But the intragroup selection mechanisms that supported this behavior would not provide a means of consolidating the position of the species after its expansion. It would thus risk failure because of internal conflict and destruction of its environment and food supply.

The prevalence of population-limiting species evidences the long-run success of group strategies that protect internal order and the habitat. The expansive societies of man, including those of modern civilization, can be interpreted as involving an experiment of the other type, an experiment whose outcome is still in question. Societal behavior leading to short-run success in expansion may be inconsistent with maintenance of systems of societal control required for success in the long run. This theme relates to the interpretation of man's present position.

NATURAL SELECTION AND FORESIGHT
AS ALTERNATIVE MEANS OF ADAPTATION

In the naturalistic view, the origin of life and its evolution to its present state, including present-day man and his culture, have resulted from a very long game of "trial and error," of random variation and selection. This process has built orderly and wonderfully complex systems that are functional and that look to the human mind as if they reflected purpose.

Similarly, highly systematized patterns of individual behavior can derive from conditioning—which is variation plus selection operating through mechanisms of the nervous system—and from the application of cultural patterns derived by a parallel process. In this area also, failure to understand the power of the mechanism of variation plus selection leads to the interpretation that systematic or seemingly purposive human behavior must be "rational" or planned. This assumption has led to the argument that institutions and systems requiring such human behavior are not feasible—and that theories assuming it are not realistic—because man is not "rational."

With reference to political systems, failure to understand the effectiveness of variation plus selection leads to the view that the only key to order is planning. This approach includes a set of policy prescriptions stemming not from naturalistic evaluation of the performance of alternative institutions but from the erroneous diagnosis that the alternatives are such planning and disorder.

Despite this basic error in thought that attributes the order of the universe to human foresight, or its analogue of godly foresight, there is no doubt that human foresight does play a role in the adaptation and performance of man within the framework of natural selection. The efficiency and rapidity of adaptation within the rules of any society derives in part from the foresight of the individuals and groups in visualizing the outcome—within the existing societal rules—of alternative actions. Yet more important, the formation of the societal rules themselves may reflect the foresight of societal leaders. Thus the adaptation of societies to nature's requirements in the case of man has not depended entirely on trial-and-error selection among societies but has been derived in part from the foresight of societal lawgivers who diagnosed the consequences of alternative systems of societal rules and chose those that, they hoped, would lead to success.

In determining the fate of a particular society or civilization, foresight and the role of the lawgiver can be at least temporarily decisive. Past societies that have risen to great eras have been interpreted as reflecting the effects of unusually efficacious sets of societal rules, which imposed on the actions of individuals and groups in society a principle of selection or reinforcement yielding a societal performance that met nature's criteria for a rise. In many cases the underlying formulation of societal rules appears to reflect the foresight of a limited group in society, or even of an individual lawgiver. Thus the performance of ancient Athens was influenced by the set of cultural rules formulated or perpetuated by Homer, and the city prospered for a time under the political rules defined by the lawgiver Solon. The invincibility of ancient Sparta for 500 years was attributed by the ancients to the extraordinary set of societal rules attributed to the lawgiver Lycurgus. The rise of Rome seems to have depended on efficacious cultural rules derived from the earlier history of its dominant group, and its later fall has been interpreted to reflect the loss of this set of rules and the inability to replace it by another.

Within this framework, the lawgivers responsible for the

burst of increased economic efficiency in the West during the past two centuries were the physiocrats, the classical economists, and the political philosophers of the eighteenth century, whose work underlay the creation of an open political system that fostered change and efficiency. Economic, legal, and cultural rules also existed that limited the birth rate and the rate of population increase in Europe. But this system of societal rules never dealt satisfactorily with population limitation and dealt scarcely at all with preservation of the environment. Its provisions relating to growth in efficiency have been importantly changed in response to the subsequent swing in prevalent political beliefs. Thus the view can be taken that this system of societal control is no longer adequate and is being undermined in any case.

In such an interpretation, the hope for survival of this society would be the appearance of a new lawgiver or class of lawgivers, who would define societal rules that would preserve the civilization through another era. The adoption of such a new set of societal rules, however, involves political hurdles that could be impossible to surmount. Perhaps few societies can thus reform themselves.

The lawgiver must take a naturalistic approach to society and to the performance required for its survival. The historical lawgivers met this criterion. Their rules were oriented toward societal performance—not appeal to human ego, individual self-realization, or the fulfillment of the individual conscience. Even before modern science, they were scientific in that they involved a realistic conception of the kind of performance a society must generate if it is to survive, as well as the kinds of societal rules that would produce that kind of performance. Whether a society formulates and adopts such a set of rules, whether it drifts into impotence and decay from adherence to societal rules generating an increasingly inadequate societal performance, or whether it adopts, because of their psychological appeal or persuasive presentation, societal rules that destroy the effectiveness of the society—this is the basic issue determining the fate of an individual society or civilization.

DETERMINANTS OF LIVING STANDARDS

The focus of this book, as of the theory of economic development, is explanation of the time path of the standard of living or of real income per capita. The approach taken here is to interpret the course of economic well-being over time as determined by the systems governing three aspects of societal performance: (1) the rate of change in economic efficiency, (2) the rate of population growth, and (3) the rate of destruction of national resources and the physical environment. These systems interact not only with one another, but also with the international systems that impinge upon them.

An increase in economic efficiency tends to increase living standards. An increase in population tends to increase total output but may either increase or reduce living standards. (The latter effect would be probable in most present-day nations.) A degraded environment implies reduced living standards, but the actions that damage the environment may, in an immediate sense, temporarily increase living standards; in like manner, actions to preserve the environment would reduce the current living standard.

Moreover, changes in the standard of living affect the behavior of population. An increase in living standards reduces the death rate by providing the medical means to delay death. It also doubtlessly affects the birth rate, though in ways that are more difficult to represent even crudely.

Population growth may require the use of less efficient land or more costly natural resources. Additional crowding and growth of urban areas may involve costs that are an offset to efficiency growth. By adversely affecting living standards and narrowing the economy's bill of goods, population growth may narrow the variety of productive processes and the opportunities for efficiency improvement. Additional crowding and pressure on natural resources may entail additional costs to prevent environmental deterioration or to offset adverse effects on living standards.

This conceptual framework can explain not only different rates of improvement in living standards among different nations and different eras, but also stable and worsening conditions of life. Among possible cases are: (1) improvement in economic efficiency fully offset or more than offset by population growth, resulting in no improvement or worsening in per capita output; (2) deterioration in economic efficiency, resulting in reduction in living standards and, under some conditions, in population; and (3) increase in living standards that is then arrested or reversed by cumulative deterioration of the physical environment.

INTERACTION AMONG EFFICIENCY CHANGE, POPULATION, AND THE ENVIRONMENT

Major dependencies among the three systems determining the course of living standards are depicted in Figure 3.2.

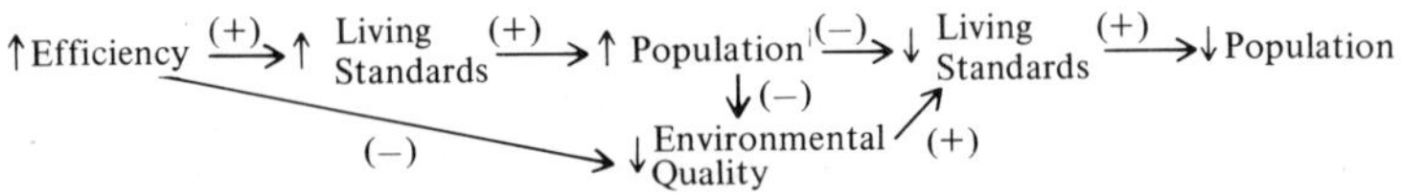

FIGURE 3.2 Dependencies Among Systems Governing Economic Development

Improvement in economic efficiency leads to an increase in real output and to increased living standards. In many cases, however, such improvement leads to population increase, which tends to reduce living standards (the minus sign indicating the opposite direction of changes in the cause and the effect). The developments that increase economic efficiency and living standards in many cases lead to destruction of the physical environment, which, after a lag, also adversely affects living standards. Less-favorable living standards check population growth. If sufficiently severe, a decline in living standards may result in famine and widespread disease and disorder, thus leading to large population reduction under most unhappy conditions.

A somewhat more inclusive illustration of the network of dependencies is given in Figure 3.3, abstracting now from the time dimension. The core relationship, included within the shaded area, shows the positive effect of efficiency change on living standards. A positive effect in the other direction is also asserted, at least over a range that is relevant to many societies. An increase in living standards favorably affects further efficiency change by improving health and education and making available a wide range of consumer goods, including those that can be produced at rising efficiency by advancing technology.

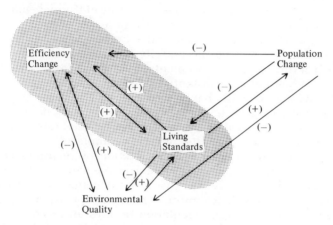

FIGURE 3.3 Feedbacks Affecting Economic Development

In the most favorable case, economic development arising from this positive feedback loop continues indefinitely. Population and the condition of the environment are stable. This case of economic progress with stabilized population and environment is considered later in the text as a policy target.

Commonly, however, increase in living standards leads to population growth and environmental destruction. Let us review some of the additional dependencies in this more complex system. Increased economic efficiency has the direct effect of increasing (making larger than they otherwise would be) real income and real income per capita. Such improvement in living standards, however, has some effect in delaying death, through improved nutrition and medical care. The quantitative strength of this dependency might vary widely from case to case, being weakest in affluent societies where nutrition and medicine are already nearly as favorable as permitted by existing knowledge. An increase in living standards also operates through some mechanisms to increase the birth rate, particularly by improving the health of parents and the quality of prenatal care.

It is often argued that an increase in living standards will eventually reduce the birth rate because it leads to wider acceptance of middle-class values. The role of this dependency is more debatable. In the West, an increase in living standards was for a time associated with a decline in the birth rate. However, this will not necessarily happen in all cases. In much of the world, improvement in living standards in recent decades has had no substantial effect in reducing the birth rate and may actually have increased it. The Great Depression lowered the birth rate, whereas the postwar affluence, at least initially, raised it again. The causal relations in question here are uncertain and probably complex.[17]

What of causation in the other direction, of the influence of population on per capita income and the rate of efficiency change? In most relevant cases, the dependence of living standards and efficiency improvement on population size is a negative one. A larger population implies lower per capita income unless the additional population is associated with at least a proportionate addition to total real output. In most cases, increase in population leads to a less than proportional increase in output because of limitations of land, natural resources, capital goods, educational facilities, management skill, and other factors.[18]

By limiting per capita income, population growth may adversely affect the rate of improvement in efficiency. Increased income per capita—at least over some range—is fa-

[17] The view that an increase in living standards cannot be counted on to reduce birth rates in Asia is expressed by Gunnar Myrdal in *Asian Drama* (New York: Twentieth Century Fund, 1968), p. 1463. The dependence of the birth-rate decline in the West on factors not existing in most other societies is pointed out in the next chapter.

[18] Adverse effects of rapid population growth on efficiency improvement are discussed in Ansley J. Coale, "Population and Economic Development," in Philip M. Hauser (ed.), *The Population Dilemma* (Englewood Cliffs, N.J.: Prentice-Hall, 1963), pp. 46–69.

vorable to efficiency improvement because it permits higher standards of health and education and broadens the bill of goods of the society beyond basic agricultural products and housing, thereby broadening the frontier along which improvements in production methods can occur.

The third system involved in the network of dependencies defines the rate of deterioration of the physical environment. In ancient as well as modern times, the process of improvement in economic efficiency accompanied by increased living standards and population growth has led to deterioration of the environment. To some extent, this deterioration is a direct result of the changes in production methods—industrialization, irrigation, and use of pesticides. To some extent, it is due to the increase in living standards or to developments inseparably associated with it: use of nonbasic consumer goods, urbanization, and increase in demand for foods and fuels. A population increase damages the environment by increasing the demand for food and space, which leads to overutilization and destruction of agricultural land, to exhaustion of natural resources, and to pollution.

Environmental deterioration limits increases in efficiency and improvement in living standards, perhaps reversing the latter by imposing additional costs that must be offset in the production process. Certain resources disappear; thus the maintenance of even a given population and living standard becomes ever more difficult.

If the interaction system involved only efficiency change and changes in living standards, it would be a positive feedback loop, potentially extending economic progress without limit. But both population and the physical environment add negative feedback loops, act to check improvement in living standards, and set a boundary to economic progress. Improvement in economic efficiency that leads to population increase and environmental destruction cannot continue indefinitely. Here man confronts the constraints of nature.

ALTERNATIVE TIME PATHS AND OUTCOMES

Interactions involving efficiency change and population growth—along with exogenous disturbances and episodic events in the society—occur over a period of time, the outcome depending on the quantitative dependencies and their lags. The number of possible cases thus becomes very large and their interpretation complex and beyond the capabilities of casual thought. It is useful to define a set of time patterns that can serve as reference points for subsequent discussion.

In one such pattern, increase in economic efficiency occurs without population growth or environmental destruction, as represented by the inner system in Figure 3.4. A

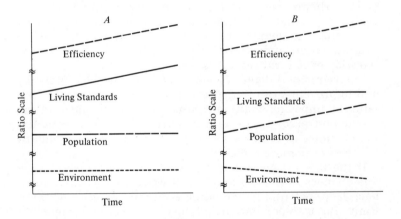

FIGURE 3.4 Illustrative Time Paths of Economic Development

schematicand nonquantitative depiction of such a time path is given in panel A of Figure 3.4. Economic efficiency increases at a steady relative rate. Because population does not change, the improved efficiency is reflected in increased living standards. Because the environment is not deteriorating, the process can continue without any definable limitation.

Literal stabilization of the physical environment is impossible as long as man is mining fossil fuels and minerals. At some future time, the recycling of materials and use of atomic energy with improved control over its pollution effects might permit something approaching a literal stabilization of the physical environment, though this achievement might also require a level of population much lower than the existing one. In the meantime, perhaps a stabilized environment can be thought of as one involving improvements in some respects that offset a worsening in others.

This time path is not hazardous and in that sense is a reasonable target for a risk-avoiding policy program. No cumulative problems to be solved in the future and no obvious impediments to sustainability of the course arise—so long as the improvements in economic efficiency and the increase in living standards do not undercut the societal control systems on which the success depends. Moreover, if the rate of efficiency growth slowed or even halted, the result would be only a slowing or halting of the rate of improvement in living standards, and not a deterioration of living standards or the destruction of the civilization.

The opposite to this favorable pattern is the one shown in panel B of Figure 3.4, a course that is close to the one prevailing in India and some other societies. Here improvement in efficiency is accompanied by proportionate population growth and also by environmental destruction. The increase in output thus made available is reflected not in an improvement of living standards but in population growth. The quality of life is at the bare subsistence level for a substantial proportion of the people and is not improving; the environment is being destroyed; the population is growing to levels that may prove unsustainable.

The course is a hazardous one. It cannot be continued indefinitely, for both environmental destruction and population growth must be halted at some point. Yet a slowing in the rate of growth in output, especially of food, will lead to starvation of the growing population. If some of the negative effects of environmental destruction operate with a lag and the past improvements in efficiency cannot be sustained in a deteriorating situation, the whole course may be retraced. The population may be reduced by famine, and the methods of production in the deteriorating society will revert to the primitive ones of earlier times. What will not be reversed is the environmental destruction, which will leave the society worse off than at the outset, requiring a final population smaller than the initial one.

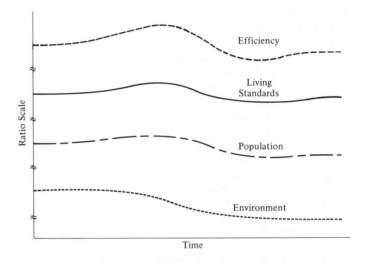

FIGURE 3.5 The Rise and Fall of a Civilization

A sequence of progress and decay something like the typical historical case is depicted by Figure 3.5.[19] An increase in economic efficiency leads to an increase in living standards and also to lagging population growth and accelerated environmental destruction. The changes in the society lead to loss of the relevance and effectiveness of the societal structure that underlay the initial increases in efficiency, causing slowing of improvement in economic efficiency. This slowdown, plus the growth of population and environmental destruction, leads to reduction in living standards, which aggravates societal disharmony and leads to further reductions in the effectiveness of societal controls over individuals and groups, with

[19] See the characterization with reference to early civilizations in Harrison Brown, *The Challenge of Man's Future* (New York: Viking, 1954), pp. 14–22.

consequent reductions in efficiency. Societal deterioration
and decline in living standards lead to a decline in population
because of starvation and disorder. The society may stabilize
again at a low level of efficiency and population in its depleted
environment, or the dynamics of deterioration may carry it to
extinction, resulting in its replacement by another society.

Such a drama of the rise and fall of a society is an old idea.
Adam Smith's view of two centuries ago remains suggestive:

> *The liberal reward of labour, therefore, as it is the effect of increas-*
> *ing wealth, so it is the cause of increasing population. To com-*
> *plain of it, is to lament over the necessary effect and cause of the*
> *greatest public prosperity.*
>
> *It deserves to be remarked, perhaps, that it is in the progressive*
> *state, while the society is advancing to the further acquisition,*
> *rather than when it has acquired its full complement of riches, that*
> *the condition of the labouring poor, of the great body of the people,*
> *seems to be the happiest and the most comfortable. It is hard in*
> *the stationary, and miserable in the declining state. The progres-*
> *sive state is in reality the cheerful and the hearty state to all the*
> *different orders of the society. The stationary is dull; the declining*
> *melancholy.*[20]

MODERN ECONOMIC DEVELOPMENT: WHAT IS DIFFERENT?

How does modern experience relate to this pattern? The
major Western nations are in a stage of rising efficiency.
Population growth continues, the additional population in
some cases becoming increasingly burdensome with the pass-
ing of each decade. Destruction of the environment continues, occurring in the past two decades at a rate unlike anything that happened or could have happened in the past.
Unless something new enters the picture, the coming phase
will involve growing costs of crowding and steeply accelerated costs of environmental destruction.

The crucial questions are: (1) whether or not population
growth and environmental destruction can be halted before
they lead to societal decline or at least decelerated enough to

---

[20] Adam Smith, *An Inquiry into the Nature and Causes of the Wealth of Nations*
(New York: Random House, 1937), p. 81.

remove the immediate hazard of a fall, and (2) whether the hazard of such a fall is still a century or more in the future or whether it is close at hand.

Those societies in which economic development has involved a great increase in population, with living standards still near the subsistence level, are widely agreed to be close to a fall. Some observers believe that famine and deterioration in societies that include a large proportion of the earth's population are likely to be very serious within a decade.[21] The reliance of these societies on food imports that cannot be increased sufficiently to keep pace with the growing population may make this outcome inevitable.

The current rise is more extensive than any earlier one, involving societies that cover a large portion of the earth's surface. Moreover, the incomparably greater technological achievements imply kinds of environmental damage that were not possible before—exhaustion of resources of fossil fuels and metals, chemical poisoning, global pollution of water and air. Together these factors imply that if there is a general fall, if economic development proves self-limiting and abortive, the fall will be unlike anything seen before.

> *We are quickly approaching the point where, if machine civilization should, because of some catastrophe, stop functioning, it will probably never again come into existence. . . . Our ancestors had available large resources of high-grade ores and fuels that could be processed by the most primitive technology—crystals of copper and pieces of coal that lay on the surface of the earth, easily mined iron, and petroleum in generous pools reached by shallow drilling. . . . As our dependence shifts to such resources as low-grade ores, rock, seawater, and the sun, the conversion of energy into useful work will require ever more intricate technical activity, which would be impossible in the absence of a variety of complex machines and their products—all of which are the result of our intricate industrial civilization, and which would be impossible without it. Thus, if a machine civilization were to stop functioning as the result of*

---

[21] William and Paul Paddock, *Famine—1975!* (Boston: Little, Brown, 1967). The improvement in agricultural yields that began in the late 1960s as a result of the successful development of new varieties of grain provides a basis for at least pushing back this gloomy timetable.

some catastrophe, it is difficult to see how man would again be able to start along the path of industrialization with the resources that would then be available to him. . . .

Our present industrialization, itself the result of a combination of no longer existent circumstances, is the only foundation on which it seems possible that a future civilization capable of utilizing the vast resources of energy now hidden in rocks and seawater, and unutilized in the sun, can be built. If this foundation is destroyed, in all probability the human race has "had it." [22]

POLICY AND ECONOMIC DEVELOPMENT

In terms of this theory, how should a society—assuming it has such self-control—set about to increase its standard of living? The risk-avoiding policy program involves the following steps.

First, a system of population control should be established that will prevent an increase in living standards from causing a population increase. More ambitiously, the population-control system should bring population to a point on an optimal time path and thereafter maintain it on this path. The system of population control must be such that it will not be undermined or nullified by selective changes in population or by changes in society that will be caused by increases in living standards.

Second, a parallel system of environmental preservation should be established, which also must continue to be effective under the changing conditions to be brought about by rising living standards.

After these steps have been completed, a set of societal rules favorable to increase in economic efficiency should be established. This set of rules also must cause continued increases in efficiency in the changing conditions that will be brought about by rising living standards. At least, it must not be a self-destructive system that will lead to an increase in efficiency and living standards followed by loss of societal coherency, mutually destructive activities, and decline in efficiency.

These conditions are not easily met. Neither the knowledge to define the required societal actions nor the political

[22] H. Brown, *op. cit.,* pp. 222–223.

capabilities to bring them about are readily available. But the validity of this policy program as an intellectual reference point is not reduced by the fact that it is not easily attained.

As evaluated in terms of this theory, the kinds of economic development programs and foreign aid programs that have predominated in the past two decades are highly risky; indeed, they are almost certain to produce an unfavorable outcome in some societies. The expected outcome of temporary increases in the goods and services available to a nation because of externally imposed and unsustainable increases in efficiency or as a result of foreign aid—unaccompanied by systems of population control and environmental preservation—is an increase in population that, after a time, places the society in a position worse than the one from which it started.

A more optimistic interpretation of such a policy package, of course, arises from the theory of economic development. If there is a coherent process of economic development that once begun is self-feeding, that automatically provides continued increases in efficiency and automatically limits further population growth, then the policies in question are quite safe. Once jogged, or pushed, or pulled through the take-off, the society will be safe, on the one-track road of progress. Because such progress is the natural and expected state of human societies, anything that will shake a nation out of its traditionalism or backwardness may be helpful in getting it through the take-off. Due to the fact that the alternatives are standing still or enjoying unending and automatic progress, it is not necessary to be fussy as to just what is done to the patient; the more that is done, the greater is the chance of the shift from stability to progress.

These are two quite coherent and internally consistent ways of looking at the phenomena in question. They lead to two quite different interpretations of the effects of policy programs. They are inconsistent with one another. They cannot both be true.

CONCLUSIONS

Living standards depend on interactions within and among the societal systems governing efficiency change, population growth, and environmental destruction. Accurate depiction of these processes will permit predictions of the future course of events and estimation of the influence of alternative policies on the course of events. If theory can define future time paths associated with different sets of policies, an effort can be made to achieve the policies required to avoid disaster by permitting modern society to meet nature's criteria for survival. An exploratory discussion of the factors involved in these interacting systems in given in the chapters that follow.

The theory outlined here depicts the outcome as depending on complex interaction processes like those involved in other aspects of natural selection, and as ultimately depending on whether or not a society meets survival criteria defined by nature. This approach contrasts with theories in which the outcome of the process is predetermined and favorable. Real and important issues are posed, both for theory or knowledge, and for policy.

CHAPTER 4 / Population and Living Standards

In determining living standards and the quality of life, the system that determines population has the decisive role. Even given the most effective conceivable performance with respect to improvement in efficiency and environmental preservation, population growth at rates within human capabilities still could assure a degraded quality of life and the destruction of civilization. A poor performance with reference to population can assure failure irrespective of what is accomplished in other connections. On the other hand, a sufficient reduction of population could lead to a high standard of living and a favorable quality of life even though no further improvements occurred in economic efficiency. Because of its decisive influence over the outcome, population is properly at the center of the theory of living standards.

The inherent difficulty of population control is a second reason for giving special attention to population. To grow in economic efficiency requires only the continuous operation of selection in favor of more efficient ways of accomplishing economic tasks. To preserve the environment requires, at least in the simplest cases, only certain taboos and prohibitions. The control of population in an uncertain environment, however, requires an elaborate homeostatic control system, or a feedback-control system, that necessarily has a pervasive influence on the way of life of the species.

The control systems required to deal with population pose special problems that make them difficult to evolve through selection or to create through foresight. Population control involves a conflict of individual interests and group interests, as well as a potential conflict between the short run and the long. Systems of population limitation can be inherently self-destroying, by leading to selection in favor of those who violate their rules. Although limitation of population has survival value in the long run, in some circumstances more rapid population growth confers power in the short run. In view of these difficulties, it is not surprising that man's failings in population control pose the basic threat to the survival of civilization.

NATURALISTIC THEORY OF POPULATION

Recent contributions leave population theory in an unsettled state. They indicate that the role of homeostatic mechanisms in regulation of population is much greater than earlier had been realized.[1] Fully to fill in the details of the theory and to collect and interpret hitherto neglected information on human population-control systems will take decades. However, the outline of the theory is clear enough for present purposes.

The fact that higher animals utilize homeostatic, group-oriented population-control systems, rather than relying on external forces to limit their population, seems well established. Limitation by external forces, in general, would not operate sufficiently quickly and would not be sufficiently density-dependent to preserve the population of the species at the level required if the species is to defend its domain, preserve adequate food per member, and preserve its habitat.

[1] V. C. Wynne-Edwards, *Animal Dispersion in Relation to Social Behavior* (Edinburgh: Oliver and Boyd, 1962).

POPULATION BEHAVIOR OF ANIMALS

The higher animals have genetically conveyed population-control systems involving response to group density or to the size of the territory available to the individual. The particular mechanisms used are diverse and complex. Wide-ranging fish and birds use a communal breeding ground of limited size, individuals unable to find a nesting space not being permitted to breed. Some animals claim a territory of a size that is genetically defined and defend this territory against intruders. Again, those unable to claim a territory do not breed, and in some cases, because of lack of food or shelter, they fall prey to disease or predators. Other species respond to crowding by stress symptoms that lead to neglect of the young and a high mortality rate, to a reduced breeding rate, or to destruction of the young and other physical conflicts among members. The behavior, however, is density-dependent and does not continue when numbers are reduced to the appropriate level. These density-dependent mechanisms have been evolved through group selection; the groups and species that lacked them lost out through natural selection to those that had them.

The rationing system for the spaces available commonly involves a dominance hierarchy in which adults are preferred to the young, and physical prowess is valued, but actual physical conflict and damage to group members is avoided or economized. In many cases, the dominance hierarchy is established through ceremonial contests, the participants being keyed by their instinctive control systems to accept the outcome without mortal conflict. The rationing system is clearly hierarchical, or antiegalitarian. The handicapped and the deviant do not survive. Such selection at the individual level serves the function of maintaining and improving the quality of the species.

The means of achieving the required pruning of population is closely related to territoriality and the dominance hierarchy. The adults unable to gain a breeding ground are genetically keyed to accept the fate of being nonbreeders; or the individuals unable to gain a satisfactory territory accept exile to an unsatisfactory one and fall prey to disease or predators. The latter act as the executioners for the population-limitation system but do not perform the essential regulating function. In some cases, the patterns of feeding the young are such that when the food supply is inadequate, only the strongest survive—the others, again, being keyed to accept their doom. In some cases, the animals are their own executioners, responding to stress symptoms that derive from excessive density.

It is essential that the pruning of population be carried out in such a way as not to damage the health and effectiveness of the individuals who are to survive and in such a way as not to damage the habitat. The instinctive keying of the rejected individuals to accept their fate without contest ensures that this requirement is met.

POPULATION BEHAVIOR OF EARLY MAN

We know that human populations through most of history were stable or grew very slowly. It appears that this growth reflected population-control systems closely parallel to those of other mammals. Primitive peoples were organized into local bands, tribes, or clans with well-defined territories. Group selection favored those peoples that limited population in ways not destructive to the surviving group. The principal methods were conventional rules for abstention from intercourse, abortion of the unborn, and infanticide.[2] These methods were supplemented by head-hunting, cannibalism, and other types of institutionalized warfare and feuding that raised the death rate. In some societies, religious sacrifice and witchcraft may have been a significant factor limiting population growth.

Because this control system was conveyed by culture rather than genetically, practices varied among local groups and regions of the world. Cultural taboos involving abstention from intercourse during lactation of the previous child, which com-

---

[2] Wynne-Edwards, *op. cit.,* p. 492. An early and long-neglected contribution on population limitation among primitive peoples is the work of A. M. Carr-Saunders, *The Population Problem: A Study in Human Evolution* (Oxford: Oxford University Press, 1922).

monly was prolonged for several years, were common. Other occasions for abstention defined by culture and religion also prevailed. Abortion seemingly was widespread in some parts of the world. Infanticide in some cases was explicit and thoroughly institutionalized; in others it involved a conventional neglect or exposure of children under defined conditions.

These population-control systems tied into tribal culture and the tribal system of territoriality; therefore, they naturally broke down or required adaptation when improvements in economic efficiency led to larger units and to the modification of the tribal culture. However, many of these population-control systems persisted into historical times. The use of infanticide by the ancient Greeks is well documented. Institutionalized neglect of female children and other forms of infanticide were common in India until they were extirpated by the British. Such practices commonly were seen by Christian Europeans simply as barbaric, savage, or inhumane—their functional nature not being understood.

POPULATION CONTROL IN EUROPE

The population-control systems of primitive man, as was noted previously, derived from group selection and closely paralleled those of other mammals, though the control system was defined by culture rather than genetically as in animals. In both cases, it was largely self-enforcing, but the group participated in enforcement as needed. The system centered around the local group as a whole.

The quite different kind of population-limitation system that developed in preindustrial Europe is important for several reasons. The fact that such a system does not exist in other parts of the world is a reason why future population behavior should not be expected to trace the earlier path taken by Europe—as, indeed, it has notably not been doing. Moreover, the European system of population limitation provided the background for the thought of the classical economists and Malthus—that is to say, the background for the fundamental thought on this subject that still influences us. Finally, so far as this system of population limitation persisted into the nineteenth and even the twentieth centuries, judgments as to the future behavior of population in the West depend in part on judgments as to its continued operation, its replacement by some other system of population control, or its erosion and destruction without replacement.

This system of population limitation was distinctive in that it did not depend entirely on the local group, the dominance of which had been reduced by urbanization and increased mobility. This system of population limitation was thus a radical departure from the discipline of individuals by a territorially based group, the system derived through group selection. It rested to a unique extent on family self-interest and foresight, including concern for the conditions of life of one's children.

The individualistic nature of the system was tied to private property, one's income being dependent on his own productive efforts and property. The communal economic systems of primitive peoples required group-oriented and group-enforced systems of population limitation. This system was tied, rather, to individualism and private property.

The hierarchy of economic classes, including such occupation-oriented ones as the guilds, was an essential element in this population-limitation system. The economic status and other prerogatives of individuals depended on their position in this hierarchy, which depended on their performance, and that of their ancestors, in limiting family size. In contrast to the population-control systems of animals and primitive man, there existed a class, the lowest group in this hierarchy, that was subject to no superior system of population limitation and whose numbers were limited by want, starvation, and disease. The system was sensitive to preservation of the economic and political institutions that maintained this hierarchy.

The mechanisms by which numbers were limited were perhaps unique in the experience of living creatures. The rise of Christianity and the introduction of new ideas concerning morals made unavailable the principal earlier means of limiting numbers—abortion, infanticide, human sacrifice, and ritualized warfare—although these continued to play some role, despite their nonrespectability. But a major means of limiting numbers was an extraordinary abstention from sexual intercourse based on the delay of marriage until an advanced age or abstention from marriage, coupled with severe penalties for childbirth out of wedlock. Conformity to Christian conceptions of the sanctity of life thus was gained largely through a unique system of sexual repression.

The system has been characterized in this way:

> *Before the development of modern industry, Europe was already distinguished from the other great civilizations by the control that its family system imposed on the rate of population growth. Men were induced to put off assuming parental responsibilities until they had acquired the means to care for a wife and children. This meant in many cases that they never married. . . . As a result of this personally onerous but socially effective system of birth control, Europe's population generally did not press as heavily on the subsistence available to it as in the Asian civilizations; compared with China or India, Europe was relatively free of great famines. And at the beginning of the modern era, the continent was still relatively sparsely populated.*[3]

The existence of this system of population limitation in Europe, and its role in maintaining the living standards of most people above the subsistence level, were emphasized by the classical economists and their predecessors. Adam Smith assumed that the wages of the lowest class in a society in equilibrium would be at the subsistence level. The "iron law of wages" would apply, population in this class being limited by the high death rate, especially among children. He also took for granted, however, the fact that, in all other classes of a society, birth limitation was practiced and was the basis for preservation of living standards above the subsistence level.[4]

[3] William Petersen, *The Politics of Population* (New York: Doubleday, 1965), p. 126. The contrast between the Asian and European patterns is also emphasized by Myrdal: "As is suggested by the broad trends of crude birth rates in India and Ceylon . . . the fertility of the peoples of South Asia does not seem to have changed appreciably during the past several decades, probably centuries. Such high levels of fertility have not ordinarily been found in western Europe during recorded history." Gunnar Myrdal, *Asian Drama* (New York: Twentieth Century Fund, 1968), p. 1423.

[4] Adam Smith, *An Inquiry into the Nature and Causes of the Wealth of Nations* (New York: Random House, 1937), pp. 78–81.

The ideas later associated with Malthus were well developed
and widely influential by the middle of the eighteenth century. Schumpeter attributes the first full statement of the
Malthusian principle of population to Giovanni Botero in 1589
and refers to many statements preceding that of Adam Smith.[5]
Malthus' contribution was only to systematize and dramatize
a set of ideas that predominated in European thought by 1750,
before the industrial revolution.

The writings of Robert Wallace offer a striking illustration
of the prevalence of these ideas and the seriousness with
which they were taken. He proposes (anticipating Marx) a
system of state communism as the ideal society, but then de-
clares it to be unattainable because it would eliminate the
existing checks on population growth. His position was thus
characterized by Godwin: "But after having exhibited this
brilliant picture, he finds an argument that demolishes the
whole, and restores him to indifference or despair, in 'the
excessive population that would ensue.' "[6]

This limitation of population in Europe, on which so much
seems to have depended, thus was not achieved without cost
or pain; it was not a free gift of progress. Deferment of marriage and sexual activity and the forgoing of marriage were
widespread. In England between 1840 and 1870, the average
age at marriage of clergymen, doctors, lawyers, merchants,
and similar "gentlemen" was about 30 years. In Ireland—the
extreme case of European marriage deferment and avoidance—the practice also prevailed among the working class.
In 1946 in Ireland, the average age at marriage was 33 years
for males and 28 for females. About one person in four remained single at age 45.[7] So far as birth limitation within
marriage was required in addition to deferment of marriage,
the principal means seem to have been *coitus interruptus,*

[5] Joseph A. Schumpeter, *History of Economic Analysis* (New York: Oxford University Press, 1954), pp. 254–258.

[6] William Godwin, *Enquiry Concerning Political Justice and Its Influence on
Morals and Happiness* (Toronto: University of Toronto Press, 1946), II, 515.
The reference is to Robert Wallace, *Various Prospects of Mankind, Nature and
Providence,* 1761. The exchange is referred to in Schumpeter, *op. cit.,* p. 256.
See also A. M. Carr-Saunders, *op. cit.,* Chap. 1.

[7] Petersen, *op. cit.,* p. 129.

abstention, and covert abortion, with infanticide still undoubtedly playing some role.[8]

A system of behavior involving such personal deprivation can only have persisted in response to severe disincentives to the begetting of large families. The pain and misery of early marriage and a large family must have been even greater than that of enforced celibacy. The logic of the system is effectively spelled out by Malthus. For classes above the lowest, early marriage meant the hazard or the certainty of demotion to a lower status in society, to a less-satisfactory pattern of life. At the bottom of the scale, the choice was an onerous one:

> *The laborer who earns 18 pence a day and lives with some degree of comfort as a single man, will hesitate a little before he divides that pittance among four or five, which seems to be but just sufficient for one. Harder fare and harder labor he would submit to for the sake of living with the woman that he loves, but he must feel conscious, if he thinks at all, that should he have a large family, and any ill luck whatever, no degree of frugality, no possible exertion of his manual strength could preserve him from the heart rending sensation of seeing his children starve, or of forfeiting his independence, and of being obliged to the parish for their support.[9]*

The limitation on the begetting of children outside of marriage was enforced by harsh penalties against mothers of illegitimate children, this as "the most obvious and effectual method of preventing the frequent recurrence of a serious inconvenience to a community, appears to be natural, though not perhaps perfectly justifiable."[10]

The foresight of potential parents was supplemented, or

---

[8] Goran Ohlin, *Population Control and Economic Development* (Paris: Development Center of the Organization for Economic Cooperation and Development, 1967), pp. 66–67. Malthus refers to "the custom of exposing children, which, in times of distress, is probably more frequent than is ever acknowledged by Europeans," in explaining why early marriages in China do not lead to a more rapid rate of increase in population. Thomas Robert Malthus, *Population: The First Essay* (Ann Arbor: University of Michigan Press, 1959), p. 21.

[9] Malthus, *op. cit.,* pp. 23–24.

[10] *Ibid.,* p. 71.

stiffened, by social rules and laws prohibiting marriage by those not in a position to support their children. Mill observed, "It is not generally known in how many countries of Europe direct legal obstacles are opposed to improvident marriages." Mill lists laws in various areas prohibiting marriage until the husband can support children or can support them at his station of life. Moreover, "where there is no general law restrictive of marriage, there are often customs equivalent to it"—prohibition by guilds of marriage of apprentices, the Italian practice of permitting marriage only to one son, permitting marriage only when a house is available, and so on.[11] This elaborate secular system for the enforcement of celibacy interacted with that of the Catholic Church, which removed large numbers of both men and women from the ranks of parents.

When preventive checks do not sufficiently operate, the positive check—"by which I mean the check that represses an increase which is already begun"—inexorably operates. The improvident father *does* watch his children starve. Again, this check operates mainly in the lowest class in society, the penalty for excessive parenthood in upper classes being demotion to a lower class but not necessarily to such extremity.[12]

Thus a high death rate from starvation and bad health, given a cyclical nature by the irregularities of plague and famine, does what is not accomplished by the preventive checks. Although disease may spread and also affect the upper classes, the operation of these forces is confined largely to the lowest classes, to those who have not elevated themselves from this status. The foundation of the incentive system discouraging births was the wretched existence and high death rates of the lowest classes in society. Belief in the importance of this incentive system to the preservation of civilization led the classical economists, humane men though they were, to oppose systems of relief that alleviated the hardship of the poor without putting some check on their procreation.

The basic dilemma cannot be more clearly stated than it was by Mill:

[11] John Stuart Mill, *Principles of Political Economy* (New York: Appleton-Century-Crofts, 1881), pp. 430–436.

[12] Malthus, *op. cit.,* p. 25.

Society can feed the necessitous, if it takes their multiplication under its control: or (if destitute of all moral feeling for the wretched offspring) it can leave the last to their discretion, abandoning the first to their own care. But it cannot with impunity take the feeding upon itself, and leave the multiplying free.[13]

The increases in living standards resulting from the industrial revolution and the era of emigration from Europe posed a threat to this system of population limitation. Happily, reductions in the death rate were accompanied or shortly followed by reductions in the birth rate. There was not a population explosion. The reason was that the patterns of population limitation used by the upper classes were, to an increasing extent, adopted by the working class. This limitation was accomplished in some areas, as in Ireland after the potato famine, mainly through delayed marriage; in other areas it seems to have reflected for the most part the effectiveness of primitive means of birth control and illegal abortions in limiting the number of children within each marriage. Many members of the working class used the improved opportunities as had the upper classes to improve the quality of their life rather than to increase their numbers.[14] If the decline in birth rates in Europe during the industrial revolution occurred by extension of the prevailing birth-limitation practices developed during preceding centuries, then there is no reason to expect it to occur in societies in which such centuries-old practices of birth limitation do not exist.

What factors led Europe to develop a system of population limitation that seems to be unique among the major societies of recorded history? Surely one factor was Europe's individualistic philosophy and family system. The core of the European system was the principle that a man should not marry until he could support a family in accordance with his expected station in life. This attitude contrasts with the Asian pattern in which "a bridegroom is usually not expected to be able to take care of a family immediately; this responsibil-

[13] *Ibid.,* p. 447.

[14] The persistence of the European system of population limitation that had been discussed by Malthus, and its adaptation to changing circumstances, are described by Alfred Marshall in *Principles of Economics,* 8th ed. (London: Macmillan, 1947), pp. 182–192.

ity rests on an extended family, at least in the beginning."[15]

The European pattern of population limitation may also have derived in part from the peculiar nature of medieval Europe, with its hierarchy of roles in which each person had his place. This was not a dichotomy of very rich and very poor but a complex system of roles in which many had something to lose by failing to live up to the requirements of their station. Other societies did not share this background and did not evolve a population-limitation system of the European pattern. With reference to population, it seems necessary to interpret various societies as following different paths of development, and not as being simply at different points on the same path.

THE POPULATION EXPLOSION

The long-run picture of human population growth is one of extraordinary acceleration. The human population is estimated to have reached one-quarter of a billion persons about 2,000 years ago. This population doubled in about sixteen centuries. The next doubling took about two centuries, the earth's population reaching 1 billion around 1850. The next doubling, to 2 billion persons, took eighty years, and was completed by about 1930. The next doubling is estimated to take about 45 years. The time required to add a half billion people to the earth's population has declined from the sixteen centuries for our first doubling to about six or seven years at the current level and rate of growth of population.[16]

This population growth has reflected different factors during different eras. By his transition from a hunting to an agricultural life, man modified his effective environment in a way that permitted an enormous expansion of population. The industrial revolution, spread through colonialism beyond

---

[15] Myrdal, *op. cit.,* p. 1433.

[16] See Harold F. Dorn, "World Population Growth," in Philip M. Hauser (ed.), *The Population Dilemma* (Englewood Cliffs, N.J.: Prentice-Hall, 1963), p. 11; Annabelle Desmond, "How Many People Have Ever Lived on Earth?" in Larry K. Y. Ng (ed.), *The Population Crisis* (Bloomington: Indiana University Press, 1965), pp. 20–38.

the West, and the subsequent enormous increase in efficiency in agriculture also increased productive efficiency. In the West, with its low birth rate and rate of population growth, much of this increase in efficiency for a period of more than a century was reflected in improvement of real incomes and living standards. However, in other areas it seems to have been reflected largely or entirely in accelerated growth of population at an unimproved living standard.

The enormous improvement in medical knowledge and insecticides that has occurred within the past century (much of it effective outside of the West only within the past twenty years) has resulted in a decline in death rates of unparalleled abruptness in some areas. This decline has involved a similarly extraordinary rise in the rate of population growth. The most striking example is Ceylon's reduction in death rate of 34 percent in one year and 53 percent in nine years, largely as a result of malaria control.[17]

Since World War II, much of the world outside the developed West has been subjected to a phenomenal decline in the death rate that "is largely 'autonomous' in the specific sense that it is not connected with any preceding or concomitant rise in incomes and levels of living, or even in urbanization or education."[18] In general, this decline has not been accompanied by a decline in the birth rate, nor is it accompanied by any of the circumstances that were associated with decline in the birth rate in the West. It is, therefore, a unique episode in population experience.

The past record includes long eras of roughly constant population for societies, as well as many earlier episodes of the rise and fall of the population of societies. The population of India appears to have been unchanged over the 200 years before the British colonial development. Ceylon seems to have had a larger population in the twelfth century than in 1850.[19] If population growth is to be halted in the modern

[17] Kingsley Davis, "The Amazing Decline of Mortality in Underdeveloped Areas," *American Economic Review Papers and Proceedings,* 46 (May 1956), 307.

[18] Myrdal, *op. cit.,* pp. 1391–1392.

[19] *Ibid.,* p. 1394.

world before it reduces living standards or destroys the basis for orderly government, there apparently must be a great reduction in effective birth rates.

BEHAVIORAL THEORY OF THE BIRTH RATE

The average number of children per couple and the birth rate are defined by the response patterns of the potential parents and the environment to which they respond. Factors to which people respond include cultural norms, legal and economic arrangements, and the costs and benefits of having children.

The proposition that people as parents respond systematically to their environment, we recall, does not require explicitly calculated decisions. In any culture, at least some people do give reasoned consideration to the consequences of sexual activities with reference to additional births. Behavior not formed through an explicit process of verbal rationalization may yet be systematically responsive to people's "feel" for the way the behavior will work out.

In an immediate sense, the number of children desired may be governed for many parents by social norms rather than by an independent decision, but these norms must be responsive, after some lag, to the results of social experiments illustrating the kinds of lives led by parents with different numbers of children.[20] Major classes of factors affecting the number of children desired by parents are of four types: (1) the net economic cost to the parents of having a child; (2) the perceived utility of a child as, as it were, a consumption good; (3) opportunities that must be forgone because of an additional child; and (4) the location of power over the decision as between husband and wife.

The range of possibilities and actual experience in the economic cost of children is evidently very large. A child may be a financial asset in cases where little is expected of parents

---

[20] A review of the psychological literature dealing with the desire to have children is not inconsistent with this interpretation. See Frederick Wyatt, "Clinical Notes on the Motives of Reproduction," *Journal of Social Issues,* 23 (October 1967), 29–56.

by way of the upbringing of children, where child labor pre-vails, and where the children provide old-age support to par-ents. At the other extreme, the upbringing of children ac-cording to upper-class standards in some modern societies involves a large financial outlay; in addition, labor done by children is insignificant, and little or no old-age support from children is expected.

Although the economic cost of children depends partly on social or class norms, it also depends heavily on government policy. Such government policies include (1) enforcement of standards of child care, (2) compulsory education, (3) limita-tion or prohibition of child labor, (4) imposition of the cost of education and health care of children on parents rather than on the population in general through taxation, (5) absence of tax concessions or other subsidies to parents in relation to the number of children, (6) absence of legal enforcement of sup-port of parents by children, and (7) provision, through insur-ance or other means, of old-age support and assistance with large health expenses or other contingencies. Practice in these connections differs widely among existing societies.

Conditions also vary widely among societies with relation to the satisfactions derived by parents from various numbers of children, the opportunities to do other attractive things that must be forgone in order to have a larger family, and the ability of the wife to give effect to her interest in limiting family size. Government policies also affect many of these aspects of the context in which parents make decisions re-garding family size.

In the tribal society, the individual parents were involved in a cultural system generated by group selection that oper-ated as a homeostatic system of population control. They had, it seems, little choice; deviant behavior was not tolerated. Modern society does not have such stringent systems of cul-tural control, leaving greater scope for variation in individual behavior. This behavior, however, still comprises a sys-tematic response to the environment—the set of cues, or the payoff matrix defined for parents by the society's laws, cul-tural norms, and government policies.

The existing situation with reference to birth limitation is anomalous in this sense: Induced abortion is almost everywhere proclaimed to be immoral and is actually illegal, with imposition of severe criminal penalties in some cases. Yet this illegal abortion is a major basis for birth limitation in the West and much of the world. In five countries of Western Europe, it is estimated that there are as many illegal abortions as live births. In Latin America, rates of illegal abortion seem to be even higher, in one country running to perhaps three times the number of live births.[21] Thus for these societies, including the Western nations, to begin obeying or enforcing their own laws against induced abortion would result in an abrupt rise in the birth rate.

FACTORS DETERMINING THE DEATH RATE

Life expectancy at birth is estimated to have been about 30 years in Greece, Rome, and Egypt during a period of about 500 years around the beginning of the Christian era. By 1900 it had risen to 45 to 50 years in North America and Western Europe. Since then it has increased approximately another 20 years. The increase in the expectation of life at birth in the most advanced societies during the past half-century has been as great as in the preceding nineteen centuries.

Still, the decline in the death rate in the West was not as abrupt as in other parts of the world in the post–World War II period. In many areas of the world, the expectation of life at birth increased in twenty years from something like the medieval level of Europe to something approaching its modern level.[22] In the West, the decline in death rates reflected the advance of knowledge, the improvement of living standards, and the development of medicine and technology. This process was contingent on the limitation of births.[23]

---

[21] *The Christian Science Monitor,* May 3, 1969, p. 10. See also Jerome M. Kummer, "The Problems of Abortion: The Personal Population Explosion," in Larry K. Y. Ng, *op. cit.,* p. 208; William and Paul Paddock, *Hungry Nations* (Boston: Little, Brown, 1964), p. 97.

[22] Dorn, *op. cit.,* p. 11.

[23] On the other hand, accidental factors were important in this case also. The reduction in the death rate as a result of smallpox vaccination parallels that from control of malaria after World War II. The reduction of Europe's population by the Black Death of the fourteenth century has been credited with

In the absence of offsetting developments, the reduction in deaths caused by diseases will accelerate population growth. The result will not necessarily cause additional problems with regard to disease prevention, but it will bring additional problems with regard to food supply and the prevention of starvation and famine. Curbing malaria with DDT is inexpensive, but producing food for a growing population in many societies can be done only at increasing cost—or at a lower standard of living—and population growth may push the society, as it were, from a disease boundary onto the starvation boundary.

No dramatic further reductions in death rates because of disease control are now foreseen. The question is whether falling living standards, lack of food, and societal disorganization will replace the positive check on population from disease, or whether these problems can be prevented by birth limitation, along with increase in economic efficiency and improvement of environmental preservation.

SELF-DESTRUCTIVE SYSTEMS OF POPULATION LIMITATION

It was noted previously that local groups of animals and tribal man rigorously enforced their population-control systems against would-be violators. Consider, within the framework of natural selection, what would happen were this not the case. In a tribe communally sharing food, let us say that a minority group is permitted to violate the tribal rules of birth limitation. The size of the minority group increases, requiring further limitation of births by other members of the tribe because of the population density thus created. Over time, the group not limiting population overpowers or obliterates the population-limiting group. Subsequently, of course, it goes on to overtax its habitat and obliterate itself.

---

helping to set the stage for economic progress by limiting population density and easing northern Europe's soil destruction. William and Paul Paddock, *Hungry Nations* (Boston: Little, Brown, 1964), p. 195. The weakening effects of its sixth-century plague, however, left the Byzantine Empire unable to defend itself against Islam and thus prevented the reconsolidation of the Roman Empire that might otherwise have occurred. See Josiah C. Russell, "That Earlier Plague," *Demography*, 5 (1968), 174–184.

Population limitation within any survival-related group, it appears, must be universal. Otherwise, intergroup selection will favor those violating the population-control system, leading to destruction of the system. In the modern world, a common idea is that limitation of births and family size should be voluntary, that each individual has an inherent right to have as many children as he wishes. The proposition is also advanced that the most intelligent and educated people, being the ones most concerned over excessive population and environmental destruction, should take it upon themselves to have small families or even to have no children at all. This would be a self-destructive system in which the intelligent and concerned are eliminated from the society while the ignorant, the unconcerned, or those satisfied with a low quality of life over-reproduce themselves and come to dominate the society.

If the standards of living of the various nations are closely tied together through free immigration, systems of obligatory foreign aid, or the inability of nations with high standards of living to defend themselves against attack by poor nations, the same principle applies on an international level. For a nation to adopt a rule of population limitation and thereby increase its standard of living is for it to write its ticket to oblivion, as this behavior will only result in replacement of successors of its population by immigrants or invaders from other nations that do not limit population. If the survival-related group consists of all mankind, limitation of population thus requires a universal mandatory system of birth restriction.

The factor that permitted the development of population-control systems through natural selection, of course, was the separation of local groups into discrete territories, each becoming a separate survival-related group. Natural selection among these groups led to the development of systems of population control. A difficulty is that such a principle of territoriality does not exist within the modern nation. Thus the survival-related group is not a local group confined to a limited territory but becomes the nation as a whole. In terms of the logic of natural selection, this loss of localism, of a very large number of small experiments among which selection can operate, is dangerous. When the large survival-related group becomes divided into subgroups that gain power by increasing the numbers of their members, the expected outcome is failure.

APPLICATION OF FORESIGHT: POPULATION GOALS

The fate of individual societies in the past—at least for periods of time running to centuries—appears to have been influenced by the contributions of lawgivers, who applied foresight to design institutions that would produce the societal performance required for survival. Because no operating institutions are currently serving as control systems to bring about the behavior of population required for the survival of existing civilization, and because natural selection cannot bring them into existence in a single case or in time to save this civilization, a favorable outcome depends on the role of the lawgiver being fulfilled in this case. This section considers goals such as a lawgiver would seek to define. The next section considers institutions and policies that might serve—if their implementation were politically possible—to bring about the required behavior of population.

The idea that a population may be so large or so small in relation to available resources as to be detrimental to the society is an old one, well developed by the ancient Greeks.[24] This idea implies a concept of an optimal population, one that is neither too large nor too small.

Such an optimal population must be defined with reference to (1) a given physical and social environment and (2) a given preference function or set of goals. When the environment and the set of opportunities that it defines are changing over time, then, with given goals, the optimal population also will change over time. What is to be defined, then, is an optimal time path for population.

---

[24] On the historical development of this idea, see Joseph J. Spengler, "The Economist and the Population Question," *American Economic Review,* 56 (March 1966), 5–12. A statement that has stood the test of time remarkably well appears in A. B. Wolfe, "The Optimum Size of Population," in Louis I. Dublin (ed.), *Population Problems in the United States and Canada* (Boston: Houghton Mifflin, 1926), pp. 63–76. The approaches of Carr-Saunders and Wynne-Edwards referred to earlier use the concept of a population that is optimal with reference to species survival.

The goals underlying an estimate of optimal population require specification. Alternative criteria for defining optimal human population can be distinguished as follows:

1. The number of people inhabiting the earth should be maximized without any constraint as to living standards.

2. The size of the population should be maximized at some initial or predetermined standard of living.

3. The population should maximize the military and political power of the nation.

4. The population should maximize some index of the absolute and relative standard of living of the upper classes.

5. Each religious and ethnic group within the population should produce the group behavior that is optimal in relation to the power aspirations of the group or—another criterion—of a leadership elite within the group.

6. The population should maximize the probability of species survival under natural selection. To make this criterion operational requires a specification of the time horizon. A population that is favorable for the short period may be excessive for the long run.

7. Finally, the population should maximize the average standard of living, or the *quality of life.*

Past discussions seem to have involved confusion or inconsistency regarding the implicit criteria of optimal population. A common approach has been to evaluate population in terms of its implications for the power of the nation, without noting that the population that is optimal in terms of this criterion is not necessarily the same as the one that maximizes living standards.

Also relevant to the definition of a population that is optimal at any point in time are the rules regarding environmental preservation. The more rapidly any particular generation is permitted to destroy the environment, the larger will be its optimal population, because costs of its actions will fall not upon this generation but upon future generations.

A final factor to be considered is the effect of improvement of knowledge on optimal population. Figure 4.1 shows two optimal population paths. Movement to the right involves passage of time and improvements of knowledge of the kind experienced in the past century. Optimal population defined according to the maximum-numbers criterion (at the subsistence level or any constant standard of living) is upward sloping. The improvement in knowledge makes it possible to sustain a larger population at a given living standard.

But this same change in knowledge implies reductions, rather than increases, in the optimal population defined with

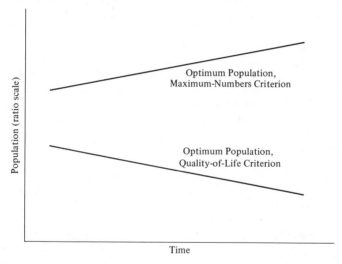

FIGURE 4.1 Population Path That Is Optimal Under Different Criteria

reference to the quality-of-life criterion. The reason is that the improvements in the standard of living made possible by increases in knowledge magnify demands on resources and costs in environmental deterioration. The changes in the standard of living of the upper classes since the turn of the century have greatly increased each person's demands upon the environment: the automobile with its air pollution, gasoline consumption, need for highways and parking; air travel with the same kinds of costs; such hobbies as boating, skiing, traveling, and camping. These activities damage the environment and increase the space needed per person. They demand a smaller population if they are to be generally available.

In the present-day way of life, people interfere with one another more than they did in the horse-and-buggy days. We might be able to visualize that, apart from food problems, India with its present population density might achieve a favorable standard of living comparable with that of the United States in the 1890s. But elevating the present population of India to the present-day standard of living of upper-class Americans is unthinkable because of its implications for environmental destruction.

It has commonly been assumed that, because an improvement in knowledge permits an increase in population at a given living standard, such improvement generally overcomes or minimizes the population problem, lessening the necessity of population control. This interpretation seems too simple. Improvement in knowledge may increase the optimal population for a constant standard of living but may *reduce* the optimal population under a quality-of-life criterion.

For a nation not on an optimal population path, it would be appropriate to define also an optimal adjustment trajectory that would bring the nation to a position on the optimal path. This trajectory would depend on the various economic, social, and political costs associated with the adjustment, which may be functions of the rate at which it is made.

TARGET PATHS FOR POPULATION

The position of present-day nations can be interpreted in terms of three classes of societies, depicted in Figure 4.2. In societies of class *A,* population is near the maximum that can survive with existing organization and knowledge. Population growth is in a trajectory that, if continued, will increase population above the viable level, leading to an increase in the death rate from starvation, disease, and disorder. If these events operate with some lag, population may overshoot the maximum sustainable number (perhaps temporarily sustained by foreign food shipments) and then may require an era of absolute decline in population from high death rate, as in path A'. Many observers see certain countries as being in such a trajectory and at the point of large-scale famine and rising death rate within a decade or two. Development of the new high-yield rice has had the effect of temporarily increasing the slope of the line depicting the maximum attainable population and has thus reduced the likelihood of famine in the immediate future. Such a development does not solve the long-run problem but raises the stakes in the game, increasing the probable scale of deaths from future famines.

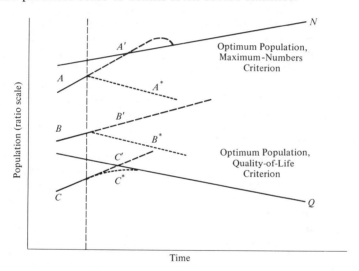

FIGURE 4.2 Actual and Optimal Population Paths

Societies with a population near the maximum sustainable at the subsistence level clearly have a population far above that consistent with the maximum standard of living permitted by present knowledge. In relation to the quality-of-life criterion, the optimal policy would immediately begin to reduce population, bringing it down at some rate to an ultimate intersection with Q (path A^*).

In relation to the quality-of-life criterion, development of the high-yield rice does not affect optimal population. If the goal is to move the society at some rate to path Q, the steepness of N is irrelevant. Indeed, any effort to take advantage of a steep N and have a period of rapid population growth would simply take society further away from its goal.

Perhaps the United States and most countries of the developed West can be placed in class B. The population is far smaller than the maximum population that could be sustained in these areas at the subsistence level. However, the population undoubtedly is higher than the one consistent with the maximum attainable standard of living. The nature of recent technological change has been such that the maximum attainable standard of living is achieved with a population that grows smaller over time. Population in these societies, however, has been rising, thus widening the gap between the actual standard of living and the maximum standard that is attainable. Indeed, the population trajectory probably has been steeper than that of N, the maximum sustainable population, implying that continuation of existing rates of population growth (path B') would eventually bring these societies to the subsistence level.

Presumably the optimal population policy for these societies also involves an abrupt decline in the birth rate sufficient to bring about gradual reductions of absolute population (path B^*), though perhaps at a slower rate than for societies of class A.

Finally, there may be some societies whose population is presently below the level leading to maximum standard of living. Australia and Canada are possible examples. In these cases, an optimal population path might involve a phase of continued growth with subsequent leveling-off of population, and perhaps later a phase of decline if the nature of improvements in knowledge continues to be such as to require declining population for the maximum standard of living.

If there were no political or social problems in transferring populations, an optimal world population policy would involve bringing countries of class C immediately up to Q and bringing about an immediate decline in population in countries of class A by transferring population from the class A countries to the class C countries. However, this shifting may not be possible or even desirable in the world's present state of thought and political organization. The dominant importance of societal control of individuals and the impediments to this control imposed by the existence within a nation of competing ethnic groups argue against such mixing of populations.

POLICY TOWARD POPULATION

On the basis of a quality-of-life criterion, the target for most societies is some defined rate of decrease in population.[25] The next questions involve the particular means to be used to limit births to the required number. An important consideration is the relative effects of the system of birth limitation on people of various classes and groups, and the long-run viability of the program.

One "natural" approach to birth limitation involves imposing on parents, through prices and taxes, the marginal social cost of additional births. According to Spengler:

Curbing population growth could prove easy in modern nations, given current contraceptive methods and knowledge thereof. It is necessary only to alter the terms of trade between gross increments to the population and other uses of the inputs involved. In essence, this might entail holding each couple responsible for all or most costs, visible and invisible, direct and indirect, of reproducing and rearing children, in keeping with at least minimal standards prescribed by the state. Should the number of births still be too large, excise taxes could be imposed upon higher-order children and upon child-oriented products and services, while if births were too few, these products and services could be cheapened through the use of subsidies.[26]

[25] In contrast to the many discussions taking the goal as one of reducing *the rate of increase* of population—or even as admitting that there might be a population problem—an increasing number of analyses have taken the stabilization of or reduction in absolute population as the goal: "A general answer to the question, 'What needs to be done?' is simple. We must rapidly bring the world population under control, reducing the growth rate to zero or making it go negative." Paul R. Ehrlich, *The Population Bomb* (New York: Ballantine Books, 1968), p. 131.

[26] Joseph J. Spengler, *op. cit.,* p. 21. See also Stephen Enke, *Economics for Development* (Englewood Cliffs, N.J.: Prentice-Hall, 1963), Chap. 20.

In this approach, a system of taxes and subsidies would be designed to confront parents with an opportunity field defined with reference to the social costs of deviations from the optimal population path. So far as these are taken as economic costs and the disincentives to excessive births are stated in economic terms, additional births become something that parents can "buy" to the extent that they are willing and able to pay the price. The resulting system is analogous to the economic system. A couple can have six automobiles if they can pay the amount required to cover their production costs. Similarly, a couple can have six children if they can reimburse society for the social cost associated with the additional births.

One application of this logic essentially involves a flat excise tax per birth, or its equivalent in other birth-related taxes. This tax would be set at the level that, given people's attitudes toward having children and the available facilities for limiting births, would bring about the socially required birth rate. The ability of couples to have children, then, would depend on their economic position. A wealthy couple could have as many children as they wished. A poor couple might not be able to afford any. The privilege of "buying" children is added to the privilege of buying consumer goods as an element in the economic game and, of course, an inducement to economic activity.

Another approach would apply concepts familiar from the graduated income tax, with its exemptions and its marginal tax rate higher than the average rate. Thus each couple might be allowed one or two births without tax, the tax on additional births being high enough or rising steeply enough, again, to limit total births to the socially desired number.

If the approach of a high marginal birth disincentive is pushed to its extreme position, becoming virtually a prohibition of additional births—say, by a tax on each birth above the second equal to five years' income—then the privilege of having births can no longer effectively be "bought" but is bestowed as a free good to each couple within the limited quotas and is effectively prohibited beyond them. Whether the disincentive for births above the permitted number is a large economic payment or whether some other penalty is required then becomes a matter of choice based on political and aesthetic criteria.[27]

Birth-limitation systems could be designed that are responsive to a wide variety of criteria. Rather than making the privilege of additional births available for the payment of a tax, or making it available for purchase, it might be made available as a reward for various kinds of specially assessed contributions to society. For example, it might be bestowed in proportion to the assessed desirability of a couple's genetic inheritance.

One implication of systems of birth limitation relying on taxes or economic disincentives is that, in the group-oriented society, the stage would be set for ethnic and religious groups to compete for political dominance by achieving a superior economic position and then using this position to maintain a higher birth rate. If a group that opposed population control in this way sufficiently increased its power, it could eliminate the system. Because of this fact, such a system would be potentially self-destructive.

It is beyond the scope of this book to explore alternative systems of birth limitation and their political, social, and economic implications. The major reference point in the following discussion will be a system in which (in deference to the point of the preceding paragraph) the birth-limitation system is egalitarian, allowing little room for variation in the number of births permitted to particular parents.

The effectiveness and acceptability of limiting births through the incentive system are affected by certain technical characteristics, as it were, of the birth process: the discon-

[27] Boulding's suggestion of issuing salable birth licenses to each woman—denominated in the "deci-child"—is of this class. Each couple can then have the standard number of children without paying a special tax. The disincentive to have more than the standard number is defined by the cost of buying more licenses—or the penalties for violating the rules of the system. Making the birth licenses salable provides consolation prizes to those who do not have children and also acts as a deterrent to those who do not really want children. Although this procedure may be desirable on other grounds, it is objectionable in that it permits groups to increase their numbers and their power in society by buying licenses and having a birth rate higher than the average. See Kenneth E. Boulding, *The Meaning of the Twentieth Century* (New York: Harper & Row, 1964), pp. 135–136.

tinuity of birth, the long lag between conception and birth, and the irreversibility of birth. Society cannot undo unwanted births but must prevent them. If the only means is by preventing conception, then prevention can scarcely be ensured in individual cases.

These considerations raise to crucial importance the availability of induced abortion as a means of limiting birth. Any particular birth can be prevented when induced abortion is available, and it is therefore possible to impose severe disincentives to excessive births. Where abortion is not available, the accidental factor would prevent assessment of severe penalties for individual births, greatly complicating the task of devising a birth-limitation system that is effective without having intolerable side effects. For these reasons, the ensured availability of induced abortion as a means of birth limitation is an essential part of effective systems of limiting birth.

The timing of operation of birth disincentives is also an important consideration. Although it is in a sense "natural," placing on parents the full social costs of rearing children has the effect of imposing the disincentives long after the birth, when the parents may be beyond any decisions about further births. Lacking perfect foresight about their later attitudes and financial capabilities, some parents would find themselves overextended. Then parents and children would both be burdened by the costs of child rearing at a time when no social purpose would be served. The effective operation of such a system would depend on people learning from experience the hazards of excessive family size and taking this factor into account when making their decisions. However, if several generations are required to learn this lesson, then this time lag is a serious disadvantage of such an approach in relation to the world's present population needs.

Although at first glance it may seem harsh and inhumane to speak of a large tax imposed at birth or before birth or to speak of a legal prohibition of above-par births, in relation to the "natural" approach of letting parents bear the costs of child rearing, the former system actually may be not only more effective but also more humane. Such is the case even though the slogan, "Parents must have free choice as to the number of their children," would seem to be met by the first approach but not by the second.

This result is, of course, no anomaly. If parents, indeed, are to be given free choice in the matter, the terms on which the choice is made must be sufficiently adverse to births to limit the average number of births to the required standard. The implication is that parents who exercise their free choice unwisely would necessarily be retrospectively burdened by heavy disincentives or punishments. Free choice without sufficient disincentives implies the absence of effective population control. Free choice with such long-lagging disincentives implies an unhappy punishment of erring parents and their children. Of course, a general cost of free choice is that it involves the opportunity to err, and to suffer for it. In this case, however, children suffer for the error of the parents. Thus any *right* of parents to have as many children as they wish—under whatever incentive system—conflicts either with the child's right to come into the world under acceptable conditions or with the society's right to prevent overpopulation.

Achieving any degree of birth limitation with minimal disutility to parents requires maximum knowledge and availability to parents of means of birth limitation. Thus, while enforcing birth limitation, the government presumably should prevent private or government agencies from interfering with free access to knowledge and means of birth limitation. Government subsidies of the means of birth control and the dissemination of birth-control information may be part of a system of birth limitation. But making available birth-control means without confronting parents with the required birth disincentives does not comprise an effective system of population control. The rationale of ensuring availability of birth-control means is not that it is itself a system of population control but rather that it minimizes the disutility with which any given degree of birth limitation can be attained.

POPULATION CONTROL VERSUS FAMILY PLANNING

"Family planning" refers to programs designed to permit parents to have the number of children that they wish to have and to induce them to make a conscious choice or plan with reference to the size of their families. It is commonly assumed that a program of population control and a program of family planning are the same thing or that a program of family planning is a first step toward an effective program of population control. However, family planning does not necessarily imply or lead to population control. If it is thought to deal with problems with which it does not actually deal, the movement for family planning may be a major impediment to effective population control.[28]

Family planning differs from population control in several respects:

1. It takes as given the number of children that parents desire to have. In much of the world, or perhaps all of the world, the family size presently desired by parents implies rates of excessive population increase. In any case, a system of population control must make family size responsive to societal needs.

2. Because it takes the number of children desired as given, the family planning approach neglects the dependence of this factor on institutions and policies that are determined by government or that could be altered by government.

3. The dependence of limitation of family size, with imperfect means of birth control, on the strength of motivation to limit births and thus on the incentive system impinging on parents is not taken into account in the family planning approach. In the absence of strong motivation to limit family size, births that are unwanted, but not *sufficiently* unwanted for parents to take action to prevent them, will continue to occur. Sufficiently strong motivation will achieve limitation of births even where the available means are far from ideal.

4. Family planning efforts have advocated only certain preferred or "respectable" means of birth limitation. The family planning proponents have not emphasized the means that seem to have been most important in limiting the birth rate in the West.[29] More importantly, family plan-

---

[28] Such an argument is admirably spelled out in Kingsley Davis, "Population Policy: Will Current Programs Succeed?" *Science,* 158 (November 10, 1967), 730–739.

[29] See Goran Ohlin, *Population Control and Economic Development* (Paris: De-

ning and planned parenthood proponents in the past have opposed induced abortion as an available means of limiting births.

The goals of the Planned Parenthood-World Population organization were characterized by its president as follows:

Planned Parenthood applies the Reverence for Life concept by placing the creation of life under the discipline of man's ethical principles and intellect—through conception control. The aim of Planned Parenthood is to assure each new infant the birthright of a warm welcome in a loving home, by enabling parents to have the number of children they want, when they want them.[30]

These goals obviously do not lead to a system of population control. The repeated references in the literature of population policy to the effect that "parents everywhere should be free to decide how many children they should have"[31] can only be interpreted as evidence of a failure to understand the population problem. "The identification of family planning with population control is an ostrich-like approach in that it permits people to hide from themselves the enormity and unconventionality of the task."[32]

Failure to distinguish between family planning and population control—and the implicit assumption that the former would achieve the latter—is characteristic of recent statements by public officials, including the Declaration on Popu-

---

velopment Center of the Organization for Economic Cooperation and Development, 1967), pp. 79–81; J. N. Stycos, "A Critique of the Traditional Planned Parenthood Approach in Underdeveloped Areas," in Clyde V. Kaiser (ed.), *Research in Family Planning* (Princeton, N.J.: Princeton University Press, 1962).

[30] Alan F. Guttmacher, "Planned Parenthood-World Population Report," in Larry K. Y. Ng, *op. cit.,* p. 304.

[31] Quotation is from the "Final Report of the American Assembly Conference on the Population Dilemma," in *ibid.,* p. 319. The planned parenthood orientation of India's large program is indicated in K. S. Sundara Rajan, "India's Population Problem," *Finance and Development,* 11 (September 1965), 144–151.

[32] Davis, "Population Policy," *op. cit.,* p. 739.

lation, signed by a number of heads of state under the auspices of the United Nations. The statement of Secretary-General U Thant in this connection takes this approach: "The Universal Declaration of Human Rights describes the family as the natural and fundamental unit of society. It follows that any choice and decision with regard to the size of the family must irrevocably rest with the family itself, and cannot be made by anyone else."[33]

The most fundamental point regarding the population problem is that *societal control over the behavior of individuals* is needed if civilization is to be preserved. The view that individuals should be given rights defined by ideology without regard for the needs of society is quite opposed to this concept.

INVESTMENT IN POPULATION CONTROL

An approach that has emphasized the social productivity of population control has viewed the problem in economic terms, comparing the rate of return from "investment in population control" with that of investment in conventional capital goods.[34] This framework provides one useful way of illustrating the negative social productivity of additional births in many societies. Thus it implicitly indicates that the existing political, economic, and social framework is not presenting to potential parents an incentive system that serves to bring individual behavior into conformity with societal requirements.

It may be instructive to dramatize the deficiency of the existing system by making the point in economic terms, but to view the problem as basically an economic one seems misleading. We are deceived by a metaphorical use of a word if we take "investment in population control" to be similar to investment in plant and equipment. Clearly, enormous amounts of funds

---

[33] United Nations Press Release, December 8, 1967. See also the 1969 statement of the UNA-USE National Policy Panel, *World Population, 1969,* and the 1969 Notre Dame address of World Bank President Robert McNamara.

[34] See Leonard G. Bower, "The Return from Investment in Population Control in Less Developed Countries," *Demography,* 5 (1968), 422–432; Stephen Enke, "The Economic Aspects of Slowing Population Growth," *Economic Journal,* 76 (March 1966), 44–56.

can be "invested in population control" without any significant reduction in the birth rate. On the other hand, a drastic reduction in the birth rate could be achieved without any such "investment" whatever. It may be helpful to note that, within some range, the standard of living may be raised more by "buying" a reduction in births than by buying a new manufacturing plant. However, the argument that a reduction in births actually can be bought the way a manufacturing plant is bought might be deceptive. The problem of population control is not an investment problem per se, but a control problem. The governing framework is political. The constraints limiting effective policy action are both political and ideological.

THE NATIONAL PROGRAM OF POPULATION CONTROL

An effective national system of population control would include these elements:

1. Definition of a target path for national population, which for most societies probably should involve some rate of decline in population.

2. Imposition of a system of birth disincentives that will bring about the required birth rate. The suggested system is egalitarian, minimizing differences in permitted births among parents. The birth disincentives should be imposed in time to prevent unwanted births rather than as costs at a much later time.

3. Interference with availability of birth-control knowledge and means should be prevented by the government; where useful, the government also should subsidize or conduct activities to make these available.

4. Induced abortion must be available as a last resort to prevent unwanted births.

5. Presumably such a system would require registration of pregnancies and births and some government accounting for children. Detailed enforcement problems would require careful thought and planning.

6. Such a program of national population limitation, of course, would be accompanied by limitations on immigra-

tion. These limitations raise a host of problems, including an implied inability of people to flee a tyrannical or a failing society. Careful thought might find means of minimizing these costs within a framework not destructive of the needs of world population limitation.

Such a population-control program differs sharply from approaches that emphasize the need for large government programs supported by foreign aid, as well as the need for dissemination of birth-control information and instruments and the "freedom of choice of parents," and neglect the crucial role of the incentive system affecting parents' desired family size.[35]

WORLD POPULATION POLICY

The adoption of such a national system of population control might most hopefully be expected in those nations having the most extensive education, effectiveness of central government, and strength and security from foreign attack. The logic of such a program is to take actions that immediately involve a psychological and political cost out of regard for the future of civilization. A national government that is not strong and stable presumably would be unable to institute or enforce such a program, especially because doing so might involve active opposition of religious or ethnic groups in the society. Finally, the nation that is insecure in relation to its neighbors may fear to limit its population because to do so would invite attack by overpopulated and impoverished neighbors or because other claims on its resources would make such an exercise of foresight unrewarding.

In view of the difficulties involved, a world system of population limitation can be achieved only through a process of initial action by the nations best endowed to take such action, followed by concerted development by such nations of an international system that modifies the incentive system of other nations in such a way as to enable or require them to move in this direction.

[35] See Ohlin, *op. cit.*, Chap. 11.

Such a program by a group of population-limiting nations might involve these elements:

First, an effective system of collective security, for protecting population-limiting nations from the territorial and other claims of overpopulated nations, would be essential. Due to the fact that the expected outcome is that the population-limiting nations would enjoy rising standards of living, a higher quality of life, and a growing freedom from overcrowding, while their opposite members would experience extreme crowding, poverty, and starvation, the situation would pose a conflict in terms of reference.

Second, the participating nations would have to create incentives for other nations to adopt population limitation. Foreign aid programs, for example, could be made conditional on such action. Advantages in trade or security assistance might similarly be made conditional. Membership in a society of population-limiting nations offering substantial benefits to members might provide such an incentive.[36] Presumably if the nations in the leadership role have applied to themselves the same standards of population control that they propose to others, some of the objections could be overcome.

CONCLUSIONS

The treatment of population in the theory of economic development must be understood in terms of the times and the attitudes from which this approach arose. The Great Depression had submerged concern about overpopulation; the stagnation doctrine had represented rapid population growth as a boon, at least in the short run. In shaking off classical economics and the binding constraints symbolized by laissez faire, the thought of the times had lifted the constraints of nature on man and had adopted an unusually anthropocentric

[36] Representative of prevailing thought is the statement that "any attempt to coerce other governments as, for example, by making aid contingent on the adoption of a family limitation program (as has been rashly suggested by some enthusiasts), would obviously be resented. No responsible statesman endorses any such idea." Frank Lorimer, "Issues of Population Policy," in Philip M. Hauser, *op. cit.*, p. 153.

view of economics. The stage was set for an era of confidence in the efficacy of planned modernization and concerted efforts to advance the backward areas of the world.

So far as there was any explicit rationale for neglecting the adverse effects of population growth on living standards and the environment, it derived from the framework of unilinear evolution and the assumption that the road at hand was the road of progress. Somewhere further down the road, the population problem—if there were one—would solve itself, or would at least prove solvable. The framework of unilinear evolution was explicitly applied to offer the argument that population could not be tampered with separately but must develop naturally according to its predetermined timetable.[37] More commonly, the argument was implicit in the very concepts of development, modernization, overcoming backwardness. Once these concepts were, through accustomization, accepted as valid, they implied that somehow the population problem would automatically take care of itself as a part of the process of development. Were this not the case, the very concept of "development" would be absurd. When the concept was accepted, its implications were, perhaps inadvertently, accepted along with it.

A simple but perhaps persuasive test of this interpretation was provided by the naturalists who, in the 1960s, pointed out the imminence of catastrophe from current population trends and the need for radical change in population policies. Implicitly they posed to the theorists of economic development the question, "How was this problem handled in your theory?" The theorists of economic development appear to be nearly empty-handed—except for the belief that the answer lies somewhere ahead, down the road of progress. On the other hand, the group of economists who have taken a naturalistic view of population have not really been believers in the theory of economic development.

The idea that some predetermined timetable adjusts the human birth rate to the requirements of progress is quite inconsistent with the naturalistic theory of population. This

[37] Harvey Leibenstein, *Economic Backwardness and Economic Growth* (New York: Science Editions, 1963), p. 151.

theory defines population behavior as dependent on group-oriented population-control systems, the counterparts of which, in the modern world, depend heavily on government policy. Consideration of the institutions and laws that have affected human population in the past supports this approach.

Application of the framework of unilinear evolution to population does not seem supportable. No predetermined timetable for population and progress has been shown to exist. Sets of laws and institutions (societal control systems) could be applied that would put population on a path consistent with maximization of living standards, as could others that would lead to disintegration of national societies within decades. The laws of nature permit societies of the first class to survive and ensure that the others will fall, but which role will be played out by existing nations remains in question.

Application of a naturalistic theory of population virtually destroys the theory of economic development, apart from its difficulties in other connections. If there is not a predetermined set of stages of population behavior through which each society advances—if different societies move down radically different paths depending on their laws and institutions that affect population (and these, in turn, are not on a predetermined timetable)—the concepts of "development" and "modernization" are seriously misleading.

CHAPTER 5 / Environmental Preservation and Living Standards

The confrontation between a naturalistic view of present-day civilization and the view underlying the theory of economic development is nowhere more striking than in their treatment of the natural environment. The naturalists warn that man is on a collision course with environmental destruction and catastrophe. But the theory of economic development tells a story of progress, advancement, modernization. It tells a human story, with little place for nature. The relation between the two approaches is reviewed in this chapter.

ENVIRONMENTAL PRESERVATION: A NATURALISTIC INTERPRETATION

Man's environment consists largely of very complex ecological systems that have been developed by natural selection. Not only plants and animals but even the atmosphere, the oceans, the weather—none of these is permanently fixed, but rather arises from interaction processes involving a multitude

of living things. Localized operation of selection has eliminated not only species but also ecological systems that are
self-destructive. Thus the natural environment is robust in
the sense that, if left to its own course, it will not explode or
destroy itself, but will continue on a path of evolutionary
change.

Because early man was governed by localized group selection, his capacity to damage the earth was limited by the same
mechanisms that applied to other forms of life. The localized
group that destroys its habitat destroys itself also. When
man's knowledge and technology permitted him to develop
nonlocalized societies and to dominate and exploit other living creatures, he became able to challenge nature to larger
and longer-lasting experiments. The society that devastates
its habitat still will destroy itself. However, as a result of
man's greater powers, the experiment now includes much of
the earth and runs for centuries. Man's achievements do not
permit him to escape from the game, but they raise the stakes.

PAST ENVIRONMENTAL DESTRUCTION BY MAN

Technological skill is not needed to cause environmental
destruction. Overgrazing by sheep and goats under the administration of man has devastated vast areas. Deforestation
and overcropping leading to erosion can be similarly destructive. The lowly rabbit, introduced into ecological systems not
accommodated to him, has been a source of great mischief.
These facts are evidence that nondestructive ecological relations are not, as it were, a free gift but are worked out through
natural selection leading to incorporation of the required control systems into species behavior. Thus it was inevitable that
when man developed large societies and outgrew his systems
of localized control, he would begin damaging the environment.

His record as a destroyer of soil and ecological systems is a
long one. The great deserts of the Middle East have been
created since Biblical times, it seems, by overgrazing. Much
of Spain was devastated by the overgrazing associated with
the economic development program of Ferdinand and Isa-
bella. The Pontine Marshes were a monument to overcultiva-

tion of hillsides to feed the growing population of Rome.[1] The highlands of Scotland were degraded a century and a half ago by deforestation to fuel industry and then by the overgrazing of sheep.[2] Environmental destruction by man is by no means a recent innovation.

THE ACCELERATION OF ENVIRONMENTAL DESTRUCTION

Recent decades, however, have multiplied man's capacity for environmental destruction. In part, this increase reflects technological advances that permit the support of a much larger population. In part, it stems from the expanded range of pollutants and increased use per person of exhaustible resources.

Growth of population, increase in living standards, and development of the automobile and the airplane have led to phenomenal acceleration in the use of oil, coal, and metals.[3] In some areas, the depletion of known underground resources has temporarily been offset or more than offset by new discoveries, but of course new discoveries of oil fields cannot be made without limit.

Apart from other considerations, the existing way of life in advanced societies will be undercut seemingly within decades by the depletion of fuel supplies, forcing some kind of adjustment. Atomic power can be used in place of fossil fuels, but even with today's limited use, the disposal of radioactive materials presents problems.

Local air pollution resulting from population growth, the automobile, and industry has contributed to a reduction in the quality of life in many cities. This kind of change in the quality of life is generally not included in usual measures of the standard of living. Air pollution is also a health hazard and source of both medical expenses and cleaning costs; more-

[1] See Fairfield Osborne, *Our Plundered Planet* (Boston: Little, Brown, 1948), pp. 144–151.

[2] F. Fraser Darling, *West Highland Survey: An Essay in Human Ecology* (New York: Oxford University Press, 1955), pp. 4–5.

[3] Harrison Brown, *The Challenge of Man's Future* (New York: Viking, 1954), Chaps. 5–6.

over, it has reduced or destroyed the productivity of agricultural land near large cities. The quantitative effect of these
costs may be substantial but they are not measured or included in conventional measures of living standards.

Pollution of water is widespread. It extends to total destruction of lakes and rivers as an ecological system and their
transformation from an asset to a liability. Major factors are
runoff of agricultural fertilizer and pesticides, discharge from
industrial plants, heating of water by power plants, and the
discharge of sewage. The treatment of sewage removes some
kinds of damage to the lakes and rivers but does not cure
others. Thus the sheer growth of population, even with improving treatment of sewage, has been a major source of the
destruction of Lake Erie, perhaps the most striking example
of water pollution yet recorded.[4] However, pollution is common and includes rural lakes as well as such renowned scenic
attractions as Lake Tahoe[5] and the Lake of Lucerne. "The
Missouri-Mississippi Basin and the Cuyahoga, Sacramento,
Delaware, and Potomac rivers are unsafe even for boating
more than 70 percent of the time."[6]

Efforts to curb local water pollution have been under way
now for decades. Their outcome and the problems they disclose suggest how difficult it will be to deal with kinds of
environmental destruction involving more difficult control
problems because of their wider extent or less-obvious damages. The effort over the past twenty years to clean up the
Ohio River, the broadest such program in the United States,
has had only limited success, marked by continued large-scale
emission of pollutants.[7] The costs of thorough pollution control are often very large. The cost of halting acid seepage
from abandoned coal mines is said to be greater in some cases
than the value of the mine when it was active. Pollution-

---

[4] "The Dying Lake," *The Wall Street Journal,* February 10, 1969, p. 1.

[5] Raymond F. Dasmann, *The Destruction of California* (New York: Collier
Books, 1966), p. 167.

[6] U.S. Department of Health, Education, and Welfare, *Toward A Social Report,*
1969, p. 32.

[7] "The Dirty Ohio," *The Wall Street Journal,* March 17, 1969, pp. 1, 14.

control regulations that are costly to industry may lead to migration to less-regulated areas, to intergovernmental "competition in laxity"—a problem that arises at all levels of government.

Prevalent systems of sewage treatment do not prevent population growth from adding to water pollution, thus requiring additional, more expensive treatment. It is estimated that to build and operate the facilities needed to treat all municipal wastes at 85 percent effectiveness by 1973 would cost $20 billion, but because of the growth of urban populations, raising treatment standards to this level would still involve municipal discharges into rivers that would be greater in 1980 than they were in 1962.[8]

The growing scale and additional dimensions of water pollution have introduced the possibility of pollution not only of the lakes and rivers but even of the oceans. Leakage from ocean disposal of atomic wastes, accumulation of pesticides carried by rivers, oil pollution from tanker leakage and offshore oil wells all appear to be escalating at an extraordinarily rapid rate. Because of the problems of enforcement of regulations on the high seas and the need for concerted action by national governments, really effective control of pollution of the oceans is especially difficult. The accumulation of evidence in the late 1960s on the contamination of fish and all forms of animal life by DDT caused increasing concern over this problem.

Yet another hazard arises from the burning of fossil fuels, which adds carbon dioxide and water vapor to the air. Since both these substances are more transparent to shortwave solar radiation than to the longwave radiation from the earth to space, this may significantly raise the surface temperature of the earth. On the other hand, increase in atmospheric turbidity has the opposite effect, reducing the solar radiation reaching the earth and acting to reduce the earth's temperature. That recent changes in climate have not been more evident probably reflects in part the offsetting tendency of the two forms of pollution. In the view of Bryson, "Since 1940, the

[8] *Toward A Social Report,* pp. 32–33.

effect of the rapid rise of atmospheric turbidity appears to have exceeded the effect of rising carbon dioxide, resulting in a rapid downward trend of temperature."[9]

Although the effects of changes in the earth's temperature are not fully known, they include changes in glaciation and in the level of the oceans. A sufficient decline in temperature for a sufficient period would presumably lead to a new ice age.

Population increase also leads to the destruction of natural beauty. Mere increase in numbers of people requires increased use of land for farms, industry, mines and oil wells, and cities. The spread of quasi-urban living over whole sections of the country and its engulfing of historical landmarks like Gettysburg and beauty spots like Estes Park has a definite impact on the quality of life.

Moreover, improved transportation brings to selected tourist attractions numbers of people that may destroy the object of their quest. The traffic jams and smog problems of the more popular national parks illustrate this point. Finally, physical destruction of lakes, rivers, and forests removes sources of natural beauty.

The effect of additional crowding on the quality of life can be seen as a matter of taste, of aesthetic principles, or of differing conceptions of man's proper destiny. To some, additional crowding is repugnant on these grounds. However, the extent to which the masses of people living in large cities share this value is perhaps uncertain.[10] It is conceivable that people accustomed to life in large cities have no desire for natural beauty, or at least will pay no substantial price to preserve natural beauty. Their attitude would not necessarily imply that the loss of natural beauty does not mean a reduction in the quality of life. It might be interpreted simply as reflecting

[9] Reid A. Bryson, "Climatic Effects of Atmospheric Pollution." Paper read at the 1968 National Meeting of the American Association for the Advancement of Science.

[10] However, a 1969 poll indicated that about half of the respondents were "deeply concerned" about environmental destruction and an overwhelming majority would prefer to live in a nonurban area. Respondents were evenly divided on the proposition that population limitation will be necessary to preserve the existing standard of living. *The Christian Science Monitor,* March 19, 1969, p. 6.

perverse selection, less-sensitive individuals having greater survival value than their more delicate counterparts and increasingly creating an environment in which their own survival advantage is enhanced.

THE ENVIRONMENT AND THE STANDARD OF LIVING

Environmental deterioration affects the quality of life by increasing the real production costs of economic goods. Soil destruction increases the cost of producing any given amount of food and/or reduces the amount of food that can be produced at any given level of cost. Depletion of fossil fuels and minerals increases their production costs and thus increases the costs of heating homes and of manufactured goods requiring such materials. These rising costs would ultimately lead to shortages in the sense that, with the level of real income they could earn, increasing numbers of people would not be able to purchase the things required to maintain their standard of living.

Among adverse effects of environmental destruction not entering into the cost of particular goods would be the psychological and economic disadvantages of breathing polluted air, being surrounded by increasingly polluted lakes and rivers, and living under increasingly crowded conditions. Unless the individual takes some action to offset such deterioration, his standard of living ultimately declines. But to offset the increasing deterioration, he needs a rising income to pay for the offsetting actions: for example, additional cleaning and replacement of clothing and other goods, and vacation trips to less-unattractive sites. At the same time, some actions that are available to offset the effects of environmental destruction will themselves become increasingly costly or even absolutely unavailable. If growing cities became increasingly unattractive as a result of air pollution, leading to a rapid growth in attempts to escape to vacation sites, these sites would become increasingly costly and might themselves be destroyed. Thus there are many ways in which environmental deterioration reduces real living standards and the quality of life.

Preventing environmental destruction does not lead to the same conclusion, but it also involves increases in production costs. The imposition of a control system to prevent environment-destroying production processes and economic activities would immediately increase the real cost of economic goods. Thus it would reduce the standard of living, perhaps on a substantial scale.

Imposition of a rigorous system of environmental preservation would also alter the relative costs of goods and services, thus requiring a change in the composition of goods consumed and the style of life. Flights on jet aircraft might have to be rationed or their effects offset by pollution-overcoming techniques so costly as to raise the price out of the range of most people. Such nonpolluting activities as arts and services would not increase in price, leading to a shift of consumption in this direction. However, the kinds of technically advanced processes that are the basis of recent rapid increases in living standards as conventionally measured are often among the main sources of environmental destruction. Consequently, a system of environmental preservation not only would immediately lower the standard of living but also might severely limit the possibilities for future increases in economic efficiency.

Because imposition of a system of environmental preservation would reduce the standard of living and damage many specific economic interests, there is a question as to the political viability of such a program even in societies with a standard of living well above the subsistence level. In a society including many people near the border of starvation, the additional costs associated with environmental preservation might have to be at the short-run cost of causing additional starvation. Similarly, cessation of malaria control through widespread use of the environment-destroying DDT in some areas would mean a large increase in infection with and deaths from the disease, since equally effective alternative programs are not now available at a manageable cost. If population continues to grow rapidly and more nations come to have more people living at the margin of subsistence, these impediments to environmental preservation will become more severe. For these reasons, the adoption of policies for environmental preservation may be contingent upon simultaneous or prior adoption of policies to control population.

RATIONAL POLICY TOWARD
ENVIRONMENTAL PRESERVATION

The rational choice of policy toward environmental preservation closely parallels that with regard to population control. Both require taking unwanted actions now in order to avoid possible severe costs later, or the use of preventive checks to avoid the operation of positive checks. Both involve uncertainty or imperfect knowledge as to the extent and timing of the adverse consequences of not imposing controls. Both are intensively involved with ideologies, religion, and group interests, so it is extremely difficult to identify the general interest or to find machinery to protect it. Finally, in both areas effective control would require a realism and tough-mindedness of thought and the adoption of rigorous world-wide systems of control.

CONTROL PROBLEMS REGARDING
ENVIRONMENTAL PRESERVATION

From the point of view of control, the modern problem of environmental deterioration is unlike anything faced in the past. Limitation of environmental destruction in the past was based on group-oriented controls and localism or territoriality, closely tied to the system of population control in a context in which environmental deterioration was local and was associated largely with overpopulation. These control systems are of limited availability in the modern world because of the decline of localism and of the nonlocal, and often nonobvious, nature of the environmental deterioration arising from modern industrial processes and consumer goods. Impediments to effective control of environmental deterioration in the modern world can be characterized as follows:

1. Some kinds of pollution are difficult to detect or to measure. Pollution of the seas and intermittent or concealed pollution of air or water may pose detection problems. Leakage from radioactive wastes deposited in the sea would also pose such a problem. International enforcement of rules against pollution, therefore, might require an elabo-

rate international system of detection and surveillance.

2. The adverse effects of some environment-damaging activities occur only after a substantial lag. Consequently, preventive action depends on knowledge and on the spread of knowledge to groups that must support the action.

3. In contrast to the kinds of environmental deterioration caused by animals and primitive man, many of the adverse effects of present-day activities are not localized, but may be felt in other localities or on a global scale. The implication is that local groups, as well as local and even national governments, may find that the costs to them (as contrasted with the total costs) of their environment-damaging activities are smaller than the costs of preventing them. This factor, plus the expected migration of business to avoid controls, implies that some kinds of environment-damaging activities can be controlled only on an international basis.

4. International control programs, especially those requiring detailed regulations and their local enforcement, pose problems that are difficult to handle within existing political institutions.

5. Further, the control problem is made difficult by the fact that environment-damaging activities are numerous, involving many aspects of production and consumption. Thus to devise and enforce the required regulations is a task of formidable complexity.

6. The lack of firm knowledge, the technical nature of the required knowledge, and the indirect and nonobvious character of the damages from environmental destruction make recognition of the problem and political implementation of control measures very difficult.

POLICY FOR ENVIRONMENTAL PRESERVATION

Presumably any program of control of environmental deterioration must originate in the advanced nations. In contrast to the population problem, the problem of environmental destruction is one in which the most damaging actions are occurring in the advanced nations. Some kinds of threat to the environment arise mainly in the United States and

Europe. Moreover, the knowledge required for estimation of hazards of environmental deterioration and techniques of control must come largely from the leading nations, and the educational background of the electorate that may be required to gain support of the electorate for environment-preserving policies is stronger there. The situation seems to call for a radically increased program of research in this area and of interest by scholars, the government, and the public in general.

Against localized pollution, local and national governments can act as knowledge becomes available. Programs to control local pollution of water and air have existed for some time, have achieved notable successes in some areas, and are gaining increasing attention. Some such programs are hampered by the need of concerted action by a number of state or local governmental units. An effective program may require substantial shifting of functions to the national government level.

The operating task of policy is the confrontation of all who engage in activities that damage the environment with an incentive system that will sufficiently limit these activities. The task is to provide a set of disincentives to environment-damaging activities that will confront the individuals and businesses with cues, incentives, and reinforcers that cause them to take actions that are consistent with societal needs. This is another problem of societal control over individuals to permit societal survival. The existing arrangements are defective in that actions detrimental to society are advantageous to the individuals and businesses that take them, leading systematically to damage to society.

The characteristic control instruments would be prohibitions or taxes on damaging activities, sufficient to limit them to a predetermined amount consistent with societal interests. As in the case of limitation of births, various means can be used, and the objective is to prevent environment-damaging activities, rather than retroactively to punish people for them.[11]

---

[11] One suggestive approach to control of waste disposal is the creation of only a predetermined amount of licenses, which then become transferable property rights. The price system would increase the value of the licenses in relation to the demand and would allocate them among competing waste

Action against pollution or environmental destruction with extranational implications requires an international agency or a group of nations acting in concert. Because at least some national governments will be unwilling or effectively unable to take the actions required, the proposed strategy is the same one discussed earlier in connection with population control. It is a strategy of leadership and learning, or of foresight combined with natural selection. Any nations meeting defined standards of environment-preserving programs should support one another against the claims of other nations, making the benefits ultimately deriving from their programs in part available as incentives to additional nations to join the group.

If environmental preservation does add to the quality of life and if some group of nations can provide the required leadership and can be resolute in presenting a rigorous incentive system to other nations, at least a part of mankind may perhaps meet nature's criteria and achieve survival of civilization through preservation of the environment.

CONCLUSIONS

The limitations of the environment at least with relation to agricultural land and population were emphasized by earlier economic theory. The scope of earlier environmental destruction by man and its association with periods of societal expansion and economic development have not just been discovered but were pointed out by Osborne as early as 1948. So where did environmental destruction fit into the mainstream of the theory of economic development?

The question is a revealing one. The limitations of the environment, its fragility and the hazard of its destruction, are curiously missing from this story. The existence of this blind spot in the theory of economic development adds to our understanding of its origins, its foundations.

---

disposers. See J. H. Dales, *Pollution, Property, and Prices* (Toronto: University of Toronto Press, 1968). Detailed consideration of alternative control mechanisms for the various classes of activity involved seems to be needed.

The theory of economic development stems from the anthropocentric strain of Judeo-Christian thought:

God planned all of this explicitly for man's benefit and rule: no item in the physical creation had any purpose save to serve man's purposes. And, although man's body is made of clay, he is not simply part of nature: he is made in God's image. Especially in its Western form, Christianity is the most anthropocentric religion the world has seen.[12]

If there is a rationale for the neglect by the theory of economic development of the natural constraint upon man's increase in numbers and exploitation of the environment, it must be the one implicit in the framework of unilinear evolution and the theme of progress. The population problem will automatically solve itself later on. The advance of technology that aggravated the problem of environmental destruction will later solve the problem; what is needed is only more knowledge. We have not solved the problem because it has only recently come to our attention, but once we recognize it we shall solve it. Given the premise of progress, these are reasonable positions. But they rest on the premise of progress, which seems to derive from the belief that man is superior to nature.

[12] Lynn White, Jr., "The Historical Roots of Our Ecologic Crisis," *Science,* 155 (1967), 1203–1207; reprinted in Paul Shepard and Daniel McKinley (eds.), *The Subversive Science: Essays Toward an Ecology of Man* (Boston: Houghton Mifflin, 1969), p. 347.

CHAPTER **6 / Determinants of Change in Economic Efficiency**

This chapter offers an interpretation of the process that underlies self-feeding change in a society's economic efficiency. It explores factors tending to make this process self-limiting. Once again, these topics are considered within a naturalistic framework and this approach is then compared with ideas emphasized in the theory of economic development.

CHANGE IN SOCIETAL EFFICIENCY: A NATURALISTIC VIEW

The economic efficiency of a society at any point of time is to be explained in terms of a historical process of societal change. Some societies improve in efficiency over time whereas others deteriorate. The condition of a society at any point must be explained by dating its position in such a continuing process. The major task is to characterize the process by which societies increase or decrease in efficiency and the factors determining the rate at which this change occurs. Steady and long-continued change in the economic efficiency of a society reflects changes in the behavior of individuals and institutions, and it is these changes that are to be explained.

THE PROCESS OF SELF-FEEDING EFFICIENCY CHANGE

The essential features of a process of self-feeding increase in economic efficiency, the common features running through the symptomatic diversity of actual experience, seem to be characterizable in terms of three functional sets of factors:

1. Productive innovation occurs, increasing the real output of the economy from given resource inputs.

2. The additional output accrues in some part to those responsible for the innovation.

3. The rewards from successful innovation motivate and finance additional innovation, and the demonstration that innovative activity is rewarded leads others to engage in it.[1]

This characterization defines an interaction process or positive feedback loop that is potentially self-feeding, "explosive," in that it does not approach an equilibrium position but can continue for a long time.

Continued productive innovation requires all three sets of factors listed. If innovation occurs but is unproductive, there is no basis for rewarding the innovators or financing additional innovation and consequently no self-feeding process. If productive innovation occurs but the gains are entirely captured by others and are not available to reward innovators or to finance additional innovation, the process, again, is not self-feeding. If productive innovation occurs and is rewarded but no one is in a position to respond to inducements to innovate, the process does not continue. Sustained innovation requires these three sets of action, these three dependencies. The list cannot be shortened.

[1] Such a concept underlies the approach of L. J. Zimmerman, *Poor Lands, Rich Lands: The Widening Gap* (New York: Random House, 1965), pp. 104–108, 115–116.

On the other hand, this list provides for all the classes of factors that are essential to self-feeding improvement in economic efficiency. Productive innovations can be made by any of a variety of agencies, by large or small private businesses, by government agencies, by cooperatives, by individuals. The innovations may involve almost any aspect of the productive process—use of more machinery, use of less machinery, production-control improvements, use of new seeds, altered irrigation procedures, improved labor supervision, production of new products, improved quality control, reduction of administrative overhead. The common functional element is improvement in efficiency—increase in outputs in relation to inputs.

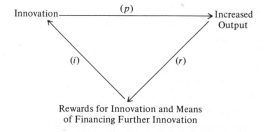

FIGURE 6.1 Feedback Loop Governing Cumulative Efficiency Change

The arrangements under which the innovator is rewarded may also be diverse. But, again, one can conceive of arrangements in which innovation will be rewarded and other conditions in which it will not, under various kinds of economic institutions. Whether it is or is not rewarded is the essential question.

The process of self-feeding innovation can be represented as in Figure 6.1. In principle, the interpretation can be quantified. The rate of change in societal efficiency depends on three factors reflecting certain aspects of the performance of the society and the lags in their operation. The three factors measure the increase in output arising from additional productive innovation (p), the proportion of this increased output accruing to those responsible for the productive innovation

(r), and the effect in generating additional productive innovation of the incentive thus provided (i). Differences among societies in their rate of increase in economic efficiency can be interpreted in terms of these three factors.

Such a characterization is useful if it divides factors affecting efficiency change into groups of close substitutes. In thus comprising groups of factors with high internal substitutability, the p, r, and i factors parallel the division of productive factors into land, labor, and capital. In a society already possessed of large amounts of labor in relation to land and capital, the marginal productivity of labor would be expected to be low. Efforts to add to output by increasing the supply of labor would be of little avail. Labor is not the bottleneck, the factor of high marginal significance.

Similarly, we might visualize a society in which self-feeding improvement in efficiency does not occur despite high potential productivity of innovation. This might happen because the proceeds of innovation do not accrue to innovators and therefore no one in the society has an incentive to innovate. If the lack of incentives is the bottleneck, efforts to increase the prospective productivity of innovation still further without altering the system of incentives may have virtually no effect on the rate of efficiency change.

Lacking such a framework, we interpret the significance for the rate of economic progress of various seemingly relevant factors on the basis of an intuitive, judgmental, or ideologically determined assessment of whether the factor is, in some absolute sense, "important" or "not important." By defining relations of complementarity and substitutability among kinds of actions that might be taken by policy, as does the production function in situations in which it is relevant, this structure provides a basis for more effective interpretation of the effects of policy actions.

This framework can be applied to cases of zero and negative as well as positive rates of efficiency change. A case of zero or near-zero economic progress could arise from a zero or near-zero value of p, r, or i or from very small values of any combination of these. Recognition of the terms of the interaction among these sets of factors, and the destructive effect of a near-zero value of any one of them, may help to illuminate cases in which negligible progress occurs although some relevant factors are very favorable.

Cases of negative economic progress not attributable to disorder or destruction of resources may also be explainable in terms of this framework. Such cases may involve a political and institutional framework conferring rewards for antiproductive innovation: for example, stealing or destroying the goods of others, concealing or exporting capital, avoiding actions required to adapt the productive process to changing circumstances. The potential for antiproductive innovation exists everywhere. The greater the incentive to such action, the greater the responsiveness of people to the incentive, and the smaller the lags in the interaction process, the greater the rate of negative efficiency change. Societal rules can lead to coherent patterns of economically destructive activity.

EFFICIENCY CHANGE IN FRONTIER AND NONFRONTIER SOCIETIES

The constraints on the ability of a society to increase its economic efficiency can be viewed as consisting of two classes, which involve the problem of *knowledge* as against the problem of *implementation.* We refer to a heuristic map (Figure 6.2) depicting economic efficiency over a long period of time for (A) the most effective society conceivable, (B) the most economically effective existing society, and (C) some economically less effective societies.

Path A measures the limit of what is potentially attainable in the prevailing state of knowledge, which is assumed to be improving over time. The most advanced existing society, represented by B, confronts constraints both of knowledge and of implementation. Other societies could elevate themselves to the same degree of advancement as the most advanced societies through a transition period of abnormally rapid increase in efficiency by applying the kind of methods already in use there. The effective constraint on economic improvement in such societies thus is one of implementation rather than of knowledge.

The implementation problem involves intellectual and analytical difficulties. To apply in one society production methods that are being used in another involves problems of

transference or application. Since the economic circumstances of various societies differ, a slavish copying may be
inefficient; indeed, the problem of transference is the problem
of choosing *what* is to be copied from a multidimensional
experience. This is a knowledge problem of a sort, but one
differing from that of the pioneering societies. The adaptation of existing steelmaking techniques to local peculiarities
is a different problem from the invention of steel.

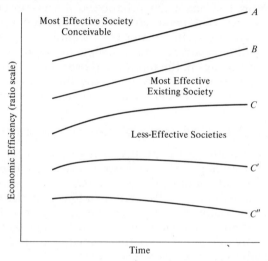

FIGURE 6.2 Frontier and Nonfrontier Economic Efficiency

   Thus the intramarginal societies have potentially available
a phase of rapid increase in economic efficiency in which they
apply the knowledge and methods already used elsewhere.
In intramarginal societies in which this application does not
occur, the question is why it does not occur. If the knowledge
exists, why is it not applied? In terms of the framework developed previously, the availability of knowledge regarding production methods that are better than those being used makes
for a high potential productivity of innovation. If the innovation does not occur, the reason must be explained in terms of
an adverse incentive system or adverse response of people and
institutions to the incentives that exist.

SOCIETAL RULES AND EFFICIENCY CHANGE

In earlier chapters, the performance of various societies with reference to their rates of population growth and environmental destruction was represented as explained by the prevailing systems of societal rules. These govern the behavior of individuals and groups within the society, behavior that then determines the course of population and of environmental destruction. The same framework applies to the aspect of societal performance now under consideration, its rate of change in economic efficiency.

In each of these areas, there is a wide range of potential performances for any given society. In the short run, population can grow at a rate constrained only by the total available food; or, with a low birth rate, population can decline rapidly. The performance of any particular society within this wide range of potential performances depends on societal rules that define the incentive system applicable to individuals in making the decisions that determine societal performance. The same logic applies to the short-run performance of a society with reference to environmental destruction. Similarly, for any given society in the short run, there is a wide range of potentially applicable rates of increase and decrease in economic efficiency. Which of these is realized depends on the cues and incentives presented by the society to the individuals and organizations whose behavior in an immediate sense determines the outcome.

The process by which individuals and organizations respond to the context defined for them by nature's laws and societal rules is that discussed in Chapter 3. The process of adaptation is accelerated by foresight and rationality but does not require them. It can occur through accidental variation in practice so long as variations that increase efficiency are rewarded or reinforced. Given this fact, learning and imitation, which also occur indirectly through revision of societal norms and roles, suffice to produce an increase in efficiency. What is in question is a process of change through selection among different patterns of behavior. The question is only what kinds of behavior are being reinforced, rewarded, or positively selected.

Within this framework, the prevalence of societies in which economic efficiency does not show cumulative increase is to be explained in terms of societal rules that oppose such efficiency change. These can be characterized in terms of the three sets of factors previously identified. In most societies, a large part of potentially available productive innovations are ruled out by societal taboos or governmental regulations. Where innovation does occur, the gains commonly do not go to those responsible for the innovation, because of a variety of institutions that are subject to a variety of justifications. Finally, in many societies those who otherwise would assume the role of innovator are deterred from doing so by cultural and political restraints and disincentives that greatly narrow the range of potential response to the existing incentives to innovation.

INTERSOCIETAL SELECTION AND INSTITUTIONS FAVORING EFFICIENCY IMPROVEMENT

Increasing efficiency is the basic theme of natural selection. The change and diversification in life forms appear to operate toward increasing efficiency in the sense of maximizing the amount of life sustained within an area. Moreover, this maximization of life operates in much the same way as the maximization of efficiency in an economic system, by ever-increasing specialization and division of labor within a structure of ever-increasing complexity. Thus it would not be surprising if natural selection favored human societies that increased in economic efficiency.

If this situation does not occur, it must be because rapid increase in societal efficiency has side effects that are damaging to the society. An interpretation of such side effects has already been reviewed. The performance of a society depends on a cultural control system by which society preserves the coherency and responsiveness of individuals and subgroups to the performance requirements that must be met for societal survival. Rapid increase in economic efficiency changes conditions in the society. This change undermines the cultural control system, leading to internal conflict and disorder that destroys the efficiency of the society, as well as to loss of control over population and over environmental preservation.

Thus a societal structure leading to rapid improvement in economic efficiency is efficacious in the short run but may be subversive over a longer period. If so, natural selection, which is geared to the long run, operates in favor of societies that play a conservative strategy, that resist increase in economic efficiency. In the past, the expansive societies have not continued indefinitely to improve in efficiency, or they would have dominated other societies. Rather, their period of rise was followed by a fall.

There must be some set of conditions under which the progressive society would not fall but would continue indefinitely to experience change with order and to operate within control systems permitting it to meet nature's requirements. One can envision this goal being accomplished by a succession of lawgivers possessed of the foresight and the power to adjust the society's control systems before that society began to destroy itself or its environment. Or one can visualize a society so structured, as if by a metasystem of control, that it is able continually to adapt itself to changing conditions while preserving the required control. But such a state has not existed in the past, and the tenure of progressive societies has been limited. With a large enough number of relevant experiments, perhaps natural selection would reach such a result, but our focus now is on the outcome of a single great experiment.

EXPLANATION OF THE SHORT-RUN PERSISTENCE OF SYSTEMS SUPPRESSING IMPROVEMENT IN EFFICIENCY

Many societies appear to have important resistances to a process of self-feeding improvement in economic efficiency. The lack of even short-run success with programs aimed at economic development of societies with low living standards illustrates this point. Therefore, some explanation is needed as to why efficiency-improving innovations are not positively selected even in the short run. The following observations are relevant:

1. Although improvement in economic efficiency can be a self-feeding process, as characterized here, and is thus a threat to a stable society, sets of rules can be developed that will sterilize this potential. Once innovation occurs, it is certain to alter the stable society, but it can be prevented from occurring on an important scale by societal rules that preclude the kinds of action in question, that deprive it of its reward, or that deactivate those who would play the role of the innovator.

2. Such anti-innovative rules, once established, commonly are supported by interests more powerful, more tangible, and more effectively concentrated than are those interests associated with the purely hypothetical gains from innovation. Thus, once established, such societal rules may be stable and resistant to disturbance. Such a pattern is like the performance of animal groups showing effective societal discipline under mechanisms developed through natural selection. These societies are highly conservative, centralist, governed by the "establishment," and intolerant of short-run innovation or violation of the societal control rules.

3. In human societies, the openness that favors productive innovation in many cases leads to societal disorder and a retreat to a more closed system within a very short period of time. Successful self-feeding innovation running for centuries seems to be the exception. Some experiments with openness and rapid change have destroyed themselves within a decade.

4. In the modern world, the effort to use foresight on behalf of economic progressiveness or economic development has in some cases not been based on a realistic interpretation of the relevant natural laws and has promoted policies that have had the opposite of the intended effects.

Many societies thus are governed by rules that preserve stability and stifle productive innovation. Only in societies with an unusually favorable set of initial rules is the disruptive effect of increase in efficiency tolerated for long. The development of the West can be interpreted within this framework as deriving from a unique set of rules that grew out of the enthusiasm for a scientific view of man and nature that prevailed in the late eighteenth and early nineteenth centuries.

POLICY TOWARD EFFICIENCY CHANGE

The central task of policy to promote positive change in economic efficiency, as the matter appears within this framework, is to create the kinds of institutions, policies, and laws that will encourage the self-feeding process described here. Because what is required is to permit the society's potential for this process to be realized, the task is in a sense a negative one involving mainly the removal of conditions that impede efficiency change.   This idea is, of course, an old one.   It was a major theme of Adam Smith.

Because it involves mainly the laws and actions of government—and institutional arrangements that depend on the support of government—policy to promote increase in efficiency is mainly a political matter.   Many positive actions taken by government also can accelerate the process of change in economic efficiency, the precise definition of these actions being a matter on which opinions differ.   But the essential role of government—and a necessary and sufficient condition for self-feeding improvement in efficiency—is the establishment of a set of favorable societal rules.   Some more specific comments on the effects of government policies are given in Chapter 7.

POLICY PROMOTING CONTINUATION OF IMPROVEMENT IN ECONOMIC EFFICIENCY

In this interpretation, improvement in economic efficiency, once established, does not automatically continue indefinitely. Indeed, in the usual case the process is a self-destructive one. This matter is one concerning which established knowledge is limited.   Within this framework, the role of policy to preserve improvement in economic efficiency would be continually to adapt the laws and institutions serving as societal control systems in such a way as to prevent growing impediments to continued improvement in efficiency and, most seriously, to avoid group conflict and loss of societal coherency that can seriously reduce efficiency. Increase in efficiency and in the standard of living require also adaptation and maintenance of effective societal control systems that limit population growth and environmental destruction.

CONCLUSIONS

The approach taken here to explain the rate of change in a society's economic efficiency is consistent with the approach taken with regard to other aspects of societal performance. These can be interpreted within the framework of natural selection, for changes in societal performance reflect the set of rules governing intrasocietal selection among individuals and organizations, what people learn, the incentive system they confront, and the payoff matrix of the game they play with the outside world.

This approach also is consistent with that of the mainstream of economics. Since the physiocrats and the classical economists, economic efficiency has been emphasized as the basis of the standard of living and societal rules have been regarded as determinants of whether or not improvement in efficiency occurs. The emphasis of this body of thought on competition or rules preventing the restraint of trade relates to the point that is here made somewhat more broadly.

The theory of economic development, on the other hand, does not emphasize economic efficiency as the basis of improvement in living standards. As noted elsewhere, the several variants of the story of economic development emphasize a variety of other factors but do not emphasize factors leading to economic efficiency as such. Efficiency is seen as a side effect of other changes—political modernization, increase in the stock of investment goods, help in the form of foreign aid, economic planning, development of the spirit of nationalism, and so on.

It is quite consistent with the theory's framework of unilinear evolution that economic efficiency should not be determined by separable factors but should be an aspect of the process of development, modernization. Population was interpreted within this same framework. But this theory then is vulnerable to a demonstration that different societies are not simply at different stages in the same process of development, that they are not on the same track but on different tracks, that the political and institutional factors determining change in efficiency differ among nations in a way that cannot be explained as involving different stages in a single process.

7 / The Political System and the Standard of Living

The theory of economic development implies that living standards are not importantly affected by political institutions. It does not emphasize differences among political systems as explaining differences in the rate of economic development or in the ability of societies to achieve the take-off. If the political system importantly affects living standards, it becomes necessary to depict alternative paths of historical change that societies may take depending on their political systems. If certain kinds of political institutions preclude economic progress or will cause it to be reflected in overpopulation and subsequent starvation, it would seem that political criteria should be used for the granting of foreign aid.

That economic progress depends crucially on political institutions is an old idea. This was a major theme of the physiocrats and the classical economists. Until recent decades, the predominant view among economists was that the central factor in the rapid economic changes and increase in economic efficiency in the West was its political system, which removed the impediments that prevented such progress in other societies.

The mainstream of modern economic theory remains consistent with this interpretation. It depicts living standards as depending on economic efficiency, which depends on economic behavior that responds systematically to an incentive system that, in the modern world, is largely defined politically. Modern price theory provides no basis for believing that economic efficiency increases continuously, irrespective of the nature of economic decisions or the framework within which they are made.

Such emphasis on political factors, however, is not consistent with the framework of single-track progress of the theory of economic development. In his key statement of this approach, for example, W. W. Rostow depicts Russian and American growth as involving movement along the same track, indicating that Russian economic change under the czars and then under communist government can be interpreted within the standard framework of economic development. Discussions of foreign aid and international economic policy assume that economic development can occur under a wide variety of political institutions. Indeed, to suggest that a nation cannot receive its dividend of economic progress under the political institutions preferred by its leaders is regarded as improper. A naturalistic approach to the determination of living standards seems necessarily to tell a different story.

THE POLITICAL SYSTEM AND THE STANDARD OF LIVING: A NATURALISTIC INTERPRETATION

The political system largely defines the rules of the game for any society and thus the incentive system, payoff matrix, or effective "environment," to which individuals and groups within the society respond. Thus it affects the nature of intrasocietal selection, what it is that individuals and groups learn, are conditioned to, and which patterns of behavior are reinforced and come to prevail. A major role is played by the formal apparatus of law, justice, and administrative regulation. This apparatus provides a long list of things that may not be done or that involve penalties. The system of taxes, from this point of view, defines a set of financial penalties attached to certain actions and thus affects the payoff matrix affecting individuals and groups. Government subsidies—or negative taxes—offer financial inducements to certain actions.

Important also is government enforcement of rules applying to dealings among individuals and groups. The definition and the security of property rights, the degree to which order is preserved, the extent to which certain groups in society have special privileges—these are all important determinants of behavior and of the performance of the society.

The exercise of power in a society is never entirely formalized or legalized. In many cases, there is a wide gap between the nominal performance of government in all its functions (administrative supervision, preservation of order, enforcement of justice) and what actually goes on. Behavior responds to the rules that actually operate rather than those that are on the books.

THE POLITICAL SYSTEM AND POPULATION CONTROL

In the modern world, population behavior is dominated by rules defined by the political system. The European system of population limitation as discussed in Chapter 4 depended on politically defined rules. The system of birth limitation based on the family depended on laws relating to marriage, penalties for childbirth outside of marriage, and legal limitations on the ability to marry. Rules of the guilds requiring delay in marriage depended on the politically defined position of the guilds. Laws relating to private property and the hierarchy of economic positions were the basis of the system.

As the ideas underlying laws and government policies changed in the nineteenth and twentieth centuries, they became more concerned with immediate humanitarian considerations and less responsive to the function of population limitation. Thus welfare programs were liberalized, income was redistributed from the affluent to the poor, and free services were made widely available. In addition, government policies had an important effect in elevating the birth rate by the prohibition of abortion and infanticide and, in many places, by the legal proscription of implements of birth control. Prohibition by European colonial powers of means earlier used to limit family size importantly affected population growth in colonial territories.

The dominant role of the political system as a determinant of population behavior is illustrated by the Japanese experience, in which a change in government policies replaced a rapid rate of population growth by stability of population, primarily by making available abortion facilities. In the senses that (1) existing political systems and laws favor population increase and that (2) political arrangements are definable that would stabilize population or reduce it, the population problem of the present-day world is a political problem.

Not only does the political system influence population, but changes in population importantly affect the political system. Differences in the rates of population growth of subgroups in the society will alter their relative numbers and thus their political power. Thus the long-run viability of a political system requires that it prevent the above-average population growth of groups in the society that would lead to its overthrow. An open franchise and prevalence of generous welfare payments and other forms of income redistribution comprise a system of rules favoring subgroups having a rapid rate of population growth. The population-limitation systems generated by natural selection were weighted against deviant groups, which were not permitted to survive or to reproduce. A sustainable system of population limitation in the modern context could not involve rules encouraging groups opposed to population limitation to increase their relative numbers and power over long periods.

THE POLITICAL SYSTEM AND ENVIRONMENTAL PRESERVATION

Preservation of the environment in the modern world depends almost entirely on rules defined and enforced through political machinery. Although past political systems have failed to prevent environmental destruction, some of their provisions may have reflected the foresight of lawgivers and selection among societies favoring those that preserved their habitat. For example, systems of land tenure that promoted the inheritance of land intact and that tied people to specific pieces of land, such as prevailed in Europe, may have been functional in preserving the land and limiting population.

Increase in economic efficiency, the rise of cities and industry, and the disappearance of this localistic system removed impediments to destruction of the environment. For example, the destruction of the earlier land-tenure system and of the clan-based political system opened the way to a commercialized exploitation of the land and resulted in the degradation of the Scottish highlands through deforestation and sheep-grazing.[1]

Thus the localistic impediments to environmental destruction that had their roots in one political system were undone by economic and political changes. The halting or deceleration of environmental destruction in a world where localism is lost and where many new and difficult-to-control means of environmental destruction have been created could be accomplished only by new political arrangements.

It may be that many, or even all, modern societies cannot create the required political rules. Past institutions for environmental preservation arose from a localistic way of life that is now lost, from group selection that is inapplicable in the short run in the modern world, and perhaps in some cases from the foresight of a lawgiver combined with the power of a chieftain or king. In a modern society in which power is gained by politicians who win the favor of the mass of people, it may not be possible to institute policies that involve a heavy present cost in the interest of future advantages revealed only by knowledge and analysis.

THE POLITICAL SYSTEM AND EFFICIENCY CHANGE

In the modern context, the political system also defines those rules of the societal game that determine whether or not the potential for self-feeding increase in economic efficiency is realized. The productivity of innovation is negatively affected by government actions that prevent the undertaking or

---

[1] F. Fraser Darling, *West Highland Survey: An Essay in Human Ecology* (New York: Oxford University Press, 1955), pp. 2–6.

limit the productivity of otherwise available opportunities. For example:

1. Regulation or licensing coupled with ineffective or misguided administration, which hampers effective operation of businesses. In such a situation, graft is likely to exist; but it may, on balance, improve the operation of the economy, for the social costs of the graft may be less than the damage done by an absolute inability to take actions necessary to the effective operation of business.

2. Uncertain availability because of exchange controls on imports and materials required for production.

3. Regulations on business operations that increase costs or reduce the expected rate of return. Examples are prohibition of or high-premium wage rates for work on holidays, nights, and so on.

4. Preemption of areas by government enterprises that cannot themselves exploit the opportunities for productive innovation.

5. Other regulations in the form of direct prohibition or limitations on advertising and promotion that have the effect of preventing private business from entering an area in which productive innovation would otherwise occur.

Although all these factors are negative in the sense that a bad situation might be improved simply by reducing government activities, others require a positive contribution:

1. Maintenance of law and order, enforcement of contracts, and protection against destruction of property or illegal expropriation by guerrillas, racial violence, and ordinary robbery.[2]

2. Provision by government or creation of an environment in which effective provision is made by private business of such services as roads, water, and reliable electric power.

[2] A neglected problem of rural lawlessness is discussed in Ithiel de Sola Pool, "Village Violence and International Violence," Peace Research Society (International), *Papers,* 9 (1968), 87–94.

3. Provision by government or through private agencies of information and research related to production and marketing in the context of the society in question.

4. Provision of government investment and enterprise in areas where this approach would be the most productive one or where a functional gap would otherwise exist.

5. Enforcement of a set of rules for economic activity that relates rewards to productive activity rather than privilege or power, preventing concentration of economic power that would undercut the political system and prevent maintenance of such rules.

Government policies that maximize the marginal rate of return to productive innovation enlarge the area within which creative change can occur and protect the innovator against activities by government agencies or private groups that would make innovation impossible or reduce its efficiency.

Government actions that are attractive from other points of view may hamper self-feeding improvement in economic efficiency by diverting the gains in output resulting from innovation so that they do not motivate or finance additional innovation. Some examples are given in the following paragraphs.

A high marginal tax rate affecting the proceeds of successful innovation is detrimental unless the proceeds from taxation of innovatory projects are used to motivate and finance further innovatory projects, which is not ordinarily the case.

The threat of future expropriation of property on unfavorable terms acts like the hazard of a future unfavorable tax rate. The threat of illegal destruction or expropriation of property has a similar effect.

Arrangements for profit sharing or for any system of wage determination involving high marginal increases in wage rates in response to business profits also has the effect of a high marginal tax rate, diverting the funds to the business' workers rather than to the government. This additional income to employees ordinarily makes no contribution to self-feeding efficiency change.

Finally, socialist economies ordinarily do not allow the proceeds of successful innovation to be made available to the manager for further innovation.

Responsiveness to the existing opportunities for productive innovation may also be importantly affected by government actions. For example, government's acquiescence in or encouragement of persecution of minorities or intrasocietal groups especially associated with business limits response to existing opportunities. The persecuted groups may respond by exporting capital to a more favorable environment and by emigrating, with lasting effect on the capacity of the society for economic development.[3] Similarly, limitations on the economic activities of foreign businesses and foreigners limit the pool of available entrepreneurship or the response to opportunities for productive innovation, as does maintenance or support by the government of an educational system and a system of information and propaganda that disparage business and work.

POLITICAL FACTORS AND DIFFERENCES IN LIVING STANDARDS

Political factors are seen by some observers as contributing importantly to the lack of increase in economic efficiency in societies that have performed unfavorably in that respect.[4] Some relevant factors are these:

[3] The prevalence of such practices is suggested in this comment by Morgan: "Among the countries of Southeast Asia, Burma, Ceylon, and Indonesia have harassed and squeezed out Chinese, Indian, and Western enterprises and emigrants. The Philippines and Thailand have squeezed the Chinese businessman but have been tolerant toward Western enterprise. Elsewhere in the world Arabs, Negroes, Irish, Jews, and many another group has been put to the squeeze. Especially in newly independent countries where nationalism is a high fever do we find minorities in general systematically discriminated against." Theodore Morgan, "Economic Planning—Points of Success and Failure," *Philippine Economic Journal,* 4 (1965), 413.

[4] An empirical study finding a substantial role for political factors in statistically "explaining" differences in growth rates among low-income nations is that of Irma Adelman and Cynthia Taft Morris, "A Factor Analysis of the Interrelationship Between Social and Political Variables and Per Capita Gross National Product," *Quarterly Journal of Economics,* 79 (November 1965), 555–578.

1. Inflationary monetary policies leading to capital flight, inability to mobilize savings for productive investment, irrational price structure, and inflation-suppressing regulations that cause economic inefficiency.

2. Detailed economic regulations—wage and price controls, exchange controls and rationing of foreign exchange, regulations on employment terms—that prevent efficiency improvement and positively promote inefficient practices.[5]

3. Welfare programs that are beyond the ability of the economy to sustain without inflation or burdensome taxation.

4. Direct and indirect government support of wage rates and employee benefits for government and industrial workers that promote misallocation of resources and limit self-feeding efficiency change.

5. Economic planning leading to wasteful projects and to poor allocation of resources.

For the politicians of the underdeveloped nation, we should like to organize an educational Cook's tour which would take in such noteworthy archaeological sites as completed factories which have never produced, housing projects which are uninhabited, unfinished water-spreading dams whose initial purpose and design have been forgotten, tracts of virgin soil cleared and now reverting to waste, superhighways used mainly by donkeys and mules, and the countless villages untouched by developmental efforts and in full decay.[6]

As Domar puts it:

Their governments are simply not yet ready to undertake the very complex and difficult task of managing their economies.

[5] An empirical study leading to the conclusion that productivity growth in Latin American countries during the past decade has been about zero and explaining the lack of improvement in average efficiency by the inefficiencies introduced by government controls is that of Henry J. Bruton, "Productivity Growth in Latin America," *American Economic Review,* 57 (December 1967), 1099–1116.

[6] Andrew Watson and Joel B. Dirlam, "The Impact of Underdevelopment on Economic Planning," *Quarterly Journal of Economics,* 79 (May 1965), 194. The authors argue that particular conditions existing in most nations with low living standards preclude efficient centralized planning.

Few governments are. Can you imagine the mismanagement, waste and corruption which would accompany an attempt by the government of my own Commonwealth of Massachusetts to take over its economy?[7]

A focal case because of its size and importance has been India, whose poor performance is widely attributed in part to specific aspects of its centralized planning and detailed regulation.[8]

6. Excessive government expenditures for nationalistic or prestige projects, government buildings, airlines, overly elaborate roads, dams, steel mills. Also large expenditures for military goods.

7. One-party government, in some cases accompanied by repression of opposition, diversion of the educational system to party propaganda and even deification of the head of state, and intrusion of partisan political considerations into government economic activities.

Both the moderate and radical wings of the nationalist elite favor the single or dominant national party, and such parties exist in many of the new nations of Africa, in several countries in Asia, and, in the case of Mexico, in Latin America as well. . . . The illiterate masses who have had little or no relation to national politics are educated to read the party literature and to become aware of national and international problems from the party point of view.[9]

8. Graft and corruption among government workers and of-

[7] Evsey D. Domar, "Reflections on Economic Development," *The American Economist,* 10 (Spring 1966), 8. See also, Gerald Sirkin, *The Invisible Hand: The Fundamentals of Economic Planning* (New York: McGraw-Hill, 1968), Chap. 7; Charles W. Anderson, *Politics and Economic Change in Latin America* (Princeton, N.J.: Van Nostrand, 1967), pp. 373–376; Lauchlin Currie, *Accelerating Development: The Necessity and the Means* (New York: McGraw-Hill, 1966), pp. 47–48.

[8] Among such evaluations are Sirkin, *op. cit.,* Chap. 7, which gives references to other sources; and Anne O. Krueger, "Indian Planning Experience," in Theodore Morgan, George W. Betz, and N. K. Choudhry (eds.), *Economic Development: Readings in Theory and Practice* (Belmont, Calif.: Wadsworth, 1963), pp. 403–420.

[9] Paul E. Sigmund, Jr., *The Ideologies of the Developing Nations* (New York: Praeger, 1963), pp. 9, 23.

ficials.[10] Some cases of large-scale stealing by the head of state or political elite.

9. Inefficiency of government service.

> *The mechanisms of the Latin American nation-state can neither provide peace and order, nor a basic minimum of public services, nor meet the challenge of new social demands, nor serve as a forum for easing the disruptions of change. Such testimony is by now commonplace. It has become part of the folklore of development.*[11]

Some of the political and ideological considerations that impel governments to extensive regulation seem to imply that the resulting bureaucracy shall be "an underpaid, paper-shuffling dead hand."[12] Appointment for political reasons of excessive numbers of government employees, who commonly are underpaid, leads to this situation.[13]

Because government in Europe and the United States in the eighteenth and nineteenth centuries was neither efficient nor honest, it is useful to ask how, in this earlier experience, the political conditions were created for continued growth in economic efficiency.

First, the West largely avoided inflation, apart from wartime, by adhering to the external discipline of metallic mone-

[10] A discussion of the pros and cons of corruption in this connection is given in J. S. Nye, "Corruption and Political Development: A Cost-Benefit Analysis," *American Political Science Review,* 61 (June 1967), 417–427.

[11] Anderson, *op. cit.,* p. 4. The author notes "the seeming paradox—that it is to the roundly condemned institution of government that so many turn to provide the crucial impetus for economic change."

[12] Such is the characterization of the historical Latin American bureaucracy in Wendell Gordon, *The Political Economy of Latin America* (New York: Columbia University Press, 1965), p. 164. The author adds, "Unable to be constructive, in considerable measure because of his lack of status, the low-level bureaucrat has reacted by being surly and uncooperative in his dealings with the public." See also p. 66.

[13] Andrew Shonfield, *The Attack on World Poverty* (New York: Random House, 1962), p. 5. Shonfield relates the problem of padded payrolls to that of low salaries for government officials, which in turn drives educated and able people to seek jobs abroad.

tary standards. In other words, the West avoided inflationary monetary policy by avoiding monetary policy.

Second, detailed government economic regulations were limited by the predominance of classical economics, with its analysis of the inefficacy of such regulations. What was new and radical in the eighteenth century, against the background of mercantilism, was the concept that economic order could exist without detailed government regulation and "planning." The rule of laissez faire saved the West from overregulation.

Third, avoidance of costly welfare programs by the West also derived from its individualist political theory and the prevailing analysis of the adverse effects on population and economic incentives.

Fourth, the analysis of classical economics that excessive wage rates cause unemployment and that the rule of competition should prevail in the labor market was carried into the political area during early Western development.

Fifth, comprehensive economic planning and an extensive role of government enterprise were also avoided as a matter of political theory. As Myrdal says of the West, "The ideological and political milieu of economic development . . . was that of the liberal interlude between Mercantilism and the modern welfare state." He emphasizes the importance of this difference between the two sets of cases:

> *The appearance in underdeveloped countries of the demand for economic development and still more the assumption that it is the concern of the state to engender development by means of planning is a new event in history, so far as the non-Communist world is concerned. . . . The industrial revolution in the Western countries did not—and, more important when we discuss ideologies, was never thought to—come about as a result of state planning in the modern sense.*[14]

Sixth, government extravagances in the West were limited by the antigovernment and antinationalist ideology of the times, though the record of the West in warfare and its costs is unfavorable.

[14] Gunnar Myrdal, *Asian Drama* (New York: Twentieth Century Fund, 1968), pp. 712–713.

Finally, the extremes of political nationalism developed in the West in the nineteenth and twentieth centuries belonged to an ideological revolt against the internationalism and individualism of the Enlightenment and the eighteenth century. If the view that development derives from nationalistic enthusiasm rather than economic efficiency is wrong, it is another perverse exportation from the twentieth-century West.[15]

A basic message of the classical economists was that economic progress could occur only by limiting the stifling government control of the economy that they saw as resulting from the mercantilist theory and from the highly centralized governments of their time. It seems likely that they were right on this point. If the government of eighteenth-century England had sought to control its economy in detail, the industrial revolution would have been slowed or prevented altogether.[16]

DETERMINANTS OF THE PERFORMANCE OF THE POLITICAL SYSTEM

The behavior of national governments frequently is treated as if political leaders were free agents exercising volitional control over the society. Then the political problem is to show government officials what needs to be done. This unrealistic

---

[15] The modern nationalistic ideological framework is illustrated by Kwame Nkrumah, "Background to Independence," in Paul E. Sigmund, Jr., *op. cit.,* pp. 182–186; Kofi Baako, "Nkrumaism—Its Theory and Practice," *ibid.,* pp. 188–196. For characterization of this ideology, see *ibid.,* pp. 3–26.

[16] The absence of detailed government economic regulation is interpreted as a major factor permitting economic development in England and Japan, in contrast to its failure to develop in China and France, in Robert T. Holt and John E. Turner, *The Political Basis of Economic Development* (Princeton, N.J.: Van Nostrand, 1966), pp. 292–308. Cameron illustrates the same point by contrasting the favorable experience of Japan and of Russia in the late nineteenth century with that of Spain, the Ottoman Empire, and earlier Russia. Rondo Cameron, "Economic Development: Some Lessons of History for Developing Nations," *American Economic Review Papers and Proceedings,* 57 (May 1967), 321.

approach has been widely commented on,[17] but it is not customary to take the next step to a systematic explanation of government behavior. Still, the behavior of a governmental apparatus must be defined by its structure, by the rules of its game, just as is that of the economy. We require a naturalistic interpretation, therefore, both of the influence of government on societal performance and of the factors determining the behavior of government.[18]

THE BEHAVIOR OF THE POLITICAL SYSTEM IN THE SHORT RUN

In the short run, government can be thought of as responding to a set of rules or as being defined by such factors as the voting rules of the society, the distribution of beliefs, the structure of subgroups and parties, the constitution or political charter and structure of government, the political traditions and norms, and the level of education and thought patterns of the electorate. This set of factors defines the principles of selection applying to potential officials and government administrations. It defines, on the average, the kind of government that will prevail. In any particular case, of course, an unusual outcome can be produced by a political leader of unusual qualities.

On this basis, certain kinds of political performance can be identified as the expected outcome of classes of political machinery. The representative government based on an intelligent, informed, and critically analytical electorate performs well but is rare. Representative government with a credulous electorate produces leaders who promise what cannot be delivered, commonly resulting in various kinds of efficiency-damaging policies. The system with voting rules leading to multiple parties, coalition governments, and an inability of

---

[17] A common view is "that the problem is essentially one of political leadership, that if the 'right people' could come to power, the problem would be solved. However, the state is not an independent variable in the equation of change. Its capacity to act is limited by the very conditions which it is urged to overcome." Charles W. Anderson, *op. cit.,* p. 367.

[18] Relevant contributions are David Easton, *A Systems Analysis of Political Life* (New York: Wiley, 1965); and Walter Buckley (ed.), *Modern Systems Research for the Behavioral Scientist* (Chicago: Aldine, 1968), Part 7.

government to make and carry out decisions is illustrated by interwar France and by Italy. Government by an entrenched clique or elite party tends to be cautious of change and protective of its power, conceals information, is inefficient because of concentration of power and inability to admit and correct errors, and is hazardous because of its ability to make large errors.

LONG-RUN DETERMINANTS OF NATIONAL POLITICAL PERFORMANCE

Over long periods, the performance of the national political system is affected by its external environment and by the principles of selection that operate among nations and among national governments. These principles are defined by the rules of the international system. In an era of warfare, military effectiveness is required for survival. If the prevailing rules lead to peaceful competition, then economic effectiveness and attractive political institutions pay off. A game of mutual subversion and conspiracy awards victory to yet another kind of government and another set of national political rules. An influential goal in earlier times was the establishment of an international order within which peaceful competition in constructive achievements would determine the survival of governments and political systems. The international political system in the late 1960s was in a state of flux, of uncertain performance and prospects.

REFORM AND THE POLITICAL SYSTEM

If political activity comprises a system or game, then political change is also a defined game. The capacity of various groups to change the system depends on their initial resources, their relation to the initial game. The final results may bear no defined relation to the intentions of the reformer and in some cases may be quite the opposite. The power to alter the initial system, therefore, is not necessarily the power to gain the desired replacement system. This fact is illustrated by the experience of the "enlightened despots" during the Enlightenment and by the present situation of the Soviet

Union and other communist nations that are exploring moves toward a less-centralized system of economic control.[19]

One difficulty is that the centralized power of the government may be adequate for maintenance of the status quo, for a defensive strategy, but not for reforms that challenge the interests and ideology of those in power. The enlightened despots were resisted by their nobility and the church, whereas decentralization in communist societies encounters resistance from within the existing power hierarchy.

A second difficulty is that once basic reform is introduced into a hitherto stable system, the process of change may develop a dynamic of its own, working out in ways not foreseen by its initiators—ways that they may find frightening or threatening. Again, both the enlightened despots and present-day reformist communist leaders find themselves wanting a certain amount of reform, but embarrassed that a first step toward reform seems to create pressures for further steps.[20]   Of course, the controllers of a centralized system who want the benefits in efficiency from decentralization but cannot accept the loss of centralized power face a basic dilemma.

Nominal control of a government may confer little power to alter the performance of the governmental system. The elected political leader usually is a player in a game whose rules he can do little to alter and according to which he must play if he is not to lose out to competitors.

The government actions that lead to elevation of living standards, as these have been characterized here, involve current costs on behalf of later rewards. Adoption of programs for control of population and of environmental destruction and adoption of a set of rules favorable to an increase in economic efficiency are not immediately appealing. In many nations, a political leader who proposed adoption of such a program would lose the next election to a party promising actions more emotionally appealing. In this connection, one

---

[19] The reasons for and nature of the decentralizing reforms of Eastern Europe in the late 1960s are discussed in Rudolf Bićanić, "Economics of Socialism in a Developed Country," *Foreign Affairs,* 44 (July 1966), 633–650; and Branko Horvat, *Toward a Theory of Planned Economy* (Belgrade: Yugoslav Institute of Economic Research, 1964).

[20] See Milovan Djilas, *The New Class* (New York: Praeger, 1957); Horvat, *op. cit.,* Part 5.

of the functions of foreign aid that is offered on a conditional basis is that it permits the recipient government to take actions that it knows are economically desirable but that it could not otherwise take for fear of jeopardizing its own political position.

One framework for political reform parallels the approach suggested here in connection with policy toward population control and environmental preservation. A group of nations whose political system and economic policy meet certain standards can offer membership—and inducements arising from the success of the group—to other nations if they meet the same standards. This arrangement sets up, as it were, an international political game encouraging constructive selection among national governments or provides a framework for reform of national governments.

But this approach, taken at the international level, poses the conflict between the present and the future: its payoff would not be immediate. Thus the problem of reform at the international level also involves the question of replacing arrangements that promise high immediate rewards but that are damaging in the longer run, with arrangements that promise little for the present but that offer the greatest promise in the long run.

OTHER INTERPRETATIONS OF THE INFLUENCE OF POLITICAL FACTORS ON LIVING STANDARDS

The modern literature concerning economic development has treated political factors within frameworks that differ from the one used here. Reference is made to several prominent approaches.

POLITICAL MODERNIZATION

A consideration of political factors within the framework of unilinear evolution that predominates in the theory of economic development leads to a concept of political modernization or political progress. It does seem common in present-day thought to view political actions that lead to economic development not in terms of a functional analysis but rather in terms of ideas as to what constitutes a modern, or proper, or advanced, political system. This tendency can be subdivided into several specific interpretations.

One influential approach depicts political modernism as involving socialism, central direction of the economy, and elimination or close regulation of private enterprise. In this view, political modernization involves an advance from the earlier and now archaic approach of laissez faire to a large and expanding role of government. The approach is supported by a number of strands of modern thought: Christian views of the immorality of private enterprise, Keynesian stagnationism, and Marxist thought.

This approach leads to extensive government planning and control of economic activity. The adoption of government planning on the basis of ideas of political modernization interacts with the ideas of economic modernization that have shaped the content of the planning. The idea that economic modernization is synonymous with industrialization and implies the use of the most advanced industrial techniques or emphasis on heavy industry has been widely influential. The counterpart of this idea is that agricultural improvement is not the road to modernization and does not merit the activities of government or even a claim on available resources. Within the previously described framework, this theory can rule out the important opportunities that exist for improving agricultural efficiency in predominantly agricultural countries, as well as lead to the creation of high-cost industrial facilities. Neglect of agriculture based on such theories of what comprises modernization has been interpreted as an important factor in the poor performance of India.[21] Theories in which improvement in agricultural efficiency is an important ingredient of overall improvement in a national economy lead to quite different policy prescriptions.[22]

Nationalism is also widely emphasized as an ingredient of

---

[21] See Anne O. Krueger, *op. cit.*

[22] For example, H. J. Habakkuk, "Historical Experience of Economic Development," in E. A. G. Robinson (ed.), *Problems of Economic Development* (New York: St. Martin's Press, 1965); reprinted in Theodore Morgan, George W. Betz, and N. K. Choudhry, *op. cit.*, pp. 5–7.

political modernism. To some observers, the development of a nationalistic approach such as has characterized the West increasingly in the present century is an element of political modernization that is helpful, if not essential, to economic development. This framework provides a justification for many policies that have unfavorable direct effects on economic efficiency: high-cost prestige industrial plants and airlines, various government expenditures, and the imposition of trade restrictions and economic controls to foster industrialization and a nationally oriented economy.

Such an emphasis on nationalism as a requisite for political modernization justifies political systems that, interpreted on a functional basis, are not favorable to an increase in living standards. If, indeed, what is required is to awaken the spirit of nationalism, then a one-party government using the press and schools to spread nationalistic doctrines may be the optimal political arrangement. From a functional point of view that emphasizes economic efficiency, however, such regimes commonly have followed policies that opposed improvement in efficiency and such an educational system scarcely promotes it.

A more conservative interpretation of political modernism associates it with institutions such as presently exist in the United States, involving representative government, the universal franchise, and the welfare state. Once again, during its phase of limited education, lower living standards, and limited experience with representative government, the West operated with a limited franchise that was only gradually widened. In a society where the unlimited franchise leads to government administrations elected on the basis of promises of immediate rewards to an electorate incapable of analyzing complex problems, government may be unable to adopt effective systems for control of population and environmental destruction or political rules conducive to continued increase in economic efficiency.

Governments in nations with low living standards that, in terms of functional analysis, are an impediment to economic progress, are supported largely by concepts of political modernism. Interpretation of political institutions within the framework of unilinear evolution and conceptions of political

modernization or progress leads to implications quite different from those of interpretations within a framework of open
evolution or naturalistic functional analysis.

THE ROLE OF PLANNING

One view associates political modernization with the movement from laissez faire to economic planning. Within this
framework, it is reasonable to prescribe additional planning
as the means to economic modernization through political
modernization. Partially on the basis of this logic some low-
income nations with limited political experience have
adopted programs of centralized planning such as have not
been used in the leading Western nations and would not be
considered for application in the United States.

Once again, there is a modern literature that does not interpret planning within the framework of unilinear evolution
but that considers its performance under particular circumstances.[23] By and large, this literature paints an unfavorable
picture of the past and expected future performance of central
planning in nations with low living standards and raises serious questions about its consistency with continued improvement in economic efficiency in advanced nations.[24] Thus
there presently exist two quite different interpretations of the
effect of economic planning on economic efficiency. One
views such planning as political modernization or progress
and evaluates it favorably; the other gives a functional interpretation and a much less favorable evaluation.

LAND REFORM

A specific example of a political action that can be viewed
within either an ideological or a functional framework is

---

[23] For example see Andrew Watson and Joel B. Dirlam, *op. cit.,* pp. 167–194;
Theodore Morgan, "The Theory of Error in Centrally-Directed Economic Sys-
tems," *Quarterly Journal of Economics,* 78 (August 1964), 395–419; Gerald
Sirkin, *op. cit.*

[24] See Branko Horvat, *op. cit.;* Rudolf Bićanić, *op. cit.;* Yevsei Liberman, "The
Soviet Economic Reform," *Foreign Affairs,* 46 (October 1967), 55; Michael
Gamarnikow, *Economic Reform in Eastern Europe* (Detroit: Wayne State Uni-
versity Press, 1968).

"land reform," or the division of large tracts into small ones preferably owned by the tiller ("Emotionalism! Thy Name is Land Reform. Every facet of the subject is coated with passion"[25]). As viewed within a framework of political progress or modernization, land reform commonly has been interpreted as a crucial step forward for the backward economy, or even as an essential prerequisite of economic progress.

Yet when the matter is viewed functionally in relation to economic efficiency, the outcome is less certain. In some cases, it seems, such parceling of agricultural land may not only reduce efficiency in the short run but may hamper future progress. While the United States was

> pushing Land Reform for Latin America, its agricultural technicians and scientists were rapidly making peasant farming obsolete. While the drive throughout Western Europe, the United States, and the British Commonwealth was toward consolidation of uneconomic-sized units and the creation of ever larger units, Latin America was to march in the opposite direction.[26]

CONCLUSIONS

The distinction between frameworks of open evolution and unilinear evolution seems to apply meaningfully to the political determinants of the standard of living. Within an ecological framework or a framework of open evolution, the national political system defines the incentive system to which individuals and organizations respond and thus also their behavior, which determines the performance of the society with reference to change in economic efficiency, environmental preservation, and population control. The key to an effective economic performance is a political system defining societal rules that will call forth an effective economic performance.

Within this approach, the performance of the political sys-

---

[25] William and Paul Paddock, *Hungry Nations* (Boston: Little, Brown, 1964), p. 240.

[26] Lauchlin Currie, *op. cit.,* p. 66. See also the Paddocks, *op. cit.,* Chap. 15.

tem also must be interpreted in a systematic way. The behavior of the national government is determined largely by a set of rules defining the terms of competition among potential governmental leaders. Thus some political charters will guarantee, on the average, a political system that produces an adverse economic performance. The external environment to which the national government adapts is determined in part by the international political and economic system. The most basic political reform is to create an area of the world within which the rules of international relations are conducive to the survival of national governments that will create the environment within which the behavior of individuals and organizations will result in controlled population, a preserved environment, and increases in economic efficiency.

A more prevalent view interprets the relation of political factors to economic development in terms of unilinear evolution and concepts of modernization of political institutions. The political institutions and the framework for economic activities resulting from this approach can be interpreted as a major cause of the lack of increase in the living standards of some nations. Moreover, such an anthropocentric approach to political institutions does not seem to provide a basis for control systems that will permit modern man to meet nature's criteria for the survival of his civilization.

CHAPTER 8 / Religion, Culture, and Living Standards

The theory of economic development emphasizes culture in the limited sense that the take-off involves the shift from a traditional culture or traditional society to changing institutions that are an aspect of economic development. But an interpretation of the influence of culture on living standards not tied to the framework of unilinear evolution could depict differences in culture as causing societies to take different paths with respect to population, environmental preservation, and change in economic efficiency.

Similarly, the theory of economic development does not emphasize differences in religion as explaining differences in living standards among societies. Yet this seems a potentially important explanatory factor, and some theorists have ascribed to it a substantial part of differences in living standards. Religion affects living standards in several ways, by directly influencing behavior, by affecting attitudes toward man and nature, and by affecting political ideas and thus the prevailing political system. This chapter offers some observations about the place of culture and religion in a naturalistic theory of living standards.

RELIGION AND CULTURE AS DETERMINANTS
OF LIVING STANDARDS

Religion and culture affect people's attitudes and thus their behavior and the performance of society, which determines living standards. The Protestant ethic, the set of ideas that reached its height early in the economic development of England and the United States, seemed to be particularly favorable to economic progress. The attitudes prevailing during this period may be characterized in terms of four factors:

1. An injunction to effort, to self-improvement, to achievement, with economic achievement and accumulation of wealth regarded with favor.

2. Rejection of luxurious living, frivolity, conspicuous consumption—the implication being that successful economic achievement led to accumulation of wealth.

3. An individualistic orientation that not only made the individual responsible for his own strivings but also discouraged the quest for preferment through accumulation of power and its use against others.

4. Absence of hereditary castes or other closed systems of role differentiation that would prevent individuals from contributing to economic activity on the basis of their abilities and drive.

This system of religious and cultural values can be contrasted with others that are unfavorable to economic improvement:

1. A passive or resigned attitude toward the world, which discourages effort and achievement.

2. An otherworldliness that regards the material conditions and the achievements of this world as unimportant.

3. An emphasis on conspicuous consumption of wealth as the means to satisfactions.

4. An extensive set of behavioral constraints defined in religious terms. An all-embracing concept of what activities

are good and bad that gives religious notions priority over purpose-oriented behavior.

5. An anti-individualist orientation.

6. An interpretative framework leading to excessive expectations, unattainable aspirations, and thus to rejection and destruction of institutions that make effective use of the opportunities that do exist.

7. More generally, attitudes or an interpretative framework leading to an unrealistic picture of man's relation to nature and of the consequences of his actions and policies.

The direct effects of such values and attitudes relate mainly to the capacity of a society for self-feeding improvement in economic efficiency. However, they also affect the political system and government policies and in this way also affect the possibilities of population control and environmental preservation.

Religion and culture can confer on actions certain rewards or punishments that join those determined in other ways to define the total incentive system to which people respond. Penalties in the afterlife assigned to certain actions illustrate the point. A religion or cultural system that dominates the thought of a group may thus overrule or modify the incentive system defined by available economic opportunities and the political system.

The ability of a religion or cultural system to prevent economic change, however, is fragile unless supported by power. If potentially rewarding opportunities for economic innovation exist, the religion or culture may be unable to prevent their exploitation by recalcitrant individuals or foreigners. If the rewards for this behavior are sufficiently great, the force of example may lead to widespread change in behavior, which reduces the power of the religion or culture or forces it to adapt to the new situation. Where a religion or culture affects government policies that can be enforced even against foreigners and heretics, greater resistance to change can be engendered.

Behavior with reference to family size has been especially influenced by religion and culture. Moreover, government policy affecting population and environmental preservation depends on the prevailing view of man's relation to nature, which in most societies is heavily influenced by religion and culture. In this connection, the naturalistic or scientific view of man's relation to nature can be viewed as a competitor of various religious and cultural views.

RELIGION, CULTURE, AND THE BEHAVIOR OF POPULATION

Different cultures and religions present to individual parents different norms or goals as to family size. In Catholic Latin America and in some Asian cultures, a large family is viewed as a boon and a testimonial to male virility. In some segments of Protestant and Jewish culture and religion, the norm is a small family, each member of which is educated and motivated for high achievement and a high standard of living.

Apart from such definition of norms, the means of birth limitation that are available to individuals are proscribed by some cultures and religions. The position of the Catholic Church in opposing abortion and most means of birth control is the most striking case in point. These differences in religion and culture appear to be reflected in significant differences in average family size. Thus religion and culture are in the present-day world significant determinants of the rate of population growth.

If such is the case, an argument is thus presented against interpretation of population within the framework of unilinear evolution. Specifically, doubt is cast on the proposition that, at a certain stage of economic development, population growth automatically will slow down. It appears, rather, that the whole time track for population should be expected to differ among societies that have basically different religions and culture. To argue the contrary requires either the denial that culture and religion affect the birth rate or the argument that culture and religion automatically are changed in a uniform manner in the process of economic development. No basis for accepting either of these propositions seems to have been provided.

Religious and ethnic groups operate in a special manner as

an influence on population when they compete with one another for power and dominance within a national society. In such cases, selection operates systematically in favor of groups with a certain population policy. Which set of group rules will be rewarded depends on the political system of the society. If power is earned through economic affluence, it will go to the group that limits family size. The egalitarian society with the universal franchise will award power to the group with the highest birth rate. The first political system makes ethnic and religious groups the organizing units for a system of population limitation, whereas the second one operates to the opposite effect.

It may be that the type of population-control system required for continued increases in living standards in the modern world can arise only from a naturalistic view of man and nature. If so, the extent to which various religions and cultures oppose the scientific approach is important. There appear to be substantial differences in the degree to which existing religions and cultures oppose the scientific view of man and nature.[1]

The influence of culture and religion on environmental preservation is governed by similar considerations. In contrast to earlier societal religions, the modern messianic religions are anthropocentric and do not play a positive role in environmental preservation. Religions have not actively opposed policies for environmental preservation. Their negative influence on ideas and policies perhaps is no greater than that of ideologies of secular anthropocentrism, including those based on the idea of progress or economic development. However, insofar as long-run success requires adoption of rigorous systems of environmental preservation based on a naturalistic view of man's relation to nature, religions that oppose such a view may prove to be a decisive impediment to environmental preservation.

---

[1] One study finds membership in Protestant and Jewish groups more favorable to acceptance of the scientific approach and involvement in scientific activities than membership in the Catholic group. See Gerhard Lenski, *The Religious Factor,* rev. ed. (New York: Doubleday, 1963), pp. 280–284.

RELIGION AND CULTURE AS DETERMINANTS OF EFFICIENCY CHANGE

Well-established religious and cultural systems that exert substantial control commonly are conservative or resistant to change. This characteristic may have survival value, as change commonly alters conditions and undermines the power of the religion or culture. One way of preserving the existing situation is to impose impediments to innovation, including innovation that increases economic efficiency.

Because such religious and cultural systems contemplate a static situation rather than one of progressive change, they view the distribution of income in terms of dividing a fixed pie according to rules of equity or morality. The concepts of proper income distribution to which this view gives rise commonly are not favorable to rewarding productive innovation and therefore impede a self-feeding increase in economic efficiency. Finally, in some cases religious and cultural systems denigrate business and economic activity among their own members and may be the basis of attacks on outsiders who engage in them.

RELIGION, CULTURE, AND SOCIETAL CONTROL: A HYPOTHESIS

In the naturalistic interpretation of the rise of human civilization, the control systems on which early human societies depended for survival were conveyed by integrated complexes of culture, religion, and political arrangements. Through these group-oriented control systems, rather than through instinctive behavior patterns like those of animals, man controlled his population, preserved his habitat, and achieved an acceptable degree of economic efficiency. Economic systems involving complex specialization of roles and division of labor, with arrangements for assignment of roles and distribution of income, were conveyed in this way. The development of such cultural-religious-political complexes that were efficacious in enabling man to meet nature's criteria for survival was achieved through natural selection among localized societies with different cultural systems.

This situation was exemplified by the ancient Greeks and Romans. Their religions were indigenous "native cults" that were seen as essential for the effectiveness of the society.[2] The execution of Socrates for religious heresy thus was not an act of religious fanaticism such as later became common, but was rather a response of society to subversion. An attack on the societal gods and beliefs was thought to lead to destructive behavior, the treachery of Alcibiades and Critias being viewed as cases in point.

Christianity was a radical departure from such societal cults with regard to societal control over individuals. Christianity was an international or universal religion, not oriented toward a particular society. Its doctrines reflected not the gradual accretion of beliefs but a supposedly supernatural revelation. Whereas the earlier cults can be interpreted as having survived in part by contributing to group coherency and adaptation to nature's criteria for survival, the messianic religions traded mainly on their direct emotional appeal and were basically anthropocentric. Finally, the Hebrew religion and Christianity were based on the idea of progress and the ultimate exaltation of an elected group, which had not been a predominant theme in earlier thought.[3]

Thus early Christianity was attacked by the Roman government not out of religious exclusivism in the modern sense but because it was seen as revolutionary and subversive, a threat to the organization of society. As Gibbon stated, "The Christians incurred the supposed guilt of an unnatural and unpardonable offense. They dissolved the sacred ties of custom and education, violated the religious institutions of their country, and presumptuously despised whatever their fathers had believed as true or had reverenced as sacred."[4]

---

[2] Characterization of religion and culture in these terms is given in William Howells, *The Heathens* (New York: Doubleday, 1956), Chap. 1; Bernard G. Campbell, *Human Evolution* (Chicago: Aldine, 1966), Chap. 10; Max Gluckman, *Politics, Law and Ritual in Tribal Society* (New York: New American Library, 1965).

[3] The contrast between Christianity and the earlier societal religions is discussed in Howells, *op. cit.,* Chap. 1.

[4] Edward Gibbon, *The Decline and Fall of the Roman Empire,* I (New York: Modern Library), p. 448.

Even where a religion gained a monopoly position in subsequent experience, as the Catholic Church did in many nations, such monopoly did not give the church the functional role of the earlier societal religions. Christianity remained an international religion, rather than one related to the organizational needs of the particular society, and an anthropocentric religion not serving to adapt man to nature's requirements for survival. But such monopoly religions, like the earlier societal cults, are resistant to change and thus oppose improvements in economic efficiency. The dominant role of the Catholic Church, for example, has been interpreted as the major explanation for the lack of economic improvement in Ireland and as a factor contributing to the limited achievements of Latin America.

In the modern world, the nation commonly incorporates competing religious groups. In many nations, conflict among religious groups is an important impediment to societal coherency and effectiveness, as illustrated by the contest between Hindus and Moslems in India, between Catholics and Protestants in several nations, and among tribal groups in Africa. Moreover, such religious groups provide a framework for competition to achieve dominance through a high birth rate in regions where the political system confers power upon numbers.

In this interpretation, religion in man's earlier history formed a part of a complex of institutions that served as his control system and permitted him to meet nature's tests for survival. The development of international, messianic religions paralleled other aspects of the loss of localism and the rise of anthropocentric beliefs. Freed—for some centuries, at least—from the discipline of natural selection, these religions told man a flattering story of his dominion over nature. They contributed to behavior of modern societies that made them highly expansive and successful in the short run. The popular appeal of anthropocentric religion is an impediment to acceptance of a naturalistic view of man's relation to nature, which may be the only basis for policies that will preserve civilization.

The development of secularized religions or anthropocentric ideologies meeting the same emotional needs involved this same potential problem. The concept of man's inexorable betterment, of which a particular version is the concept of economic development, can be interpreted as deriving from this body of thought. In this interpretation, localized religions that served to adapt man to nature have been replaced by nonlocalized religions that tell man he is above nature, this being one aspect of the high-stakes game in which modern man is challenging nature, to the jeopardy of his survival.

The era of rapid economic change in the West was the period in which the initial enthusiasm over science among the elite that then possessed power reduced the dominance of anthropocentric religion:

> *In the chilling proximity of rationalism and worldliness religion, in the established and fashionable churches, lost all the glow and fervor of emotion that distinguished it in earlier ages. Mysticism and zeal were distrusted and hated. . . . In consonance with this spirit preachers endeavored to make men energetic in business, moderate in pleasure, upright, charitable, and honorable. In comparison with the moral urge, even matters of cult, ritual, and church government, so passionately disputed in other times, sank into the background. . . . Not coldness and skepticism, however, but superstition and fanaticism were commonly regarded as the chief enemies of sound religion.*[5]

An interpretation of the role of culture as a determinant of living standards can be offered that closely parallels that for religion. In localized societies shaped by natural selection, culture and religion were inseparable. Development of the international, anthropocentric religions left a residue of culture associated with ethnic groups. This residuum contributed to societal coherency, although its conservativism opposed economic change. Societies retaining ethnic homogeneity, such as the British Isles until recently, France, and

---

[5] Preserved Smith, *The Enlightenment: 1687–1776* (New York: Collier Books, 1962), pp. 387–388. This redirection of religion was not, of course, permanent. As Smith characterizes the romantic reaction (pp. 394–395): "From cold moralism they fled to hot, mystical experience. . . . Oppressed by too much sanity, they welcomed the relief of hysteria and absurdity."

the Scandinavian nations, continued to derive some benefit from a common inheritance of culture. Such mixed societies as the United States operated effectively so long as one cultural group played a dominant role and others accepted this role and became "Americanized."

But ethnic groups, like religious groups, provide a possible basis for destructive competition where such competition is encouraged by the prevailing rules. The 1950s and 1960s saw a rise in these divisive tendencies in a number of nations. In the individualistic ideal of the Enlightenment, such ethnic attachments did not matter, for each educated person became a "citizen of the world." But education has not proved to have this effect. Mutually destructive, nonlocalized contests among ethnic groups in modern nations pose a threat to societal coherency and effectiveness.

As culture and religion developed through natural selection as man's control system, man simultaneously developed through natural selection instinctive behavioral predispositions that made these control systems effective. Religion and culture could control man because he was instinctively geared to accept such control. These instincts led him to associate himself emotionally with the tribal culture and religion, to look down on outsiders or to hate them, and to adhere to his group. This emotional pattern had survival value so long as the culture and religion were adaptive and the competing groups were localized.

But where localism is lost and religious and ethnic groups are mixed together in a national society, the emotions that tie men to such groups and lead them into contest with others do not sustain the society but reduce its effectiveness. A basic theme thus is that the conditions now existing in many societies change the group-oriented emotional predispositions of man from a means of preserving societal coherency and effectiveness, which it was at an earlier historical stage, to an instrument of internal division. The cosmopolitan society is suited to the ideal man of the Enlightenment, the rationalistic citizen of the world. But education has not made this man predominant. Recent experience emphasizes the importance of the emotions that once bound man to his tribe and that now tie him to groups whose contests may be destructive.

CONCLUSIONS

The development of religion, like economic development, often is viewed within a framework of unilinear evolution, as reflecting man's progress. Man is seen as progressing from the primitivism of polytheism to the stage of monotheism and then, according to some students of the subject, on to the final stage of humanism.

As they bear on man's ability to meet nature's criteria for survival, however, these changes may involve retrogression rather than progress. The polytheistic societal cults apparently belonged to control systems that adapted man to nature, permitted him to limit his population, preserve his environment (except in the case of expansive and urban civilizations), and maintain a degree of societal coherency and economic efficiency. Monotheistic religion was anthropocentric; it told man he was above nature and led him into destructive intrasocietal conflicts. Although they are basically anthropocentric, supernatural religions retain a Being who is superior to man and define rules for man to follow; they are willing to impose discipline on man's behavior. Potentially their doctrines have some flexibility with regard to matters of earthly policy.

Within this framework, the most surely destructive religions are the versions of humanism that tell man he is above the need for discipline, that his task is only to realize himself, or that progress—group self-realization—automatically will uplift him and solve his problems.

Another set of beliefs—a religion in the sense of offering an explanation of man's origins and relation to the universe—is naturalism, or science. The eighteenth century's enthusiasm for science helped shape the rules that led to the industrial revolution and what has since become "economic development." The thinkers who defined the conditions underlying this process saw it coming to a bad end because of the resulting growth of population. They did not expect man to implement effective control over his population. The knowledge generated by modern science emphasizes the need for population control and environmental preservation if civilization is to survive. It also contributes to a definition of the conditions

under which rules could be established that would facilitate
achievement of these goals. But insofar as anthropocentric
religion and ideology are competitors of the scientific view of
man and nature, their predominance may prevent adoption
of the required policies.

CHAPTER 9/ Education and the Standard of Living

An increase in government expenditures for education is widely viewed as the key to economic progress. Education may be thought of as providing the general intellectual skills and the technical knowledge required to implement advanced methods of production. In earlier thought, education was seen as essential for an effectively functioning representative government and therefore as a political prerequisite for economic progress. In the modern concept of economic development, an increase in the educational level can be thought of as a part of the process of modernization by which nations lagging on the road of progress correct their backwardness by emulating the advanced nations.

To fit the framework of unilinear evolution, "education" should be a standard product, performing the same functions and having the same effects in the various societies. Many observers have pointed out that such is not the case. What passes under the label of "education" in various societies differs greatly. Thus all education cannot be equally efficacious. In fact, some education may oppose economic progress.

Functional analysis of the influence of education on living

standards involves two basic questions: (1) What knowledge, beliefs, skills, and attitudes is it most efficacious to teach the members of this society through formal procedures, and what should education mean in this society? (2) How much of this education should the society employ, and what are efficient means of achieving this education?

In truth, the asserted function and content of education in such leading nations as the United States have undergone important changes in the past. The education now prevailing in the United States and England differs from that of the era when rapid increases in economic efficiency began. During the 1960s, the productivity of the system of education prevailing in the West was increasingly questioned. Higher education, it was pointed out, serves in part as a vehicle by which the educated advance themselves over others in ways that do not increase their social productivity. Higher education sometimes inculcates antisocietal values. This situation raises the basic question of how education is controlled.

Nations unable to afford the waste of an inefficient educational system or the disruption of a subversive one face difficult choices in making effective use of education. Educational modernization, in the sense of copying current Western institutions, is subject to objections that parallel those applying to the emulation of present-day Western political institutions. If education is the key to increasing living standards, what is involved is not simply a matter of *more* education but rather a complex policy problem.[1] This problem ties into others discussed here. It relates to societal control over individuals and institutions and to the need to meet the performance standards required of the successful society.

[1] Both the great potential benefit of education under ideal conditions and some of the shortcomings of the education actually conveyed in low-income countries are characterized in United Nations, Department of Economics and Social Affairs, *1965 Report on the World Social Situation* (New York: United Nations, 1966), Chap. 4. A characterization of an actual, as contrasted with the ideal, university system in a low-income country is given in Robert Keatley, "Vietnam Universities Versus Reformers," *The Wall Street Journal,* September 26, 1967, p. 16. See also William and Paul Paddock, *Hungry Nations* (Boston: Little, Brown, 1964), Chaps. 9–11 and the references cited there; and Gunnar Myrdal, *Asian Drama* (New York: Twentieth Century Fund, 1968), Chaps. 31–33.

INFLUENCES OF THE EDUCATIONAL SYSTEM
ON LIVING STANDARDS

The prescription for an educational system favorable to increases in living standards arising from the theory developed in this book can be characterized in this manner. If an increase in living standards depends on the ability of the society to control its population, preserve its environment, and provide a set of societal rules leading to continuing increase in economic efficiency, the major task of formal education is to convey the societal rules, beliefs, and values that underlie an effective performance in these connections. Since this performance depends on societal systems for shaping individual behavior, the system of formal education must convey these systems. In a society with a culture, institutions, and values not favorable to an increase in living standards, it is questionable how far the system of formal education can go in creating them.

A second function of the system of formal education is to convey the knowledge needed to perform certain jobs. This knowledge extends from such widely needed skills as reading, writing, and arithmetic, to training in such professions as medicine and engineering and such applied skills as farming. Much of this information can be conveyed through on-the-job training or through learning systems not formalized in the way now predominating in high-income nations.

Moreover, if the effective society in the future must, by calculation, shape policies and rules adapting it to nature's performance criteria, as in the case of population control, and if the adoption of such policies depends on popular vote, the educational system will have to convey the scientific interpretation of man's relation to nature from which such policies must stem. This places the educational system in conflict with prevailing religions and ideologies.

In addition to the content of education, there is the question of the means by which education is accomplished. A costly education diverts economic resources and educated manpower from other uses and thus impedes an increase in living standards. If education is financed through taxes, an expensive educational program may significantly hamper a self-feeding process of improvement in economic efficiency by diverting resources from the financing of economic innovation.

Formalization of education, although it may in some cases be essential for efficiency, raises problems for societal control over the content of the education. Where the content of education is governed by a class of educators, by the members of a profession, by self-perpetuating faculties of universities, or by religious or ethnic groups, the content of the education may not correspond to societal needs. Education may sometimes be the means for reforming a society, but it also can contribute to perpetuating the society's problems and deficiencies.

THE INVESTMENT-IN-HUMAN-CAPITAL APPROACH

Efforts at quantitative measurement of the rate of return to "investment in human capital" received much attention in the 1960s.[2] If the rate of return to society from investment in human capital in the form of education can be estimated, the argument can be made that this form of investment ought to be pushed to the point at which its rate of return equals that in other forms of investment. This approach, however, involves several difficulties.

First, it assumes that the social rate of return to education can be estimated from the cross-sectional relation between differentials in education and income. This approach, as applied, appears to give inadequate weight to factors that cause income to be correlated with education but that do not measure the social productivity of education. In general, these factors involve (1) the superior ability and motivation of the educated over the uneducated, and (2) their superior status in the power system. The latter reflects both the initial advantages of those who are selected for above-average education and the power derived from the ingroup status conferred by the education. In other words, even though the education taught nothing whatever that added to the student's ability to

[2] Central contributions are Gary S. Becker, *Human Capital* (New York: National Bureau of Economic Research, 1964), and *Journal of Political Economy,* Supplement, *Investment in Human Beings,* October 1962.

work effectively, we should expect the educated to have higher incomes than the uneducated.

Some efforts have been made to separate these dependencies, to derive a measure of the effect of education on income, after controlling for other factors, but this attempt poses problems that cannot be satisfactorily solved. The separate effects on income of differences in the sex and age distribution of the educated and uneducated classes, for example, can be estimated to some degree of satisfaction.[3] Controlling for ability evidently poses problems that cannot be fully solved. With additional data, we can increasingly control for ability measured in certain defined ways, such as the results of intelligence tests. But it is widely conceded that ability is multidimensional; the ability that is relevant to economic performance consists largely of motivation, energy, persistence, and other qualities not measured by IQ. But if the relevant ability cannot be measured adequately, then controlling for this factor and separately estimating the effects of education on income are difficult.[4]

The most difficult problem from a methodological point of view, however, is the influence of differential terms of competition, or exercise of market power, by the educated and uneducated groups. It seems clear that if physicians were limited to their present numbers and exercised their present legal and institutional prerogatives, their incomes would be high even though their education was of little value and their abilities were mediocre. His education confers on the physician a license to practice medicine, a function for which patients are willing to pay well, and limits the number of such licenses. The same is true for lawyers, teachers, and other professionals. The problem, then, is to disentangle the effects of the knowledge gained through the education from the effects of the market power that it conveys with admission to elite professions or occupations—a virtually impossible task.

Where limitations of access to economic activities engaged

---

[3] Even these measures pose difficulties. Insofar as the educated and uneducated form noncompeting groups, the internal cross-sectional income distributions of the groups cannot be taken as determined by the same factors.

[4] See Becker, *op. cit.*, Chaps. 3, 4.

in by the educated are formal (as in explicit educational requirements for certain professions), it is possible, in principle,
to estimate roughly the extent to which these requirements
are excessive or unnecessary and how much of the income of
insiders is to be attributed to these arbitrary educational requirements. But then questions are raised as to how greatly
the quality of service would be affected by lower educational
requirements, and what quality of service is necessary or appropriate.

The problem becomes yet more intractable when the preferred position of the educated comes about not through any
formally defined educational requirements but through informal preference showed by educated people to other educated
people, even with reference to positions that do not require the
education. This situation leads to what might be termed an
"education prejudice," the effects of which are similar to those
of racial prejudice in limiting the opportunities of the inferior
group relative to those of the superior group, of altering the
rules of the game, the terms of trade, between them. Quantitative analysis of this matter seems well beyond the capabilities of existing methodology. Yet the effects of such side effects of education may be important.

In low-income countries, where the role of higher education
as a qualification for admittance to an elite status is established even more firmly than in most Western nations, the
error in inferring the social productivity of additional education from the income advantage of the educated is especially
great. The existence of the "educated unemployed," a situation that has existed in India since the era of British rule,[5]
evidently implies that the marginal social productivity of enlarging the numbers educated in the existing way within the
existing societal rules may be zero (negative after allowance
for educational costs), even though the educated employed
enjoy large incomes.

The socially productive course is to reduce or eliminate the
use of education as a basis for market power, thus eliminating
superfluous educational requirements and encouraging the
employment of people on the basis of their ability to perform

[5] Myrdal, *op. cit.,* p. 1642.

the jobs.[6] Education then could be designed to provide the needed knowledge and skills, which might be very much less expensive than the education associated with the formation of an educated elite. In short, the educational policy favorable to economic progress might involve substantial reductions in certain kinds of education. Despite its high private rate of return, such education may have a negative social productivity.

A second point with reference to the investment-in-human-capital approach to evaluation of education is that different kinds of education are not sufficiently distinguished. "Education" covers a wide variety of activities of marginal social productivity that may range from high positive to large negative values. Thus to treat education as a homogeneous commodity may be seriously misleading in the context of the comparative analysis of societies with widely diverse educational systems.[7]

A final point is that the investment-in-human-capital approach evaluates education in relation to the existing society rather than the emerging society. The effect of the investment-in-human-capital approach on interpretation of the role of education in economic progress thus may be mischievous. As Myrdal illustrates:

Economic historians have regularly paid a great deal of attention to education and educational reform when seeking to explain why the rate of economic development has varied in different epochs and in different countries. . . . But none in this tradition has tried to put educational reform into the conceptual strait jacket of a quantity of financial investment, accounted for in a capital/output ratio. This is the only innovation in the newest economic approach.[8]

---

[6] See S. M. Miller, "Breaking the Credentials Barrier," in Theodore Morgan and George W. Betz (eds.), *Economic Development: Readings in Theory and Practice* (Belmont, Calif.: Wadsworth, 1970), pp. 269–275.

[7] The error thus resulting from measuring education on a cost basis within the investment-in-man framework is emphasized by Myrdal in his criticism of this approach. *Op. cit.,* p. 1535.

[8] *Op. cit.,* p. 1545.

EDUCATION AND ARISTOCRATIC VALUES

One of the factors impeding an increase in living standards in societies with an aristocratic tradition is a value system in which prestige attaches not to successful work but to social status, which may be associated with the avoidance of work. This cultural system acts to deny society the contribution of a group of its most educated and some of its most talented members. Its indirect effect is to spread the attitude that work is demeaning, that social rewards are earned in other ways. The educational system may support and propagate these values. A problem in some newly independent countries has been the transfer to professions and government jobs of the prestige that had attached to the foreign administrators who held power in the society during the colonial era.[9]

The effect of these attitudes is to direct the efforts of the young away from productive activities toward a quest for a position that confers status or privilege. Economic activity, business activity, may be regarded as especially demeaning. More broadly, this social philosophy, if it may be so termed, is not oriented toward *performance,* toward productivity. This system is one in which a person's merit depends not on what he contributes but on his connections, the position he has managed to attain. Such competition for power and position is a zero-sum game that does not lead to improvement in economic efficiency.

THE EDUCATED AS AN ARISTOCRACY

Not only may education, even in the modern world, inculcate aristocratic values, but the group in the society that has received higher education may regard itself as an aristocracy,

[9] Myrdal points out the link in India between education and the aristocracy, which then carried over to an association with the British ruling class (*op. cit.,* Chap. 31). He states that because of these associations, the educational program requires a "radical break with the past" (p. 1624). Moreover, "the downgrading of manual work, and, in particular, the practice of using education as an excuse to avoid it, is a very serious obstacle to development." He also observes that "this attitude constitutes a large part of the problem of the 'educated unemployed' " and that it is prevalent in some degree everywhere in South Asia (p. 1646).

"a class of persons holding exceptional rank and privileges." The result is that members of this class tend to avoid occupations that have low status and to demand prestige, power, and income commensurate with their imagined position in the world.[10]

The effect may be to create a new aristocracy that differs from the old in details of its privileges and the means by which entrance to the class is gained, but that is basically of the same pattern. Its position, like that of its precursor, rests on the use of power rather than on performance as measured within an open system.[11]

Where the real objective of higher education is to justify the status of a neoaristocratic group, the form and content of the "education" are necessarily affected. The goal is not to give students the skills needed in the performance of work but to justify their claim to status as a superior class; therefore, the efficient education cultivates the qualities that were regarded as distinguishing the aristocrat and that serve the same function in the modern world.[12]

---

[10] A related point is made by W. Arthur Lewis: "An oversupply of educated people creates great frustrations, stimulates excessive migrations to the towns, and results in political turbulence." He notes that "India is one of the best educated underdeveloped countries, but not conspicuously the most successful in economic development." See his "A Review of Economic Development," in *American Economic Review Papers and Proceedings,* 55 (May 1965), 7. These points, of course, relate to the content as well as the amount of education and also to impediments within the society to making effective use of educated people and rewarding them commensurately.

[11] A stimulating discussion of such considerations in United States education is given in Thomas Sowell, "The 'Need' for More 'Education,' " *AAUP Bulletin,* 52 (December 1966), 380–384.

[12] The Paddocks' characterization of the Chilean system of higher education is: "Only the aristocratic features of the German educational philosophy program were adopted; the quite practical aspects that developed German technical efficiency and scientific brilliance were excluded as being plebeian." *Op. cit.,* p. 154.

A commenter on the educational system of Ceylon observes that ". . . the kind of education sought and provided continues to be strongly humanistic and elitist, with the result that the products of education, not being absorbed in satisfying employment, become a disappointed and alienated group of angry young men and women." J. E. Jayasuriya, "Educational Dilemmas of a Developing Country—Ceylon," *Journal of Social Issues,* 24 (April 1968), 201.

ANTIPROGRESSIVE EDUCATION

When the educational system is controlled by a group dedicated to preservation of the status quo or to maintenance of its own power position, the result is education that is antiprogressive in content. Schools run by a ruling oligarchy generally will convey ideas regarded as conducive to preservation of the existing power system, which usually will not encourage imaginative thought or the acquisition of intellectual tools that might introduce dangerous thoughts.

Where the school system is controlled by a church, it is expected to convey the doctrines and values of the religion. In many cases these doctrines are opposed to open systems, to individualism, and to the "selfishness" that is seen as existing in an open system. Thus the values communicated in such an educational system also may commonly be opposed to improvement in living standards.

UNIVERSITIES AS CONVEYERS OF REVOLUTIONARY DOCTRINES

Leading universities in some societies are under the control of self-perpetuating faculty and student groups that make them a medium for the propagation of Marxist doctrine and a source of revolutionary activity. By promoting disorder and making it impossible to achieve a government with an effective consensus and an ability to plan and act, such "education" may preclude economic progress.

COSTLY, INEFFICIENT EDUCATIONAL SYSTEMS

The foregoing points concern the content of education —ideas, attitudes, and practices conveyed to students that are adverse to economic improvement. Another negative effect of education is its costs. These costs are of three kinds: (1) the physical resources diverted to school buildings and books, (2) the services of teachers, which comprise in some cases a crucially scarce resource because of the limited number of people possessed of similar knowledge and skills, and (3) the time of the students, who, at least in the higher levels of education, would otherwise be contributing to production.

One unfavorable aspect of this diversion of resources is its effect in holding down real income per capita, thus limiting the ability to save and invest. Insofar as trained people contribute a scarce resource—a potential bottleneck factor in economic progress—their diversion to the teaching function may have a high marginal cost.

Finally, education financed by government expenditures is a drain on mobilized resources. The marginal productivity of these resources may be higher than for other resources because of the difficulties of raising government revenues through taxation. Another aspect of this point is that, given the kinds of tax systems in effect, the collection of additional taxes may hamper improvement in economic efficiency by reducing both the incentives to productive innovation and the flow of funds available internally to finance additional innovation.

This negative effect of the cost of education requires a quantitative analysis. In some cases the commitment of additional resources to education may markedly accelerate improvement in living standards. On the other hand, surely there are educational systems so expensive that their implementation in some societies would, by themselves, suffice to make economic progress impossible. Efficiency in education and limitation of the cost of education to a level suited to the position of the society are essential in low-income nations.[13]

EDUCATION IN NATIONS WITH LOW LIVING STANDARDS

In many nations, a large proportion of the population receives little education. Rates of illiteracy in the early 1960s were about 65 percent in the Near East, 85 percent in Africa, and 45 percent in Latin America. South Asia had about one-third

---

[13] As Myrdal states, "There is great wastage in all forms of education in South Asia; much of it is plain miseducation—given modernization and development as the goals, the wrong types of abilities and the wrong attitudes are imparted or preserved. This implies that improvement of education requires a better use of resources, not simply an increase in the volume of resources used for that purpose." *Op. cit.,* p. 1535.

of a billion illiterates, their number increasing by 7½ million a year.[14]   To provide United States–style schools, teachers, and elementary education for these enormous numbers of people is not feasible.   The sheer magnitude of the problem implies the need for new approaches.   If population growth were halted, and if the resources available for education could be used efficiently, there might be some hope of altering or improving the situation.

Existing elementary education varies widely among countries but ordinarily is subject to substantial deficiencies in nations with low living standards.   The content in some cases is traditional and stultifying to the mind, and urban-oriented in rural areas.   Teaching is often far from adequate, and the better teachers are concentrated in urban areas and more attractive locations.

In higher education the difficulty in a number of low-income nations seems to be one of misguided education more than quantitative deficiency.   Indeed, in some societies, such as Egypt and India, excessive resources are perhaps being devoted to higher education.   This diagnosis, which is widely accepted, implies that what is required to promote economic progress in low-income societies is not a greater amount of advanced education of the type now being provided but rather a radical reform of the content and control of advanced education.[15]   A major impediment to such reform, and in some societies an impediment that undoubtedly precludes such reform for the foreseeable future, is the political power of the educational system and its supporters.   This factor poses the characteristic problem of political reform, that even though certain leaders realized the need of radical educational reform, they would be unable to accomplish it within the existing political system.

---

[14] William and Paul Paddock, *op. cit.,* p. 160.

[15] "The South Asian peoples are not merely being insufficiently educated; they are being miseducated on a huge scale.   And there are important vested interests, embedded in the whole attitudinal and institutional system, that resist or warp policies intended to overcome both deficiencies."   Myrdal, *op. cit.,* p. 1649.

SUGGESTIONS ON EDUCATIONAL POLICY
FOR LOW-INCOME NATIONS

A suggestion that is at least indicative of the kind of approach required for elementary education in low-income nations is discussed by the Paddocks. It involves teaching by television, plus examining and choosing students for more advanced education through correspondence-school methods.[16] With this approach, all students would have access not only to the best and most effective teachers in the country but also to courses developed abroad and then adapted to the local illustrations and translated into the local language. In the crucial areas of science and mathematics, courses could be prepared for use throughout the world. Grading and commenting on the work of students, which could be done in major centers where the educated people insist on living, would pose some problems. But these are problems of administration and management that have been dealt with by correspondence schools in the advanced countries.

The apparatus needed for this approach involves mainly the set of TV courses, the grading-evaluation apparatus operating through correspondence, TV stations, local viewing rooms that need not be elaborate or expensive, and local monitors to supervise and administer the program, who need not be extensively educated. The potentialities of economies of scale in this approach are great. With effective administration at the center and the rather limited amount of funds required, the system can be extended to enormous populations. In contrast to the idea of recruiting and effectively training the army of teachers required to bring universal education to the low-income nations, inducing the teachers to live in remote areas, controlling what they teach and maintaining standards of performance, building the required number of elaborate schools, this approach seems to offer some hope.

The apparatus thus established for elementary education could be extended at slight additional cost to provide a framework for offering universal opportunities for evening adult

[16] *Op. cit.*, pp. 163–172.

education. The contribution to the low-income society of tapping the potential of those who are now in their teens, or in their twenties or thirties, could be great. It is difficult to conceive of any other approach that would bring this opportunity within the realm of possibility. This approach also could be extended into the area of secondary education and could be made the basis for offering special occupation-related or strictly vocational courses to be taken by anyone with minimum educational prerequisites. Learning activities that are job related might be handled in part through subsidization of programs managed by employers, an arrangement that if carefully contrived can be conducive to efficiency and relevance.[17]

A program for the secondary and university levels is implicit in the discussion earlier in this chapter.[18] The general theme is that the program should be strictly oriented toward preparing students to perform constructive roles in an effective society. It implies fundamental reform of existing institutions of advanced education, in ways that cannot be closely patterned after predominant movements in advanced education in the high-income nations. In many cases, the most practical approach may be gradually to withdraw financial support from existing institutions that cannot be reformed, relying on institutions established on a new model and with a new system of control.[19]

---

[17] This is among the recommendations of the Committee for Economic Development, *How Low Income Countries Can Advance Their Own Growth* (New York: Committee for Economic Development, 1966), pp. 32–35.

[18] See also the Paddocks, *op. cit.,* Chaps. 10, 11.

[19] Myrdal's diagnosis is similar. He also believes that expansion of the existing schooling on the secondary and higher level is not productive. "The enormous amount of miseducation at these levels is caused not only by the scarcity of properly trained teachers and generally low quality standards, but by the wrong orientation of schooling" *(op. cit.,* p. 1816). To gain resources to modernize education at this level, he proposes halting the increase in enrollment or even reducing it (pp. 1816–1817).

Although such an approach is in line with the comments of many observers on these systems of schools, it is radical in relation to the existing power system. Existing national and international agencies probably are incapable of adopting such programs. For example, Andrew Shonfield argues that UNESCO has been prevented by its bureaucratic control process from con-

In this interpretation, the basic problem posed by education is, again, that of societal control.[20] Education is an important and difficult aspect of the problem of achieving a system of societal control consistent with economic improvement. In this view, qualitative reform of education, together with reform of societal rules so that the rewards are to performance rather than power, is what is required.

Such restructuring of education, however, must be accompanied or preceded by a restructuring of the society's politically defined rules of the economic game. If the economy rewards individuals on the basis of power and status, an effort to build a school system oriented to economic performance can only fail.[21]

CONCLUSIONS

The view that man is proceeding up a single path of progress yields a simple and encouraging formula for education. Economic development in the West has been accompanied by continued increases in the number of years of formal education. Thus one way to modernize a backward economy and advance its development is to increase formal education as rapidly as possible.

Interpretation of education within a functional model of societal performance does not support this optimistic view.

---

tributing the kind of educational reform needed in less-developed societies, in part because it could not deal with "the initial refusal of many of the old universities of South America to teach modern economic techniques." *The Attack on World Poverty* (New York: Random House, 1962), pp. 220–221.

[20] Myrdal concludes that "effective reform of almost every kind *must assume a firmer governmental control of educational institutions,*" but at the same time emphasizes the lack of effective control in the past and the impediments to its attainment. *Op. cit.,* pp. 1659, 1820, and Chaps. 31–33.

[21] Of the notion of simply diverting students to vocationally oriented schools, Jayasuriya observes, "It is more easily said than done, for education is but one facet of a complex situation in which sociopsychological and economic factors are woven in an intricate web, and educational change does not seem possible except in the context of simultaneous changes in these factors." *Op. cit.,* p. 201.

The basic difficulty is that what passes under the label of "education" is not a standard product but varies widely from society to society. It can oppose as well as promote rising living standards.

The approach developed in this book depicts the contribution of education to living standards as depending on education's role in achieving and maintaining efficacious societal control systems with reference to population, the environment, and the increase in economic efficiency. Thus the apparatus of formal education becomes one element in a broader system of societal control over individuals.

If success in the great adventure of modern man requires the conscious adoption of societal policies based on a scientific view of man's relation to nature, and if such policies cannot be imposed by a narrow elite but require the assent of the general public, the educational system must be the means of teaching the general population a scientific view of man. Far from being automatic, the fulfillment of this function by education poses a most difficult problem of control. Indeed, we confront the basic difficulty of modern man, that to meet nature's criteria for survival he must adopt a naturalistic view of his relation to the universe. If the schools are to teach this lesson to the mass of men, the question of who controls the schools becomes crucial.

CHAPTER 10 / Economic Slack, Economic Opportunity, and Inflation

Among impediments to improvement in economic efficiency are two conditions that are in a sense the opposite of one another. The first is inflation, which usually leads to currency overvaluation, exchange controls, price controls, protection of favored industries, and, in some cases, flight of capital. The second is general economic slack in which factories are idle, workers are unemployed, and business losses reduce the capital base of the society. A variant of these conditions is a "dual economy" in which a protected industrial sector thrives within a limited domain, but chronic economic slack, unemployment or underemployment, and lack of economic opportunity seem to afflict another sector—generally the agricultural and handicraft areas.

This dichotomy of difficulties, as it were, has generated a dichotomy of interpretations and of prescriptions for policy. "Monetarists" emphasize the damage done by inflation, which is attributed to growth of total demand resulting from an excessive expansion of the money supply. They prescribe limitation of growth in the money supply as an essential in-

181

gredient of a policy program to create an environment favorable to economic progress.

But "antimonetarists" or "structuralists" argue that the monetarists' prescription leads to economic slack, thus damaging economic growth and causing hardship and political unrest. They see inflation as reflecting factors other than, or in addition to, excessive monetary expansion, although there is no close agreement on the identification of these factors.

This dichotomy of views—at least in the simplified versions of the views of participants—is widely recognized as unproductive. Dealing with it seems to require recognition that the subject involves two kinds of behavior and thus potentially two classes of policy. One is the policy toward the behavior of total demand that is emphasized by the monetarists. The other branch relates to the price-push tendencies of the economy, impediments to access to markets, the exercise of economic power, and the politically defined rules of the economic game.

Representing the phenomena in question as reflecting the joint behavior of these two aspects of the economic system provides a basis for synthesis of monetarist and structuralist ideas for defining policy strategies not based on an either/or diagnosis. It also illuminates another area of discussion, the basis and meaning of the division of some economies into two parts—dual economies—characterized by different performance and economic opportunities.

THE EFFECTS OF ECONOMIC SLACK AND INFLATION ON EFFICIENCY CHANGE

Before considering the causes of inflation and of economic slack, we review the effects of these conditions on efficiency change. Economic slack and underemployment of resources adversely affect efficiency change by reducing the expected return from innovatory projects.

An episode of economic slack or depression adversely affects the rate of return to innovative investment. Moreover, businesses that provide such innovation may be ruined and their capital destroyed during economic contraction. Susceptibility of an economy to periods of recession or depression increases the hazard of innovations involving investment because of the risk that these innovations may fail during such a period. Thus the expected rate of return to productive innovation will be lower, the greater the frequency of periods of economic slack. The economic hardship associated with recession or economic slack also may reduce the capacity of the society for orderly and constructive political decisions.

Although it is in some ways the opposite of economic slack, inflation also damages the capacity of the society for productive innovation. The adverse effects of inflation are partly a result of inflation itself and partly a result of the government policies and economic controls commonly instituted to check the inflation or conceal its unfavorable effects. Unfavorable effects of inflation on economic efficiency can be characterized as follows:[1]

1. Inflation discourages the mobilization of the society's wealth for the financing of economic production, encouraging the flight of capital abroad and the holding of wealth in forms chosen as a hedge against inflation. These conditions are a major impediment to continued improvement in economic efficiency in many nations.

2. Investment through bonds, savings accounts, loans, and other forms of credit denominated in money requires high nominal rates of interest under conditions of inflation if the lender is to receive any return on his investment—or is even to avoid losing command over wealth. For example, if the value of money is declining at a rate of 20 percent a year, the lender must get an interest rate of 20 percent just to do as well as he would by holding unproductive goods. Usury laws and other impediments to high nominal interest rates generally preclude rates that are realistic in an inflationary situation. Consequently, the flow of funds through debt markets is severely limited, preventing development of the institutions that serve this function in the high-income

---

[1] This treatment draws on Committee for Economic Development, Inter-American Council for Commerce and Production, *Economic Development of Latin America* (New York: Committee for Economic Development, 1966), pp. 24–26.

economies. Credit extended under illegal terms is an inefficient channel, and one resulting in a poor allocation of capital. Government allocation of credit under the unrealisti-
cally low real interest rates engendered by inflation may
lead to severe misallocation of investment, including that
associated with the dual economies.

3. Inflation increases economic uncertainty, thus damaging
the quality of allocation in general and discouraging innovative projects and foreign investment. The degree of
variation in the rate of price increase usually is greater in
nations experiencing rapid inflation. Deceleration of inflation can cause the usual damages of economic slack,
whereas acceleration leads to drastic government policies
or to a political overturn. The consignment of wealth to
uses best serving as a hedge against such political and economic hazards makes it largely unavailable for the financing of efficiency-improving activities.

4. Increase in the price level results in increases in the effective tax rate in systems with progressive taxation unless
offset by continued readjustment of the rate schedule,
which commonly does not occur. The result may be tax
rates so high as to encourage evasion and to discourage
legitimate investment in innovative activities that would
give rise to conspicuous income. High marginal tax rates
on the proceeds of successful innovation limit the incentive
to such activities and the means of financing them.

5. Inflation leads to shifts in the structure of prices and
wages that then give false cues to economic decisions and
result in misallocation of resources and inequality of economic opportunities.

6. The irrational redistribution of wealth and income associated with inflation and the obvious injustices created by
it undermine political amity and are not conducive to a
political environment in which reasonable decisions can be
made.

7. Inflation coupled with the lagging wage rates of government employees creates resentment and discourages efficient and honest administration of economic controls.

The economic controls used to limit the symptomatic costs of inflation are specifically responsible for conditions that damage economic efficiency in some societies.

First, price and wage controls, as usually administered, lead to uneconomic prices, a false set of cues to economic decisions, obvious inequities, and evasion and disrespect for law.

Second, failure to reduce sufficiently and continuously the external value of the national currency leads to currency overvaluation and balance-of-payments deficits. These are met by import restrictions and exchange controls, which then have important effects on economic efficiency and progressiveness. Currency overvaluation and cheap imports lead to an excess demand for imports and usually to an irrational system of import rationing. In areas where imports are excluded by trade barriers, protected development of domestic industry occurs, some of which is expensive and inefficient. The development of such industry constitutes a reduction rather than an increase in economic efficiency. As further controls are imposed to protect these high-cost industries and as other industries are required to buy from them, the reduction in efficiency may be firmly incorporated into the structure of the economy.[2]

Additionally, irrationalities in the structure of import restrictions, which are very difficult to avoid in a comprehensive system of restrictions, may be costly in preventing importation of spare parts or small amounts of investment goods required to complete projects or to keep existing projects operating. The hazard that a project will thus be severely damaged by unavailability of some badly needed item is a deterrent to innovation.

On the other hand, the goods are uneconomically cheap for those with access to imports at the official exchange rates. Thus the incentive system confronting those making decisions in favored industries that are given access to foreign exchange induces them to substitute cheap foreign machin-

[2] That such a pattern of development has been an important impediment to improvement in economic efficiency in Latin America in the post–World War II period is argued in Henry J. Bruton, "Productivity Growth in Latin America," *American Economic Review,* 57 (December 1967), 1110–1115.

ery for domestic labor. Rational response to this set of inducements—this distorted set of price cues—leads to intensive
use of imported machinery and to unemployment of labor—to
the dual economy.[3]

In this interpretation, the environment most favorable to
improvement in economic efficiency is one that combines approximate price stability with absence of economic slack.
This requirement leads to the question of whether or not price
stability and economic opportunity are consistent and to an
effort to define the conditions that will bring about their simultaneous existence.

THE DETERMINATION OF TOTAL DEMAND

One important determinant of the performance of an economy is the behavior of total demand or money expenditures
for the final output of the economy as measured by gross national product. When total demand grows more slowly than
the full-employment output of the economy, the result must
be rising unemployment and economic slack or a declining
general price level. If price stability is necessary to create a
favorable environment for improvement in economic efficiency, then such a favorable environment requires growth of
total demand at just the right rate, one neither too fast nor too
slow.

What determines the actual rate of growth of total demand?
As it applies to the high-income nations, the theory of total
demand in recent decades has been the subject of disagree-
ment among economists. The gist of the argument can be
represented in terms of another dichotomy: The Keynesian
approach represents total demand as not closely responsive to
monetary and financial factors, as dependent on exogenous
changes in investment opportunities and in fiscal policy, and
thus as not subject to any mechanisms that systematically
adjust it to the growth needs of the economy. At worst, the
prediction is chronic deficiency of growth of total demand,

[3] *Ibid.*

secular stagnation. At best, the prediction is an indeterminate growth rate of total demand requiring close ministration of fiscal policy to tune it to the needs of the economy.

In contrast, a neoclassical—or neo-neoclassical—approach represents total demand as closely responsive to monetary and financial factors, especially to the rate of growth of the money supply. The behavior of the money supply is determined by the politically defined monetary system and monetary policy of the economy and, more broadly, by the international monetary system, the system defining the growth rate of international monetary reserves. Such a theory implies that an appropriate monetary system and monetary policy will suffice to produce a growth rate of total demand that is attuned to the needs of the economy. With no hazard of secular stagnation or of indeterminate behavior of total demand, detailed and direct government control over expenditures is not needed to bring about an appropriate behavior of total demand.[4]

It has been widely conceded that whatever its validity as applied to the "mature economies" of the West, the Keynesian theory had little applicability to the low-income economies. The wide variety of experience generated by these economies with their diverse monetary policies, including long-continued and rapid inflation seemingly explainable in terms of rapid monetary expansion, provided convincing counterexamples to the Keynesian view that total demand does not respond to monetary policy. The approach taken here is rooted in the postwar experience and in dynamic theories of total demand that represent monetary and financial factors as ordinarily having an important influence on the rate of growth of total demand.

The interaction system governing total demand depends on the behavior of individuals, businesses, financial institutions, and governmental units with respect to expenditures for final output and the financial adjustments associated with them.

[4] See, for example, Darryl R. Francis, "The New, New Economics and Monetary Policy," *Federal Reserve Bank of St. Louis Review* (January 1970), pp. 5–9; J. M. Culbertson, *Macroeconomic Theory and Stabilization Policy* (New York: McGraw-Hill, 1968), Part 4.

Government actions play a central explanatory role because of their independent variation, because they behave differently in different cases. As an arbitrary economic institution, the monetary system can readily be varied by political means and historically has been an important independent variable in the interaction system governing total demand.

The relevant class of model involves an unstable response pattern of total demand. That is, an upward swing in the economy appears to be self-feeding, a case of expansion giving rise to further expansion. This instability of total demand particularly involves destabilizing responses of investors, but also seems to require positive feedback from the monetary system or from monetary policy. Such feedback has been a common condition in monetary systems involving bank-created money.

Economic fluctuations can be represented in terms of an interaction system that is unstable within the boundaries of a corridor. The ruling monetary systems contribute importantly to an explanation of both the intracorridor instability and the boundaries of the corridor. The instability requires positive monetary feedback associated with bank-created moneys. The boundaries reflect the fact that this positive monetary feedback exists only within some zone. Beyond this zone, the balance-of-payments constraint places a limit on the positive monetary feedback and, in this way, places a boundary on the economic expansion or contraction.[5]

In this interpretation, the ruling monetary system also explains the long-run average rate of growth in total demand. In halting self-feeding movements of total demand in either direction, the monetary system governs the slope of the corridor of fluctuation and the trend rate of growth of total demand. Insofar as the boundary points for national monetary fluctuation depend on the nation's holdings of international

[5] See Gottfried Haberler, "Monetary and Real Factors Affecting Economic Stability: A Critique of Certain Tendencies in Modern Economic Theory," *Banca Nazionale del Lavoro Quarterly Review,* 9 (September 1956), reprinted in R. A. Gordon and Lawrence R. Klein (eds.), *Readings in Business Cycles* (Homewood, Ill.: Irwin, 1965), pp. 130–149; J. R. Hicks, *A Contribution to the Theory of the Trade Cycle* (New York: Oxford University Press, 1950); Culbertson, *op. cit.,* Chaps. 3, 8, 9.

monetary reserves, the actions of nations in general depend on the rate of growth of international monetary reserves. If these reserves grow rapidly, nations in general are able to have a rapid rate of increase in the national money supply without feeling short of monetary reserves and without feeling the need to halt economic expansion. The international monetary system, therefore, affects the behavior of total demand in the various nations.

Historically, the behavior of the international monetary system was erratic, for it depended on world gold output and on the spread of the international gold standard and the monetary demand for gold. The result was protracted periods of world inflationary and deflationary pressure. These periods were not self-feeding without limit, however, for they finally resulted in political responses, in efforts to revise the international monetary system. The demonetization of silver as international monetary reserves in the late nineteenth century, the development of the gold-exchange system after World War I, the recent reform of the International Monetary Fund all illustrate efforts to correct an inappropriate rate of growth of international monetary reserves.

The explanation of the Great Depression arising from this interpretation attributes it not to the exhaustion of investment opportunities in maturing economies but rather to positive monetary feedback over an extraordinarily wide range because of the collapse of the international monetary system, the gold-exchange system built up during the 1920s, and the failure of the United States monetary system.

CONTROL OF TOTAL DEMAND

In this interpretation, variation in the behavior of total demand—periods of excessive total demand and inflation alternating with periods of deficient total demand and economic slack—is caused largely by politically determined factors. When nations insulate their domestic total demand from the international economic system by trade restrictions as well as by variations in exchange rates and exchange controls, responsibility for the behavior of national total demand falls more completely on national government policy. The con-

tinued severe inflations that have characterized some economies seem explainable in terms of large increases in the
money supply together with large government deficits.

This interpretation implies that total demand is potentially
controllable.   Indeed, its misbehavior reflects politically
based policies.   There are problems of knowledge in determining *exactly* what ought to be done with monetary and
fiscal policies to achieve any defined behavior of total demand, and it may be politically impossible in some cases to
take the actions thus defined.   However, it is important to
recognize that the customary powers of governments not only
give them control over total demand but also make them, in
fact, the authors of the principal misbehavior of total demand.

ECONOMIC SLACK, PRICE PUSH, AND THE
AGGREGATE SUPPLY FUNCTION

Nations differ in the degree to which their productive potential is actually utilized and in the availability of economic
opportunities to workers and to owners of factories, stores, and
land.   In many cases, there does not seem to be enough opportunity to go around.   Many workers are unemployed, are employed at undemanding and unrewarding activities, or do not
work a full work-year.

Yet other economies (postwar Germany, for example) not
only produce employment for all resident workers but also
have enough opportunities left over to provide jobs for large
numbers of imported workers.   One reason why poor societies
are poor is that the available resources are not used.   Further-
more, one reason why such societies are not progressive is that
the climate of lack of opportunity is not conducive to progress.
Therefore, a question importantly related to our subject is,
"What is economic slack and what causes it?"

ECONOMIC SLACK

The conventional interpretation of economic slack is that it
results from deficient total demand for the output of the econ-

omy. Just as the fact that a single factory is working part time is explained by the fact that there is not enough demand for its output to permit it to work full time, so the part-time operation of a whole economy seems explainable on the basis of a deficiency of demand for output in general. Then is not the cure for economic slack an increase in total demand such as can be brought about through monetary and fiscal policies?

Some economies that suffer underutilization of resources simultaneously have inflation. Inflation, or a pushing up of prices of goods and services in general, implies an *excess* of total demand. If total demand buys the output of the economy at rising prices, it must be more than sufficient to buy them at stable prices. But why is it that total demand does not increase output and opportunity instead of increasing the price level? If economic slack can coexist with inflation, something more than deficiency of total demand must be involved. Economic slack must be at least a two-sided problem.

PRICE PUSH AND THE AGGREGATE SUPPLY FUNCTION

The behavior of total demand determines the money value of new output taken off the market during any period and thus determines the combination of change in real output and in the general price level. But an increase of total demand of 5 percent might be reflected in a 5 percent increase in price level with no increase in real output, a 5 percent increase in real output with no increase in price level, and so on. Any particular economy shows a positive association between change in real output and in price level. In the short run, more rapid price increases are associated with fuller utilization of the economy and price reductions or stable prices are associated with unemployment. For an economy of given institutions and policies, such systematic dependence of the rate of price change on the degree of resource utilization can be characterized by an *aggregate supply function,* as illustrated in Figure 10.1.[6]

[6] These aggregate supply curves are closely related to the "Phillips curve" but are more comprehensive in that they relate to the price level rather than to wage rates and to the employment rate rather than the unemployment rate.

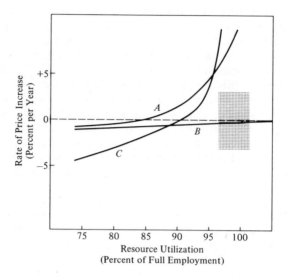

FIGURE 10.1 Aggregate Supply Curves

These three aggregate supply curves differ from ordinary supply curves in two ways. First, they relate to the supply of goods and services resulting from the output of the economy as a whole rather than to the supply in a particular market. Second, the behavioral function is dynamic in that it relates not to a set of alternative price levels but to a set of rates of increase in the price level over an interval of time. The function is also dynamic in the sense that because reference is made to growing economies rather than stable ones, it is convenient to measure output not in absolute units but in terms of a percent of potential output, for potential output in a growing economy is steadily changing. Still, these curves are analogous to supply curves for individual markets, and the reasons why they should be expected to be upward sloping are similar.

See A. W. Phillips, "The Relation Between Unemployment and the Rate of Change of Money Wages in the United Kingdom, 1861–1957," *Economica,* New Series, 25 (November 1958), 283–299.

The diversity of experience among particular societies with reference to economic slack can be represented (not explained, but represented) in terms of different aggregate supply curves. The society that simultaneously experiences large economic slack and inflation has an aggregate supply curve such as *A,* which lies high on the diagram. The society represented by *A* produces 5 percent a year inflation even when operated with 4 percent unemployment, or at 96 percent of potential full employment. To produce price stability in this society requires large economic slack.

The society that, with price stability, can employ not only all its own resources but some of those of neighboring societies as well has a low-lying aggregate supply curve, such as *B.* This curve depicts a society in which the price level still does not rise at 105 percent of full employment; and when the economy is less-intensively utilized, there is some decline in the general price level.

The slope of these aggregate supply curves, as well as their height at any single point, is of interest. Thus although the society represented by *C* generates as much inflation at 4 percent unemployment as that represented by *A*—and more rapid inflation at higher levels of resource utilization—it is not so stubbornly inflationary when a larger degree of unemployment exists.

The point on its aggregate supply curve that applies to a nation at any time is determined by the behavior of its total demand. By permitting total demand to grow more rapidly through adjustment of monetary and fiscal policies, the policy makers can choose points further to the right on the applicable aggregate supply curve, involving some combination of a higher employment rate and a higher rate of inflation. The trade-off between change in inflation and change in unemployment available to the policy maker is represented by the slope of the aggregate supply curve over the relevant zone. The flatter the curve, the greater the increase in employment rate he can "buy" per unit "cost" in terms of acceleration of inflation.

The policy maker in a society with a high aggregate supply curve faces a dilemma. Given a target zone of situations involving approximate price stability and high resource utilization, the policy makers in the societies described by C and A are not offered any choice falling within this zone. To get reasonably full employment by accelerating the growth of total demand, they must accept inflation. To get price stability by limiting growth of total demand, they must accept high unemployment and economic slack.

To produce a condition of price stability and ample opportunity in these societies—the conditions defined as favorable to improvement in economic efficiency—requires revision of the set of institutions and policies that determine the aggregate supply curve.

CAUSES OF PRICE PUSH

A *price-push situation* is one that is represented by a high aggregate supply curve. It involves inflation when the economy operates with high resource utilization and abundant economic opportunity. An economy afflicted with a price-push situation does not necessarily experience inflation, but it must have either inflation or economic slack. Eliminating the price-push situation is the key to making full employment consistent with price stability. The question then arises of what causes price push, and what policies are relevant to correcting it.

If wages and prices rise when some workers and some nonlabor resources are "unemployed" in the sense of desiring employment on prevailing terms, the implication is that access to the labor market and other markets for resources is not open. If workers who are willing to work at the going wage rate remain unemployed while wage rates rise, the implication is that these workers do not have effective access to the labor market. More broadly, the existence of involuntary unemployment of resources can be explained in terms of the set of factors denying the unemployed resources access to the market.

The relevant institutions, laws, customs, and ideas are numerous and complex. Among factors limiting access of unemployed workers to the labor market and permitting wage push are natural immobilities or imperfections of wage structure that prevent the unemployed workers from filling the vacant jobs, seniority provisions, union membership, restrictive apprenticeship programs, employee-determined qualifications, legal minimum wage rates, and customs and ideas making it nonrespectable to work or to hire others except on terms more favorable than can be earned under full-employment conditions. Similar mechanisms operate in markets for professional services, such as those of physicians and teachers.

Given a wage rate higher than is consistent with full employment, the existing employment must be rationed, which is done according to the particular arrangements involved in enforcement of the higher wage rate. Usually the least-advantaged workers, those with a low probable marginal productivity, become the unemployed. Faced with a choice among candidates for employment at a wage rate that is independently fixed, the employer will prefer the better-educated, more able, and higher-status workers. The more open the labor market, the lower the society's aggregate supply function and the smaller the likelihood of a wage-push problem.

Constraints on access to markets paralleling those in the labor market also exist in the case of other inputs. Limitations on business competition play a parallel role in excluding prospective businessmen who would be willing to contribute at a markup below the going one. The exclusion devices used by business to preserve high markups have an effect on the aggregate supply function similar to those applied in the labor market.

Unemployment also may be "structural" in the sense that the unemployed resources are qualitatively unable to meet the particular demands that exist. Such mobility problems are especially important in nations experiencing a large urban migration on the part of inexperienced workers with little education. However, these structural problems do not necessarily prevent employment of workers (1) if the demand for labor is indeed strong and (2) if the workers are allowed to and are willing to work at wages commensurate with their productivity.

Limitations on the terms of employment of labor also may affect the rate of unemployment of capital goods. Ordinarily, factories and machines can be employed only when labor is available to work with them. Potentially, however, most capital goods are available for use day and night throughout the year. The proportion of this potential employment that is realized depends primarily on whether or not law, custom, or union contract provisions require the payment of large wage premiums for working night shifts and holidays. Such provisions may reduce the effective employment of many kinds of capital goods by 50 percent or more.

Some low-income nations have a high rate of "voluntary" unemployment of labor and capital goods as a result of numerous holidays, short workweeks, and nominal "employment" of workers in activities yielding little output. This point is made by Currie:

> . . . a large proportion and, in some of our countries, even the majority of the workers are, economically speaking, virtually unemployed. These are the people engaged in a primitive type of agriculture, as well as the workers in small towns who are dependent upon this form of agriculture. To this total may be added many more workers in towns and cities which have no industrial base. Owing to the frequent holidays, the minority who have regular employment probably work no more than 220 days a year. It is obvious that people out of work, or working little, cannot enjoy a high standard of consumption.[7]

From this consideration, it is a short step to dealing with "unemployment" in the sense of limited effort during the hours that are spent on the job. In its output potential, a smaller number of hours of intensive work may equal a large number of hours of more casual work. Labor input in an economic sense is not readily measured in an objective way, but it may vary among nations.

A situation that can lead to a price-push problem is one in which wage rates are set so high as to be inconsistent with full employment. Setting minimum wage rates at too high a level must involve unemployment. Were this not true, there could be no economic problem. But the wages that are consistent

[7] Lauchlin Currie, *Accelerating Development: The Necessity and the Means* (New York: McGraw-Hill, 1966), p. 86.

with full employment depend on the quality of labor input and the efficiency of the economy.

Cases can be defined in which economic slack is meaningfully attributed not to deficiency of total demand but to a price-push situation. In any case in which economic slack is accompanied by inflation, the difficulty is attributable at least in part to the price-push situation. To yield a performance of the economy in the target zone, reforms of institutions and policies that lower the aggregate supply curve are required.

INFLATION AS A CURE FOR ECONOMIC SLACK

Where economic slack exists, increasing the rate of growth of total demand and the inflation rate will, in an immediate sense, reduce unemployment. Where an appropriate aggregate supply curve cannot be brought about in the short run, the best policy that can be implemented may involve some inflation. But such a policy is not fully satisfactory because of the adverse effects of the inflation.

Moreover, the short-run effects on employment of increasing total demand and inflation may not be sustainable. Where the price-push situation arises from the competitive use of power by economic groups in an effort to increase their income share, the existence of inflation in response to a price-push situation will push the aggregate supply curve higher, so that inflation tends to accelerate. Where wage push exists, as the economy becomes habituated to inflation, the demanded increases in money wages take account of past and anticipated future increases in the price level. Therefore, an effort to maintain high employment accompanied by inflation has a tendency to result in a rising aggregate supply curve and accelerating inflation.[8]

POLICY, POLITICAL FACTORS, AND PRICE PUSH

The aggregate supply curve depends on the rules of the economic game, which are determined by the power system.

[8] On this case, see Milton Friedman, "The Role of Monetary Policy," *American Economic Review,* 58 (March 1968), 10; Roger W. Spencer, "The Relation Between Prices and Employment: Two Views," *Federal Reserve Bank of St. Louis Review* (March 1969), pp. 15–21.

Whether or not particular groups of workers can escape the competition of others and gain a preferred position for themselves depends on the power system, as does the ability of existing businesses to limit access of potential competitors. Whether the economy has a privileged class and an underprivileged class, an ingroup and an outgroup, a class of employed and a class of unemployed, is, in this sense, a political question.

To maintain a preferred position, an economic group can adopt either of two approaches. It may impose a set of rules that exclude competitors, thus improving its terms of trade. For example, a labor or professional group may prevent access to its jobs through seniority provisions, requirement of union membership, apprenticeship requirements, educational or training requirements, and so on. The effect is to make the income of the protected group higher than it would otherwise be and to leave the excluded group worse off than it would otherwise be.

The second approach is to set a wage rate or income higher than would result from ordinary economic dealings, as through union bargaining or legislation. Since there is a potential excess labor supply at this wage, rationing devices must be adopted to define which particular workers will receive the limited number of jobs available at the high wage. Generally, these devices are the same as the preceding ones: seniority, union membership, educational requirements.

In either case, therefore, what is in question is the use of power to limit access to a market, which leads to (1) a price higher than would otherwise exist, (2) a smaller scale of activity (fewer jobs in the case of wage rates), and (3) the creation of an ingroup-outgroup relation by application of the devices used to limit access to the market.

When incomes are determined by the economic power of groups, the incentive system rewards acquisition of economic power and its use to gain a preferred position. Essentially, this is a system in which one gets by taking from others rather than by producing. It is not a positive-sum game. It is not conducive to improvement in economic efficiency.

The price-push condition, therefore, is one aspect of the performance of economies operating under political rules defined here as unfavorable to improvement in efficiency, for they reward economic power rather than efficiency. The power contest is carried out through competitive increases in the selling prices controlled by power groups, or by competitive imposition of restrictions to support these prices. The price-push situation is a side effect of this game.

The operation of an economy in which asymmetrical terms of dealing exist (that is, some groups do succeed in establishing a preferred or protected position) necessarily leads to a division of people (and businesses) into classes, the ingroup and the outgroup, the group that is protected and the one that is open. The division into two groups involves a dual economy.

A government program to favor certain industries through preferred terms of access to credit and imported goods and through protection from competitive imports is one basis for such a dual economy. This situation illustrates another class of use of power to define rules in which one group plays on more favorable terms than the others. A problem of rationing access to the favored group is created, thus raising the question of which business groups are given preferred treatment. Where, as commonly exists, labor in the protected sector shares in the gains of protection in high wages, a parallel problem is raised of defining who shall be admitted to the ingroup of privileged workers.

PRICE PUSH AND ECONOMIC DUALISM
IN LOW-INCOME ECONOMIES

In some low-income economies, the shortage of economic opportunity seems to take the form of a two-sector economy or an economic dualism. In a modern or industrial sector of the economy, wages are favorable and rising, new productive techniques prevail, and extensive use is made of machinery and capital goods. In an agricultural or primitive sector (which may include handicraft industry), wages remain low and perhaps show no improvement, innovation is limited and does not include advanced and capital-demanding productive processes. From the worker's point of view, the modern sector offers favorable opportunities if he can gain access to it, but access is restricted. The backward sector, on the other hand, offers qualitatively unfavorable opportunities but more open access. In some societies, a group of workers cannot effectively gain access to this sector either and is consigned to semipermanent unemployment.

This situation has been interpreted as reflecting a deep-seated dualism that is a distinctive characteristic of the low-income economy.[9] The two sectors have been viewed as reflecting two stages in economic development. The backward sector remains back at the beginning of the track, before the take-off into economic development, while the advanced sector has progressed past the take-off and into economic development. The policy problem can be interpreted as one of expanding the modern sector as a means of bringing a growing portion of the economy into a developed state.

On the other hand, this duality in the low-income economy can be interpreted as reflecting market imperfections, discriminatory government policies, and the exercise of economic power. The combination of high wages and limited access to employment in the "modern" sector and low wages but more open access in the "backward" sector may reflect factors that exclude potential entrants to the high-wage sector. The liberal use of capital in the modern sector and its scarcity in the backward sector may reflect government policies making credit and foreign exchange available on favorable terms in the favored sector of the economy and on unfavorable terms elsewhere. Imperfections in capital markets and credit institutions may also have this effect. Thus the duality may involve not two stages of progress so much as unequal distribution of opportunities in the two sectors arising basically from the power system or from political factors.

The theory that dualism involves sectors of the economy at

---

[9] Fei and Ranis posit the existence of "three major types of economic systems —agrarianism, dualism, and economic maturity," each of which requires a different type of economic theory. John C. H. Fei and Gustav Ranis, "Agrarianism, Dualism, and Economic Development," in Irma Adelman and Erik Thorbecke (eds.), *The Theory and Design of Economic Development* (Baltimore: Johns Hopkins Press, 1966), pp. 3–4. A generalized dualism is accepted in Dale W. Jorgenson, "Testing Alternative Theories of the Development of a Dual Economy," *ibid.*, pp. 45–66.

different stages of economic development leads to an optimistic view of the potentialities of policy. Labor can be shifted from the backward sector, where it is in any case redundant so its departure will occasion little or no reduction in output, to the modern sector, thereby moving the economy down the road of development. But if the high wages of the favored sector reflect its protection rather than its modernity, a shifting of additional workers into the sector without reducing the wages will not be possible. If agricultural labor is not redundant in any special sense but is simply inefficiently used, removal of labor will reduce agricultural output.

Similarly, insofar as the heavy use of capital in the favored sector reflects the subsidization and protection of that sector rather than its efficiency, expansion of the sector will be of limited feasibility and will not be a key to the general improvement of living standards. The possibilities for rapid progress that seem implicit in the interpretation of economic duality as reflecting different stages of economic development seem illusory if the duality in truth reflects protection of the favored sector.

A number of low-income economies have a high-wage, heavily capitalized sector involving branches of foreign businesses, which frequently are limited to one industry or to a narrow range of industries. This case also can be interpreted in terms of factors limiting the spread of these high-wage businesses, rather than in terms of a generalized concept of development or modernization. Impediments to access of additional labor to the high-wage sector in this case arise from the factors that prevent the expansion and spread of the foreign businesses: specialization to a particular industry, limitations on the willingness of the foreign business to commit additional resources to the nation in question, government rules limiting the activities or expansion of foreign businesses. Insofar as the high incomes earned in such foreign businesses reflect efficiency rather than protectionist policies from which they benefit, the businesses do provide a possible basis for increasing efficiency in the economy through expansion of their scale of activities, though such expansion might involve political issues.

POLICIES FOR A HIGH-OPPORTUNITY ECONOMY

The factors that are required to bring about a high-opportunity economy, in which resources are fully utilized and opportunities for productive innovation are favorable, are (1) a proper behavior of total demand and (2) an aggregate supply function making full employment consistent with price stability, one that avoids the price-push problem.

The economic slack and insufficient opportunities that often characterize private-enterprise economies reflect insufficiency of total demand to call forth full employment with the given aggregate supply curve. Commonly, this situation results from a price-push problem in which full employment could be induced in the short run only with substantial inflation.

The importance for economic progress of a "pull factor," an abundance of demand for output and labor at the existing price level, is emphasized by Currie. He refers to the enormous impact of a great pull factor on the impoverished sectors of the United States economy during World War II, when great changes in employment patterns were made in a short period of time.[10] He notes the relevance of the pull factor to the low-income economies and its inconsistency with the "take-off" theory:

> *Our type of underdeveloped country has long since acquired an infrastructure adequate to support a far higher level of production. What we are seeking here might better be called a "breakthrough" that utilizes a strong pull factor in speeding up the mobility of labor so that we may have a better chance of overcoming the drag exerted by too high a rural birthrate, poverty, and ignorance.*[11]

Currie's "pull factor" requires a strong demand for output and labor. But strong demand cannot be characterized without reference to the price-push properties of the economy. If wages and prices do not rise when total demand is in-

---

[10] *Op. cit.,* pp. 73–75.
[11] *Ibid.,* pp. 74–75.

creased, but output and employment are increased, the pull factor operates. As World War II illustrated, a sufficient pull factor, or the atypical existence of a high-opportunity economy, can achieve within a few years what would take decades, or would never be done, under other conditions. In the United States, a large number of ill-educated people were moved from depressed rural areas to the cities, from one kind of culture to another, and put to work building the complex airplanes, ships, and tanks that won the war. These people were not forced to move, and their migration reflected no wonders of planning. But they were offered opportunities that they would not have received under other conditions.

When an increase in total demand is quickly translated into increases in wages and profit margins, there can be little pull factor. The increase in total demand then is absorbed in higher prices, without increasing output and employment. Attempting to increase total demand more rapidly than the increase in prices may succeed for a time in generating some pull factor, but if the price-push rate responds rapidly, the result may be a great deal of inflation but only a transitory pull factor. The crux of an ability to employ Currie's pull factor, which seems to involve the dramatization of an important point, is the prevention of wage and price push.

POLICY AND TOTAL DEMAND

Given success in limiting price push, what is required of total demand usually is a rather steady rate of increase. This increase is defined by the rate of growth in output potential of the society, which depends upon the rate of growth in resources, including labor, and in productivity. An effective government can hold total demand close to the required growth path through monetary and fiscal policies.

Such a policy, however, requires that the government avoid using monetary and fiscal policies in ways that are destabilizing or inflationary, even when these policies offer immediate political rewards. The temptation of inflationary policies arises from the fact that their most immediate effects may be politically favorable, whereas the unfavorable consequences occur with some lag. Moreover, the potential political penalties for these unfavorable consequences may be avoided by blaming inflation on something other than the policies.

This incentive system for governments naturally leads to a bias toward government deficits, for government expenditures are politically rewarding and taxes are everywhere unpopular. An effort to finance government deficits while avoiding unpopularly high interest rates or restricted credit availability may lead to the rapid creation of money. Such policies impose no immediate and obvious costs. Their major cost, the ultimate onset of inflation, once again, may be attributable to something else, so that it does not become a political cost. Thus on balance, packages of actions that lead to inflation commonly are politically attractive in the short run.

The major domestic disincentive to such actions is an understanding or prevalent belief on the part of the public that these actions lead to damaging inflation. This constraint has been influential to some degree in most nations, but it has been sufficiently strong to limit inflation to modest proportions in but few. Where the constraint is weak, the national political system thus may confront the government administration with an incentive system leading systematically to policies that lead to inflation. The same incentive system then leads to policies designed to suppress the obvious symptomatic damages of the inflation and minimize its political costs to the government. These, as we have already noted, usually alter the economy's incentive system in such a way as to damage economic efficiency.

Under these circumstances, what is required to limit inflation is a modification of the incentive system impinging on national governments so that inflationary policies are discouraged. Metallic currencies, and particularly the gold-standard system, played this role in the past. The International Monetary Fund and the international monetary system it administers serve the same role to some extent today.

POLICY AND INFLATION

An attempt to achieve price stability solely through limitation of total demand while permitting or encouraging price-push tendencies in the economy will cause economic slack and will restrict opportunity. On the other hand, to pursue full employment solely through increases in total demand (again, permitting or encouraging price-push tendencies) will result in inflation and in consequent government actions to reduce the political costs of inflation.

An effective program of policy toward inflation and unemployment thus involves two sides. One branch of policy aims at prevention of price push, at maintaining open access to economic activities by workers, professionals, and businesses, matching workers and job vacancies, and making full employment and abundant economic opportunity consistent with price stability. The other branch of policy aims at bringing about the rate of growth in total demand that will best serve the society, given the current state of achievement with regard to price push.

If price push is avoided, total demand should grow at a rate defined by growth of the output potential of the economy and result in full employment and price stability. If price push is not entirely avoided and full employment is not consistent with price stability, the policy target must be some combination of unemployment rate and rate of inflation that is judged best to serve the interests of the society, until a policy against price push can be made more fully effective. In this case, the target for total demand is a growth rate defined by the growth of potential output at the "target" unemployment rate plus the rate of inflation adjudged to involve the smallest available evil. This interpretation, and its program, seem to include what is valid in both the structuralist and the monetarist views of inflation.

Although it is not difficult to characterize in its broad outline, such a policy program is politically difficult to carry out. Many special cases pose special problems. Localized excess demand leading to inflation may arise from an increase in foreign demand for the nation's exports, or from the construction phase of investment projects. Localized economic slack or depression tempting the government to seek amelioration through inflationary policies may stem from a decline in export demands or from the failure of high-cost domestic industries. Stabilization problems always involve some differences in the position of particular industries, areas, and economic groups. The basic point is that preservation of a set of economic incentives favorable to continuing progress in economic efficiency requires handling each of these problems in a way that does not lead to continued excess of total demand or the generation of institutions leading to price push. Given the political difficulty of this task, one can only wish that it were not so essential.

CONCLUSIONS

The relation to living standards of total demand, unemployment, and prices can be interpreted within the framework developed in earlier chapters. The class of performance of the economy that favors increases in economic efficiency and in living standards involves full employment and abundant economic opportunities associated with price stability. These conditions, however, are brought about by only certain sets of rules for the economic game.

Far from occurring automatically, these rules are politically difficult to attain. They compete against other rules that seem to offer more immediate payoff or whose seeming advantages are revealed without difficult theoretical analysis. Thus under prevailing political institutions, policies involving inflation and protected markets are common.

One way to deal with this situation is to create an international system that modifies the incentive systems of national governments in such a way as to encourage them to follow policies leading to price stability and open access to markets. This idea is not new; it was the basic logic of the gold-standard system that prevailed before World War I. The international monetary system officiated over by the International Monetary Fund does play this role in the modern world to some extent.

The aspects of economic performance and policy considered in this chapter present a quite different picture when interpreted in terms of other sets of ideas, including those associated with the theory of economic development. One such view is that inflation is inherently inescapable for a developing nation. Another is that the dual economy is to be interpreted as reflecting the coexistence of two different stages of economic development, and the key to development is to shift resources from the backward to the modernized sector of the economy.

11 / International Trade and Economic Nationalism

Living standards may be importantly affected by freedom of international trade and the rules applying to trade across national boundaries, which are determined by the policies of national governments. Estimates of the influence of various sets of rules for international trade on growth in economic efficiency in the participating nations depend on the theoretical framework within which the subject is viewed.

ALTERNATIVE VIEWS OF INTERNATIONAL TRADE

The usual argument of economic theory in favor of free international trade is simply an application of the general argument for open dealings. Under appropriate rules, these dealings form a positive-sum game from which each participant benefits. Total output and economic welfare are greatest when trade permits specialization and each economic unit concentrates on activities in which it has a relative advantage. Open dealings confront enterprises and individuals in all nations with an incentive system that leads to learning, improvement in efficiency, and economic progress.

This argument surely has some validity. For a nation of limited population and limited range of resources and climate to attempt to be economically self-sufficient implies that it must produce goods that could be much more efficiently obtained elsewhere, by concentrating on goods in which it has a comparative advantage and then engaging in exchange. Moreover, such self-sufficiency would imply that many goods that could be obtained from foreign trade would be unattainable. There seems no escaping the basic point that a high standard of living requires a market area large enough to permit specialization, economies of scale, and the provision of a wide range of products. Most nations are not large enough to realize the required scale of production within their boundaries. For these nations, satisfactory arrangements for international trade are a necessary condition for a high standard of living.

INTERNATIONAL TRADE AND IMPROVEMENT IN NATIONAL ECONOMIC EFFICIENCY

Open availability of imports favorably affects economic innovation by making available from abroad tools, machinery, spare parts, and materials that are necessary to carry out projects. The low-income economy does not produce many of the tools and materials needed in various kinds of productive innovation. The needed imports may not be elaborate or costly in relation to the conceivable gains from their use. They need not involve the most expensive and technologically advanced machines from the most technologically developed nations. Some important innovations may require only inexpensive hand tools. Great inefficiency may arise from unavailability of spare parts required to keep existing machines and equipment in operation, and marginal equipment and supplies required for multishift operation of plants. The unavailability of such goods because of import restrictions may importantly hamper self-feeding productive innovation.

Moreover, imported consumer goods provide an inducement to both workers and entrepreneurs to exert themselves in the innovative process. The thinness of low-income economy may imply that there are few things to want and that once some small degree of wealth is accumulated there is little incentive for further exertion. Availability of imported goods implies that people face attractive consumption opportunities that they are unable to realize. Such a situation may be necessary to overcome resistances to change, to motivate a willingness to participate in productive innovation.

Availability of imported goods also limits abuse of economic power by domestic groups and maintains pressure on local producers to strive for increasing efficiency to maintain their position against foreign competition. Without foreign competition, domestic businesses, through tacit agreement limiting competition, may enjoy satisfactory profits while becoming increasingly inefficient and falling ever further behind international standards of efficiency.

Finally, trade restrictions, such as those on behalf of import-substitution programs, not only have a primary effect in instituting or maintaining a high-cost—that is, inefficient—industry but also have proliferating secondary effects in causing inefficiency, or negative efficiency change.[1] Generally the government that has, through protection, produced a high-cost industry relying heavily on imported inputs begins to require the purchase of some of these inputs from domestic sources, thus creating a second layer of high-cost production. New investment, therefore, instead of being channeled into activities that increase efficiency, goes to activities that reduce the average efficiency of the economy. Incomes in the protected sector are maintained by restrictions on imports and by allocation of foreign exchange on favorable terms. Essentially, the government is using power to divert income from others to the protected area, thus permitting it to survive and to pay high incomes despite its inefficiency.

[1] Henry J. Bruton, "Productivity Growth in Latin America," *American Economic Review,* 57 (December 1967), 1113–1115. On the relation of this pattern to inflationary policies, see Harry G. Johnson, *Economic Policies Toward Less Developed Countries* (New York: Praeger, 1967), pp. 74–76.

THE INFANT-INDUSTRY ARGUMENT

The infant-industry argument holds that the pattern of international specialization and trade existing at any time is not the only viable one, or necessarily the most efficient one. The existing pattern reflects historical accidents and the timing of economic change in various nations, as well as past impediments to trade. Once established, however, such a pattern of specialization and trade tends to be self-perpetuating, because producing units in new locations cannot at first compete effectively with long-established businesses. If, after a transition period, the production would be more efficient in the new location, the basic argument for specialization and trade justifies protecting the new businesses during this period to permit the establishment of such a regional pattern of more efficient production.

Economists generally accept this argument as correct, the issue being only how to define the set of cases in which protection of new industries is justified and the kind of policies that efficiently provide the required protection. Because the high-income countries had a head start in most areas of industrial production, a basis exists for rather a broad application of the infant-industry argument to justify protection of industry in nations now embarking on industrialization.

On the other hand, not every kind of industrial production that can be undertaken with government support and protection will ultimately prove to be efficient. For a low-income country to use its limited resources to set up inefficient industries and then to keep them in operation through continued protection can be a great and continuing waste of resources or a source of economic inefficiency. If the infant-industry argument is to be applied to low-income nations, it is important to prevent its being the basis for establishment and continued protection of inefficient industries.

Unfortunately, existing knowledge often does not permit an accurate estimate of the level of efficiency the infant industry ultimately will attain. The picture has been further confused by the common belief that industrialization is desirable per se, because it constitutes modernization or economic development, or for other reasons. Such arguments and the spirit of nationalism have led to the establishment of industrial facilities that now seem destined never to become efficient. Perhaps these experimental ventures will provide information for future applications of the infant-industries argument involving a more careful and quantitative effort to distinguish industries that will, in the long run, be efficient from those that will not.

Even in the valid infant-industry case, development of the industry in its new location may require more than tariff protection. If what is required are government policies that identify and specifically compensate for the disabilities of the infant industry, such a requirement removes the case from the subject of conventional restrictions on international trade and introduces new dimensions of complexity into the question of what rules should relate to international dealings.[2]

THE TERMS OF TRADE AND THE ADVANTAGES
OF INDUSTRIALIZATION

Pursuit of industrialization by nonindustrial nations is supported by the view that the terms of trade have shifted in favor of industrial products and against primary products in the past and will continue to do so in the future. The implication is that even though industrialization reduced economic efficiency, it later would prove beneficial as the terms of trade shifted to rescue the high-cost industrial activities. Industrializing is like investing in a good of rising price.

This doctrine as developed by Prebisch[3] has been influential, especially in Latin America. Reviewers of this aspect of the Prebisch argument have generally not found it supported by the past record or by persuasive argument.[4]

---

[2] That establishing the infant industry requires more than tariff protection is argued by Robert E. Baldwin, "The Case Against Infant-Industry Tariff Protection," *Journal of Political Economy,* 77 (May–June 1969), 295–305.

[3] Raul Prebisch, *Towards a New Trade Policy for Development* (United Nations, 1964); see also his "Commercial Policy in the Underdeveloped Countries," in *American Economic Review Papers and Proceedings,* 49 (May 1959), 251–255.

[4] Robert E. Lipsey, *Price and Quantity Trends in the Foreign Trade of the United States* (Princeton, N.J.: Princeton University Press, 1963); M. June Flanders, "Prebisch on Protectionism: An Evaluation," *Economic Journal,* 74

The idea that the terms of international trade are governed by a trend that makes their future path unconditionally predictable is another proposition within the framework of unilinear evolution. A naturalistic interpretation of the terms of trade using the tools of economics leads only to conditional propositions. It is doubtful, in any case, that the terms of trade can be interpreted on the basis of such broad categories of products as industrial versus agricultural. Some easily produced industrial products, such as textiles, may be in abundant supply and their production poorly remunerated, whereas growth in population and income may bring high rewards to production of agricultural products for which some areas have a monopoly or an important advantage.

The key to high living standards thus appears to be not shifting to industrial production in general but rather shifting to particular products that will be in short supply and bring high incomes to their producers. A safe strategy in assuring a high future income is to preserve an adaptable economy with the capacity for efficient production in many different areas. By staying in a leadership position and producing goods that are in short supply or that other economies are incapable of producing, the national economy assures itself a favorable standard of living. Of course, exploitation of particular advantages of climate, resources, or national skill leads to another element in the strategy for maintaining high living standards.

This interpretation leads to quite a different policy strategy than does pursuit of economic development through industrialization. A naturalistic approach leads to a dim view of the prospects of the low-income nation that strains to set up an industrial plant that will be an inefficient producer in an industry that will be poorly remunerated in any case because other nations are doing the same thing.

(June 1964), 305–326; Theodore Morgan, "The Long-Run Terms of Trade Between Agriculture and Manufacturing," *Economic Development and Cultural Change,* 8 (October 1959), 1–23, and "Trends in Terms of Trade, and Their Repercussions on Primary Producers," in Roy Harrod and Douglas Hague (eds.), *International Trade Theory in a Developing World* (New York: St. Martin's Press, 1963), pp. 52–95; Harry G. Johnson, *op. cit.,* pp. 249–250.

THE POLITICAL FRAMEWORK, THE TERMS OF TRADE, AND THE INCENTIVE TO INDUSTRIALIZE

The terms of trade among various types of products depend not only on strictly economic factors but also on politically determined rules of the economic game. The existence of a dual economy involving different terms of access to markets and different levels of factor income in the two economic sectors necessarily affects the relative prices of the goods produced in the two sectors. Thus the relevant political rules of the economic game affect the terms of trade between classes of products when they are involved in international trade. For example, if industrial goods characteristically are produced under high-wage conditions but agricultural products are not, because access of workers to the industrial sector is limited, then industrial products will tend to be higher in price.

The terms of trade resulting from such a situation do provide an inducement to industrialization. The nation that can industrialize and sell its products abroad at prices supported by the high-wage policies of other nations can offer its workers a higher living standard than if they competed in unprotected agricultural production. Because such industrial imports would threaten the position of high-wage workers in the importing nation, the tolerance of nations for such imports is likely to be limited.

However, high wage rates and high business profits achieved through limitation of access to industrial activities also provide an incentive to industrialization of foreign countries even though these countries cannot export their products. By paying competitive wage rates and business incomes rather than the inflated ones included in the prices of imported industrial products, such countries might be able to produce some industrial products more cheaply than they could import them, even though they produced less efficiently than the exporting nation.

The argument that free international trade is efficient requires that trade and access to markets be free within the various nations. This condition is not entirely met. Thus differences in the incomes earned in various industries, which

reflect considerations of economic power and government
policy within the different nations, affect the terms of trade
of the products bought and sold in international trade.

OTHER ARGUMENTS FOR NATIONAL PROMOTION OF INDUSTRIALIZATION

The idea that economic development is the means to increased living standards and that such economic development
involves, or is synonymous with, industrialization supports
national programs of enforced industrialization. The related
idea, that economic progress involves the development of nationalism and increased planning of the national economy,
also supports this policy approach. Exploitation or bargaining theories of trade in which the small nation is invariably
exploited in dealings with the large nation provide a general
rationale for minimizing international trade and specialization.

POLITICAL REQUIREMENTS OF THE FREE-TRADE ARGUMENT

The individualistic political philosophy of the nineteenth
century led to the ideal of universal free trade and free access
to markets within national economies. The degree of nationalism prevailing in the modern world makes this an impracti-
cal or an irrelevant ideal. Moreover, insofar as the nation
must be the organizing unit for population control, environmental preservation, and regulation of economic activity, a
degree of individualism that deprived the national government of the powers to perform these functions would be objectionable. The ideal system of international trade for the modern world thus is one that preserves substantial powers for the
national government to insulate its economy from others.

Defining a rational, equitable, and efficient set of rules for
international trade under these conditions is a complex and
difficult task. Some criteria to be met by such a system can
be defined. Restrictions on international trade by national
governments should be changed not abruptly or capriciously
but only in an orderly manner. A world in which abrupt

increases in trade restrictions are possible poses a serious hazard for the small nation that embarks on a strategy of specialization of production and reliance upon exports. Such a nation may be seriously damaged by the sudden imposition of trade restrictions in the nations to which it sells.

Restrictions on international trade also should meet a criterion of symmetry. Bilateral bargaining over international trade, in contrast to open trade in free markets among individuals and businesses, gives the large and powerful nation an advantage over the small nation that is seriously dependent on international trade. Trade restrictions that embodied an asymmetry reflecting this imbalance of national power would be economically inefficient and inequitable. As noted earlier, similar effects can result from the exercise of economic power within nations in such a way that the terms of trade among classes of products and therefore the economic position of other nations that specialize in certain kinds of production are affected.

Finally, the general level of trade restrictions importantly affects the economic interests of particular nations. The small nation with resources suited to specialized production will benefit from open international trade and be severely damaged by a high level of trade restrictions that forces it from specialization toward self-sufficiency. Many low-income nations are much more dependent on international trade than are the large, high-income nations that engage in a wide range of productive activities. The damage that would be imposed on small nations is an objection to a high level of trade restrictions.

Differences in the needs and political philosophies of various nations argue for a set of rules for international trade that meet the criteria described here but that permit groups of nations to engage consistently in policies involving different levels of restriction of international trade. The working out of rational sets of rules that permit this flexibility and meet the other criteria is a task of formidable complexity, the performance of which has as yet met with only limited success.

PROPOSALS REGARDING INTERNATIONAL TRADE

Theories that associate economic development with industrialization, nationalism, or detailed planning and government economic controls recommend policies that limit international trade on behalf of insulation and industrialization. On the other hand, a theory explaining living standards in terms of economic efficiency does not present so favorable a picture of protection of industry. If industrialization does not comprise modernization or progress, the possibility must be confronted that industries established through government protection will continue to be inefficient and to affect living standards adversely.

But an argument for unrestricted freedom of international trade also encounters difficulties. If international trade is not fully free and is potentially subject to the imposition of capricious restrictions by any national government, a nation subjects itself to a hazard in gearing its economy for export markets. Imperfections of competition and the large size of foreign business units imply that the terms of trade may be inappropriately unfavorable to the nation that is small, weak, or inexperienced. Moreover, there is a limit on the scale of international trade that is consistent with the degree of government control over the economy, population, and resources that seems to be called for in the modern world. Complete freedom of international trade thus does not seem a viable program.

Another approach to international trade would attempt to create terms of trade favorable to less-developed nations as a way of increasing their income and thus hopefully stimulating their economic development.[5] Such proposals can be interpreted as involving implicit systems of foreign aid. Their evaluation thus raises questions that are discussed in Chapter 13. Approaches that emphasize the incentive effects of systems of foreign aid, however, may reach a negative evaluation of foreign aid that is implicit in trade concessions. Proposals

[5] Such proposals were made at the United Nations Conference on Trade and Development of 1964. A characterization and discussion is given in Johnson, *op. cit.*, especially Chap. 1.

for supporting prices of primary products also raise questions as to the distribution of benefits and the means to be used to exclude potential producers of the products.

One policy approach that is a special kind of compromise between free trade and restrictionism involves the development of multination free-trade areas, or areas of low internal barriers to trade. Such a policy achieves some broadening of markets and allows increased scope for specialization without going all the way to an opening of the economy to imports. Such free-trade areas among groups of nonindustrial nations with similar resources and background, however, may exploit but little of the potential gain from trade and specialization. In an unfavorable case, development of such a free-trade area that led to increase in impediments to external trade might provide the basis for a multination system of protection of high-cost industrial facilities. Such free-trade areas potentially have an important political effect in reducing the economic powers of the national governments involved. The desirability of such a program thus may depend heavily on whether or not it leads to a multination political unit that performs more effectively than the various national governments.

In addition to the theoretical problem of defining a rational policy toward international trade, there are political difficulties in implementing a rational policy. The usual conflict between actions attractive in the short run and those that are productive over the longer run emerges. Actions to protect domestic interests against imports usually are politically attractive in the short run, although over a period of years, when their indirect effects are taken into account, they may on balance be harmful. There is also a common political bias in favor of trade protection, as the more concentrated interests of producing units have more political weight than the diffuse interests of the general public in economic efficiency and—which may not be understood to be in question—higher living standards.

CONCLUSIONS

The rules and practices governing international trade are another aspect of the rules of the international game that affect the outcome of the game, economic efficiency, and living standards. High living standards depend on specialization and economies of scale, which, for small nations, depend on international trade and access to foreign markets. Thus a set of rules severely limiting international trade, or an unstable or unfair set of rules, could severely damage the possibilities of increasing economic efficiency and living standards. On the other hand, maintenance of economic powers of national governments sufficient to permit them to perform their role within the present economic and political climate of the world probably requires some departure from completely free international trade.

Defining a set of rules for international trade that can be justified as optimal in this situation, with different nations aspiring to different degrees of economic nationalism, is a difficult task concerning which much remains to be done. If, as suggested in earlier chapters, a group of nations agreed to a basic charter that involved criteria for population control, environmental preservation, and the meeting of certain political standards, a set of special rules governing trade among these nations would be a reasonable element in their common strategy to elevate the quality of life.

CHAPTER 12 / Foreign Investment and Living Standards

Foreign investment may contribute to improvement in economic efficiency in the recipient country by providing funds and imported goods for productive innovation. Foreign companies may provide an impetus to innovation, as well as technical know-how and experience. They may also introduce competition into inefficient local industries that had maintained their income through political and economic power, thereby improving the rules of the economic game and opening the way for continuing improvements in efficiency.

On the other hand, foreign investment may burden the recipient nation with heavy debt obligations to finance high-cost industry or politically motivated projects that reduce the nation's net economic efficiency. The nation's natural resources and most attractive investment opportunities may be developed by foreign companies that do not contribute to self-feeding improvement in efficiency in the national economy. Relations between foreign investors and the national government may enrich insiders to the detriment of the nation as a whole. More broadly, the economic power of foreign investors may negatively affect the national political system.

Economic theories emphasizing elevation of the capital/ output ratio as the key to economic development represent foreign investment favorably. Marxist theories depict foreign investment as involving exploitation and therefore as presenting an impediment to development. In the approach developed here, the effect of foreign investment on efficiency change in the recipient economy depends on particulars of the terms on which the investment is made, the control system that is reflects, and the effects that it has on the incentive system prevailing in the recipient nation.

EFFECTS OF FOREIGN INVESTMENT ON LIVING STANDARDS

"Foreign investment" includes certain arrangements that involve different borrowing terms and have different effects on economic efficiency in the recipient nation: government borrowing from foreign governments on a negotiated basis or by sale of securities abroad, foreign portfolio investment in businesses in the recipient nation, which may or may not involve control over these businesses, and "direct investment" by foreign businesses involving management and control.

Moreover, the effects of foreign investment have an important time aspect. For foreign borrowing as well as for other borrowing, the pleasant stage is when the borrowed funds become available. The unpleasant stage is when the debt must be serviced and repaid. In the case of foreign borrowing, these flows in both directions have two aspects—a foreign-exchange aspect and a domestic aspect. The inflow of foreign funds from the loan improves the balance-of-payments of the recipient nation, whereas the subsequent need to procure foreign currency with which to meet payments of interest and capital repayments later worsens it.

With reference to the domestic aspect, in the case of government borrowing the inflow of borrowed funds permits the government to spend money without raising it through taxes or printing it. In the outflow stage, however, if the use made of the funds does not lead to a flow of funds to the government from fees or sales, the need for funds for servicing and repayment of the loan must be met through increased taxes or through inflationary monetary increases. This problem does not arise in the case of private borrowing, for the project involving the private loan either derives funds for servicing and repayment through voluntary economic dealings or it fails, to the loss of the foreign investor.

FOREIGN INVESTMENT AND THE PRODUCTIVITY OF INNOVATION

Increase in economic efficiency is potentially improved by the introduction of foreign entrepreneurs or innovators and by the application of the new technology and management techniques supplied by foreign managers and technicians. Such foreign investment would seem to have great potential effect on efficiency change, by making available the full resources available in advanced nations of entrepreneurship, management skills and experience, and know-how of all kinds. However, the actual effect of the foreign investment depends on the rules under which it occurs, including the rules of the economic game in the recipient nation. Where these rules thwart improvement in efficiency, the potential contribution of the foreign business may be largely unrealized.

Intergovernmental loans reflect a different decision process and set of constraints. They may have no beneficial effect on productivity change because they are used to finance politically motivated projects, or they may damage efficiency because they are used to finance high-cost industry that will then be protected, at the expense of living standards. On the other hand, government investment can have an especially important effect on efficiency by undertaking projects that are not suited to private business.

FOREIGN INVESTMENT AND SELF-FEEDING INCREASE IN ECONOMIC EFFICIENCY

As a vehicle for a self-feeding process of efficiency change, the foreign firm is under a disadvantage because of its limited commitment to the economy in question. Ordinarily the foreign firm has limited goals for expansion within a nation abroad. Therefore, its know-how and its additional earnings may be withdrawn from the economy after some point, to be used in the home economy or in some other part of the world. Government restrictions on the role of foreign businesses, however desirable they may be from other points of view, encourage this behavior. Thus in terms of preserving the benefits of the experience and contributing to a cumulative process of improvement in efficiency, the domestic business that is committed to the national economy has an advantage over the foreign business.

Where domestic businesses are incapable of bringing about the innovation that could be accomplished by a foreign firm, special rules may be designed for foreign investment that will favor self-feeding efficiency change. One approach is to permit investment by foreign firms under prior arrangements to enable the gradual transfer of the business to domestic ownership and management. The foreign business also might contract to spin off specified local businesses. Another arrangement is that in which the business is owned by government or jointly by government and private owners but initially is managed by foreign managers who have the required experience and technical knowledge.

INTEREST RATES AND FOREIGN INVESTMENT

A conspicuous feature of foreign loans, especially borrowings of low-income nations from foreign governments or international agencies, is the rate of interest. In one view, loans at low interest rates are beneficial because they are generous, because they involve an element of giving. Because the low-income nation needs help, it needs gifts. In this view, loans at high interest rates are not helpful and may be detrimental and exploitive.

If the uses made of the foreign loans are taken as given, then a loan at a low interest rate involves a gift to someone in the receiving society, and perhaps the gift will contribute to economic progress. However, loans at low interest rates may be less useful than loans at economically determined rates. Loans at competitive interest rates may impose a useful constraint on the purposes for which the funds are used. "Hard" loan terms and lending criteria provide some defense against unproductive loans.

This line of argument extends to the allocation of the borrowed funds within the recipient nation. If funds are loaned by the local government to private businesses under tight repayment contracts at the going rate of interest, the funds will be used for projects that can be expected to be sufficiently productive to repay the loans. If the funds are loaned to private borrowers on "soft" terms (low interest rates without provision for tight enforcement of repayment terms), this system of allocation does not operate. There will be excess demand for funds on such terms. The loans then may be allocated in a political way, implicitly to buy votes. Graft and kickbacks form another allocation system, the nominal interest being low but the actual interest rate being the market rate, the difference going to the officials allocating the funds.

Funds thus allocated may lead to limited improvement in economic efficiency and to loan defaults that involve a repayment burden on the rest of the economy. In such cases, the element of gift in the soft lending terms does not lead to a social benefit. The gift goes primarily into graft for lending officers, into subsidies of uneconomic ventures, and into defaults on unproductive or unpoliced loans. Therefore, it may be desirable to separate loans and gifts, making loans on hard economic terms and putting gifts into a separate package. Separately given, it may be argued, the gifts could scarcely be as ill distributed as they might be when hidden in soft terms on loans.

POLITICAL ASPECTS OF FOREIGN INVESTMENT

Foreign investment involves political costs that perhaps should weigh heavily in the determination of policy, especially when the recipient is a low-income nation. With reference to intergovernmental loans, a common problem is that the project financed does not generate the tax receipts or the foreign exchange required to meet interest payments on the loan or to repay the loan. These problems may exist even though the activities financed are highly successful in terms of increasing the recipient nation's economic efficiency and real output. In many cases, however, the decision system governing the use of these loans is such that their social productivity is low.

In any case, where the loans are not self-liquidating, where living standards in the recipient country remain low, and where the government in the recipient country is hard-pressed on every front, a growing burden of interest and principal payments on foreign loans is a substantial political burden. The situation is most vexatious, of course, in those cases where the recipient government squandered the funds and a subsequent government faces the awkward choice of assuming this burden of debt repayment or defaulting on foreign loans. Where the governments of borrowing nations have limited experience and are subject to severe pressures, some burden for avoiding such situations seems reasonably chargeable to the lending governments.

To avoid sowing the seeds of future trouble, it thus may be wise to limit intergovernmental loans to the financing of projects that will generate sufficient revenue and foreign exchange for their repayment. Projects that are to be financed from abroad but that do not meet these criteria should involve gifts or foreign aid rather than loans. The past accumulation of intergovernmental loans for which the recipient governments have little capacity for repayment is a growing political burden.

Investment by foreign firms avoids at least some of these difficulties. Any income transferred abroad is derived through ordinary business transactions and does not require the raising of taxes. Unless the foreign business is engaged in exporting, however, any outpayments that it makes cause a demand for foreign currencies and may contribute to a weak balance of payments for the host nation.

The major political cost of investment by foreign firms, however, is a different one. Such investment may be widely resented in the host country. In much of the world, the idea that economic dealings can be mutually rewarding is not widely understood. Economic dealings are thought of as a zero-sum game. If the foreign business is profitable, the reasoning goes, it must be exploiting the host country. This interpretation is supported by Marxist exploitation theories of investment and, of course, by some political candidates.

Foreign businesses may in some cases bribe government officials or, through their market power and because of a lack of effective competition, may earn incomes that are properly viewed as exploitive. But even where this is not the case, the mere fact that it is widely believed to be the case may involve important political costs. In a situation where political power is to be gained by playing on the public's resentment of foreign business, the nation is not likely to achieve an effective political performance, on which economic performance depends. Moreover, the existence of foreign investment supports the interpretation that the government of the investing companies is involved in a conspiracy with the company to exploit the underdeveloped nations, causing suspicion of its motives in all actions.

In cases where such political costs do not attach to foreign investment by business, and where the local government has the capability to demand and enforce appropriate terms and disciplines on such businesses, this form of investment may seem an especially promising way to promote increased economic efficiency in low-income nations. But considering the central role of political factors in economic efficiency, when such foreign investment leads to political suspicions, a reasonable policy may be to take steps to prevent additional investment of this type and even to attempt to liquidate existing investments.

CONCLUSIONS

Foreign investment ordinarily does not lead to constructive modification in the political system and the economic incentive system of the recipient country. Thus if the initial control system in this nation is such that an increase in living standards cannot occur, foreign investment is unlikely to alter matters. If the control system of the recipient nation is favorable, foreign investment can accelerate efficiency change by making available additional resources. In this interpretation, the role of foreign investment is, at most, to contribute to accelerating the increase in economic efficiency under the conditions in which it would occur in any case.[1]

If the political system in the recipient nation is not conducive to a cumulative increase in economic efficiency, its failings would ordinarily also adversely affect the use made of foreign investment. When the overall situation is such that continuing economic progress will not be achieved, the most that can be gained from foreign investment is some temporary advantage. Irrespective of the productivity of the foreign investment, as such, if continuing economic progress does not occur in the recipient society, the burden of loan repayment is unlikely to be regarded favorably. The temptation to repudiate debts and the tendency of political leaders to rise to power by attacking foreign investors and their governments may reduce the expected effectiveness of the political system. If the failings of the society are basically political, the assumption of obligations to repay foreign loans under conditions in which these loans have not obviously aided the recipient economy adds to the burdens of and reduces the expected performance of the political system.

The outcome of any evaluation of the effects of foreign investment on economic development depends on which theory is used. The free and abundant international movement of capital may be viewed as symptomatic of an effective world economic order, implying that foreign investment, in general, is helpful to both parties and promotes economic development. This interpretation, however, is based on a political theory in which foreign investment raises no political problems. It relates more closely to the political world of the nineteenth century than to the political and ideological realities of the present.

Foreign investment seems beneficial in terms of theories in which (1) economic progress continues indefinitely once started and in which (2) getting over the hump depends mainly on having a sufficient aggregative stock of capital goods. If these theories are wrong and the fate of a society depends on the systems governing population growth, envi-

---

[1] This discussion follows the interpretation of Raymond F. Mikesell, *The Economics of Foreign Aid* (Chicago: Aldine, 1968), pp. 258–261.

ronmental preservation, and efficiency change, then foreign investment involves much less promise of benefit and a considerable hazard of mischief.

If the maintenance of effective societies depends on the preservation of political coherency in a world characterized by nationalism, as well as by ideological and other conflicts, much of foreign investment may not confer economic benefits sufficient to justify its political costs. It may be appropriate for governments of recipient nations (and where these lack the power to do so, governments of lending nations) to impose limits on the quantity of such investment, the kinds of activities subject to it, and the kinds of contracts or terms on which it can be conducted. If the terms of economic relations within a group of nations could be regularized by formal agreements, as in the case of the terms of international trade discussed previously, a defined set of terms for international capital movements that are consistent with the political realities of the societies in question could be included.

CHAPTER 13 / Foreign Aid and Living Standards

In one view foreign aid is the cornerstone of the program by which the wealthy nations, meeting their moral obligation to do so, will bring about economic development of the less-developed nations. Thus a major goal of human endeavor for the coming decade is to increase the amount of foreign aid and to institutionalize foreign aid as a tax on the wealthy nations for resources to be granted unconditionally to the less-developed nations. According to this view, the efficacy of foreign aid is beyond question. If foreign aid does not bring economic development, this only means that its amount must be increased.

A quite different story emerges from an approach that deals with the effects of foreign aid within a naturalistic framework. In such an approach, the effects of foreign aid programs depend on the terms on which the aid is granted, since these terms affect the incentive system applying to the recipient government and by affecting the behavior of government influence the rules of the economic system. Thus foreign aid need not benefit the recipient. Foreign aid may gravely damage its supposed beneficiary. In this approach, even though the tenet is accepted that high-income nations should help low-income nations, a definition of the effects of various kinds of foreign aid programs is needed before policy issues can be responsibly discussed.

A NATURALISTIC INTERPRETATION OF FOREIGN AID

Within a naturalistic approach to the subject, a nation's living standard depends on its performance, its success in meeting criteria defined by nature. This performance depends on the behavior of the society's individuals and groups, which depends on the set of societal rules to which they respond, which are largely defined by the national political system. The environment to which national political systems adapt is partly shaped by the relations among nations, by an international incentive system that affects the short-run survival of one kind of government as against another. What is the role of foreign aid in this picture?

A program of foreign aid is a peculiar set of international dealings affecting the international environment to which national governments adapt. Thus foreign aid affects (1) the behavior and survival of different kinds of national governments, (2) the political frameworks and policies of national societies, and (3) the performance of national societies, including their living standards and quality of life.

We can conceive of quite different sets of rules for the international game, which would lead to distinctive long-run outcomes. In a world of military aggression in which the low-income nation is militarily more effective, the nation that experiences an increase in living standards will be conquered by its neighbors. In an aggressive world in which military prowess results from an increase in living standards, short-run survival accrues to the progressive society. A system of mutual subversion and spoiling operations among societies leads to a low standard of living and a low population density. Within this framework, the effects of a foreign aid program depend on the way the international game is modified by the terms of the aid program. This will affect the short-run behavior of national governments and national societies and thus will also affect the characteristic long-run outcome of the societies involved.

FOREIGN AID PROGRAMS THAT LEAD TO
LOW LIVING STANDARDS

Foreign aid programs based on need or on the concept of the favored helping the unfortunate may involve an incentive system that results in a general reduction in living standards. By transferring resources from societies that are behaving in such a way as to meet nature's criteria to countries that are not, the natural selection in favor of the former is reduced.

The extreme case is a foreign aid program that equalizes living standards in all the countries involved, where effective population control does not prevail. Rates of population growth will be most rapid in those countries with no system of population limitation and the highest birth rates. The resulting population growth will reduce the common living standard to a level that limits population growth even in the world's least-demanding or least-organized societies. Moreover, there will be a continuing increase in the share of total population contributed by societies with low living standards. The population of societies that attempted to maintain the quality of life through population limitation would decline. Such societies eventually would disappear. Such a system confers survival value in the short run on the society with the lowest standards. Insofar as these low standards involve overpopulation and environmental destruction, this system is one of perverse selection that leads societies into an evolutionary blind alley.

Where the system of foreign aid does not completely equalize income but only transfers a certain part of income from successful to unsuccessful societies, it operates in the same direction but with less force. One effect is to slow the selection process, lengthening the survival period of political systems and sets of societal rules that finally will fail, raising the stakes in these unsuccessful experiments and thus the severity of their failure. If global failure is possible, such foreign aid systems increase its probability by increasing the relative short-run attractiveness of control systems and political institutions that will fail in the long run.

The damaging effects of a foreign aid program are increased if the amount of aid is made contingent not only upon the general lack of success of the society but also upon particular actions that will contribute to failure. Then the foreign aid program not only rewards failure in general but also rewards, in the short run, particular actions that will lead to eventual failure. An example is foreign aid that is contingent upon the adoption of economic planning in nations in which economic planning will affect efficiency adversely. Foreign aid to support government birth-control programs that appear to deal with the population problem but actually are ineffective may be similarly damaging.

FOREIGN AID PROGRAMS FAVORING AN INCREASE IN LIVING STANDARDS

In an immediate sense, any payment of foreign aid increases the living standard of someone in the recipient country, the distribution of benefits depending on the terms of the foreign aid program and the way it is administered. More important over a period of years than such direct effects, however, is the effect of the program on the performance of the economy of the recipient country. The most immediate opportunities for improving economic performance and living standards are through favorable modification of the recipient country's incentives to improve economic efficiency and to use funds provided by foreign aid to finance activities that will lead to cumulative improvement in economic efficiency. Foreign aid programs in which the aid is available only for purposes that have favorable effects on the incentive system affecting economic efficiency or in which the aid is conditional on the recipient government's taking actions of this type would thus increase living standards.

The key to improving living standards over longer periods of time is population control and environmental preservation. Such is the case only in an international context in which population limitation and an increase in living standards will not subject the nation to external attack. Effective programs to control population and preserve the environment involve some economic costs and important political costs in the sense of requiring onerous actions in the interest of later benefits. A foreign aid program that is conditional on achievement of a specified degree of population control and environmental preservation may, by rewarding the recipient government and nation for such actions, make them politically feasible in cases in which they otherwise would not be.

When population is not controlled and the birth rate is high, a foreign aid program that was successful in increasing economic efficiency might have the longer-run result of leaving the society worse off, with a return to low living standards and a more severe problem of overpopulation. In such cases, a rational or responsible program of foreign aid would not offer aid designed to increase economic efficiency until population control had been assured. The first step in the program would be to encourage programs of population control and environmental preservation in the recipient nation. Only when this was assured would aid designed to provide an incentive to increase economic efficiency be provided.

OTHER APPROACHES TO FOREIGN AID

An emphasis on the incentive effects of institutions and policy programs has long characterized the mainstream of economic thought. A number of economists have interpreted foreign aid within such a framework. However, much of the literature relating to foreign aid and most policies toward foreign aid have reflected other approaches. Some of these other approaches are characterized in the following paragraphs.[1]

MORAL OR RELIGIOUS INTERPRETATIONS OF FOREIGN AID

As Tawney notes, the evaluation of economic and social policies within a religious framework historically has been the predominant approach.[2] For religious leaders to offer policy advice on foreign aid and economic development based on

[1] For a general discussion of alternative approaches to foreign aid and their theoretical foundations, plus extensive references to literature in the area, see Raymond F. Mikesell, *The Economics of Foreign Aid* (Chicago: Aldine, 1968), especially Chaps. 1–3.

[2] R. H. Tawney, *Religion and the Rise of Capitalism* (New York: Harcourt, Brace & Jovanovitch, 1926), p. 228.

their sacred books and religious doctrines[3] is in line with historical practice.   If religious and scientific approaches are rival claimants for the position of authority, the question is raised as to the source of the ideas that do, in fact, underlie policy actions.

The religious approach to foreign aid is well illustrated by the clearly articulated position of the Catholic Church.   The authority of the popes in "shedding the light of the Gospel on the social questions of their times"[4] is seen as deriving from their unique understanding of God's law.[5]   Among the policies defined under this authority are those relating to economic development.   The approach stresses assistance from rich nations to the poor, and the moral necessity of foreign aid.

Pope Paul enunciates a principle of far-reaching implications: "We must repeat once more that the superfluous wealth of rich countries should be placed at the service of poor nations."[6]   This statement seems to imply that the rich nations should distinguish between their essential wealth and their "superfluous wealth," making arrangements to donate all the latter type to the poor nations.   On the Pope's authority, the consequences of failure to do so are severe: ". . . the rich will be the first to benefit as a result.   Otherwise their continued greed will certainly call down upon them the judgment of God and the wrath of the poor, with consequences no one can foretell."[7]

More specifically, the Pope urges the necessity for "concerted planning" and the establishment "of a great *World Fund,* to be made up of a part of the money spent on arms, to relieve the most destitute of this world."[8]

Pope Paul not only appears to go further than some other

---

[3] See, for example, Pope Paul VI, *Encyclical Letter on the Development of Peoples* (Washington, D.C.: United States Catholic Conference, 1967), p. 35; Walter M. Abbott, S.J., and Msgr. Joseph Gallagher (eds.), *The Documents of Vatican II* (New York: Guild Press, 1966), especially pp. 200 ff.

[4] Pope Paul VI, *op. cit.,* p. 3.

[5] Pope John XXIII, *Peace on Earth* (New York: Paulist Press, 1963), p. 6.

[6] Pope Paul VI, *op. cit.,* p. 36.

[7] *Ibid.*

[8] *Ibid.,* p. 37.   On the general question, see also Pope John XXIII, *op. cit.,* pp. 41–42; *The Documents of Vatican II,* pp. 299–301.

Catholic authorities in his views on foreign aid but also adds a general attack on "liberal capitalism"[9] and what appears to be a radical position on private property: "No one is justified in keeping for his exclusive use what he does not need, when others lack necessities."[10] This position seems to be an important departure from Pope John's support of "the natural right to free initiative in the economic field" and his view that "the right to private property, even of productive goods, also derives from the nature of man."[11]

The view that questions of political and economic policy should be governed by moral principles remains a prominent one in the modern world. So, also, does the view that moral actions are defined apart from their consequences. This approach remains influential in the area of foreign aid policy.[12]

Thus the widely accepted view that foreign aid is demanded in the name of generosity, of human solidarity,[13] involves a problem unless it can be demonstrated that the foreign aid program does not damage the recipient or mankind in general. The basic problem was posed by John Stuart Mill:

> *Apart from any metaphysical considerations respecting the foundation of morals or of the social union, it will be admitted to be right that human beings should help one another. . . . In all cases of helping, there are two sets of consequences to be considered; the consequences of the assistance itself, and the consequences of relying on the assistance. The former are generally beneficial, but the latter, for the most part, injurious; so much so, in many cases, as greatly to outweigh the value of the benefit.*[14]

"The consequences of relying on the assistance" refers to the revision of the recipient's incentive system as a result of the availability of the assistance. Where such incentive ef-

[9] Pope Paul VI, *op. cit.,* p. 20.

[10] *Ibid.,* p. 18.

[11] Pope John XXIII, *op. cit.,* p. 11.

[12] See Hla Myint, "Economic Theory and the Underdeveloped Countries," *Journal of Political Economy,* 73 (October 1965), 477–491.

[13] Pope Paul VI, *op. cit.,* p. 35.

[14] John Stuart Mill, *Principles of Political Economy* (New York: Appleton-Century-Crofts, 1881), II, p. 590.

fects are not taken into account, the net effects of giving are often harmful. On the other hand, assistance may be offered mainly with a view to its effect on the recipient's incentive system. This more subtle approach is familiar in common sense and folk wisdom. Any parent who restrains his giving to his children to avoid "spoiling" them is applying this more subtle strategy. The parallel to international giving is obvious.

That nominally well-intentioned actions are not invariably helpful is scarcely a new idea. Said Thoreau, "If I knew for a certainty that a man was coming to my house with a conscious design of doing me good, I should run for my life."

A moralistic approach to foreign aid that raises the foregoing issues may not be based specifically on religious teachings. Approaches defining the desirability or the value of actions in strictly human terms (on the basis of principles of morals or aesthetics) are implicitly anthropocentric, for they imply that the consequences of actions are defined by such human terms of reference without regard to consequences defined by the laws of nature. Much of present-day moralistic thinking about foreign aid is not specifically religious but involves the same difficulties as strictly religious approaches to foreign aid.

Another interpretation represents foreign aid as the West's obligation to recompense the rest of the world for the exploitation that it carried out earlier during the colonial period.[15] This view is partly supported by the influential Marxist doctrine of capitalist exploitation. The obligation of the West might be interpreted as involving provision of foreign aid sufficiently great to raise the rest of the world to economic equality. This theory follows especially from interpretations in which the "natural" course would have been equality of incomes, the existing inequality deriving specifically from the exploitation of the rest of the world by the West.

A naturalistic interpretation of living standards does not

---

[15] Mikesell states: "Foreign aid among the leaders of the developing nations has come to be regarded as an unconditional right. . . . Developed nations are regarded as somehow having grown rich at the expense of the peripheral nations." *Op. cit.,* p. 22.

lead to a presumption that if one society has a higher standard of living than another, the first gained its advantage by exploiting the second. The general rule of life on earth is one of differential performance. Success consists in having experienced an innovation that proved to be rewarding because of its favorable relation to the environment. Interpretations based on the proposition that inequality is evidence of exploitation thus do not derive from naturalistic theory.

If an exploitation theory were adopted, it would still involve the same problem as the moralistic approach. It would establish—on the basis of a different argument—that certain nations ought to help, or do something for, others. This theory still leaves unanswered the question of what kinds of action will help and what kinds will damage the recipient. The view that differences in living standards always reflect exploitation and thus that the more affluent nations always should give to others to the point of equalizing living standards presumably would lead in the long run to universal low living standards, population expansion, and destruction of the environment. It is a rule for destructive selection.

FOREIGN AID, PROGRESS, AND MODERNIZATION

Interpretations based on the concepts of progress, modernization, and economic development provide a basis for interpreting foreign aid as a means of accomplishing specific acts of modernization. What is "modern" is what exists in the United States and Western Europe. Any actions that get rid of "traditional," or "backward," institutions or equipment and replace them with their modern counterparts can be viewed as pushing the recipient nation in the direction of progress. The Western equipment and institutions lacking in other nations make up a list so long that almost unlimited amounts of resources could be used in "modernizing" the "backward" societies. They need factories, planning bureaus, government services, research agencies, medical facilities, modern houses—the list seems endless.

If one adopts, on moralistic grounds or on the basis of exploitation theories, the view that nations with high living standards ought to do something for those with low standards, but is not clear as to what ought to be done, the modernization approach provides one answer. Anything copied from the advanced countries can be interpreted as involving modernization, which can be interpreted as leading to progress. The amount of resources that can be used in this way exceeds the amount that could conceivably become available.

Favorable evaluation of the effects of acts of modernization derives from theories of unilinear evolution, in which modernization assuredly is progress. Within the framework of open evolution and the view of the economy as an ecological system, such transplantation of elements from one environment to another is of uncertain effect and may be unproductive or even destructive. Many investment projects in low-income nations that turned out unsuccessfully seem to have reflected in part a generalized belief in the efficacy of modernization.

Currie's criticism of the Alliance for Progress, which can claim a better-developed rationale that some other foreign aid programs, emphasizes the inadequacy of the underlying theory:

> *It is made up of a hodgepodge of objectives, suggestions, sentiments, and prejudices. . . . There is really nothing in all this that an economist would be justified in referring to as either a diagnosis or a program. It is simply an indiscriminate, sentimental, piecemeal approach to a problem that in reality merits the hardest kind of hard thinking on the part of all the partners to the Alliance, which is just what it has not received.*[16]

FOREIGN AID, TECHNICAL ASSISTANCE, AND THE TRANSMISSION OF KNOWLEDGE

A possible explanation for the low living standards of some societies and their obviously inefficient ways of conducting some of their economic functions is that the knowledge needed for improvement is not available to them. The knowledge is readily available from societies that are operating near the knowledge frontier, the interpretation would run, but the

---

[16] Lauchlin Currie, *Accelerating Development: The Necessity and the Means* (New York: McGraw-Hill, 1966), pp. 64–65. His label of the approach as "the well-intentioned sprinkler" graphically conveys his idea.

bottleneck is the failure to get the knowledge to the less-developed societies and to the particular firms, government agencies, and individuals who would use it.

This diagnosis of the limited efficiency change in nonfrontier societies provides the rationale for a certain approach to foreign aid. The role of foreign aid is specifically to make available the productive methods of the frontier societies to the nonfrontier societies, in order to break this knowledge bottleneck. The task of foreign aid, therefore, is to finance the necessary transfer of knowledge, to recruit and administer the technical experts and advisers necessary to break the knowledge bottleneck and accelerate efficiency change. This approach was explicitly the basis of the Point Four program begun in 1950, the first major extension of United States foreign aid beyond the special case of the Marshall Plan.[17] It has been an element in subsequent United States foreign aid programs and in the Peace Corps program.

Experience has been disappointing to the optimistic early expectations as to the outcome of technical assistance. The accuracy of the diagnosis is called into question. The problem with countries with low living standards does not seem to be a knowledge bottleneck. The provision of knowledge and technical assistance had surprisingly little effect. Perhaps this should not be surprising, for if knowledge were the bottleneck, the great gain from providing the knowledge undoubtedly would cause it to be provided under private auspices or by the governments of the nations in question. Technical advice can be bought, and many nations have used foreign advisers on their own initiative. The problem appears to lie elsewhere.

FOREIGN AID AND THE INVESTMENT THEORY OF ECONOMIC DEVELOPMENT

Theories of economic development emphasizing increased investment as the key to increased productivity provide a ra-

---

[17] Goran Ohlin, *Foreign Aid Policies Reconsidered* (Paris: Development Center of the Organization for Economic Cooperation and Development, 1966), p. 16. As Ohlin indicates, in practice, the program was not rigorously responsive to this rationale.

tionale for foreign aid. It is the means of financing such investment beyond what would otherwise be possible.[18]   But on the other hand if the crux of the matter is improvement in efficiency, if what prevents a society's improvement in efficiency is a perverse incentive system arising from political and institutional factors, and if there is no reason to expect the foreign aid or investment to reconstruct the incentive system, then the foreign aid may be largely wasted, and in any case will not give rise to self-feeding improvement in economic efficiency.

Approaches involving criteria of absorptive capabilities of various nations that purport to define the cases in which foreign aid would indeed lead to economic development involve a more complex implicit theory of economic development. The theory, of course, underlies the choice of the criteria. Approaches emphasizing investment lead to criteria relating to the rate of saving and investment, with some side condition at least implied that the investment should be productive.

A methodologically sophisticated approach by Chenery and Strout would establish general criteria for aid recipients, such as:

(i) growth of investment at 10 per cent a year at a minimum standard of productivity, and (ii) the maintenance of a marginal saving rate of .20 (or alternatively a specified marginal tax rate). There would be little possibility to waste aid on these terms, since the required increase in savings would finance a large proportion of total investment.[19]

The productivity of foreign aid offered conditionally on these criteria depends on whether they relate to the causes of efficiency change or to the effects or symptoms of it.[20]   In the

[18] See, for example, Jaroslav Vanek, *Estimating Foreign Resource Needs for Economic Development* (New York: McGraw-Hill, 1967), Chap. 1.

[19] Hollis B. Chenery and Alan M. Strout, "Foreign Assistance and Economic Development," *American Economic Review*, 56 (September 1966), 728–729.

[20] See the critical discussion of Mikesell, *op. cit.,* pp. 91–94. He points out that although the Chenery and Strout discussion emphasizes the role of foreign aid in improving skills and economic organization rather than saving and investment for a Phase I of development, in their model this element is lost. A

latter case, the policy in question will reward only *successful* societies, which are in any case rewarded by their own success, rather than provide the revision of incentive systems required to guide them to their success. Indeed, in this connection the foreign aid may be harmful by inducing recipient countries to adopt policies keyed to the specific criteria on which the aid is conditional, such as a large volume of investment. If foreign aid induces an emphasis on investment at the expense of efficiency, it will impede economic advancement. If the foreign aid program guides nations to ineffective policies through its specific criteria, the fact that it selectively rewards the societies that succeed—despite this fact—may still leave it harmful, on the whole.

POLITICAL APPROACHES TO FOREIGN AID

A number of prominent observers have interpreted foreign aid primarily within a political framework, some being led to support it on these grounds and others to oppose it. Mason sees foreign aid as potentially promoting economic development and permitting the continued existence of independent nations, "to keep open the possibility, and encourage the unfolding, of a process of economic and political development that offers a real alternative to communism."[21] He sees his approach as different from either the moralistic or a quid pro quo political approach, noting that

---

foreign aid program that is conditional on a set of policies of recipient governments defined with relation to increasing economic efficiency, in terms of the approach of this study, differs importantly from one conditional on levels of aggregate saving and investment. These comments apply also to the approach of J. C. H. Fei and Douglas Paauw, "Foreign Assistance and Self-Help: A Reappraisal of Development Finance," *Review of Economics and Statistics,* 47 (August 1965), 251–267, which identifies "self-help" with the incremental savings rate. See also Mikesell, *op. cit.,* pp. 87–96. Parallel comments apply to approaches emphasizing the balance of payments as a bottleneck, such as Ronald I. McKinnon, "Foreign Exchange Constraints in Economic Development and Efficient Aid Allocation," *Economic Journal,* 74 (June 1964), 388–409, discussed in Mikesell, *ibid.*

[21] Edward S. Mason, *Foreign Aid and Foreign Policy* (New York: Harper & Row, 1964), p. 51.

. . . to those who would like to envisage aid as essentially a human-
itarian effort to assist the undeveloped world without regard to
political considerations, it will seem niggardly and self-centered.
To those who regard the primary justification of aid as the bring-
ing into being of a group of countries committed to act with the
United States and the West, it will seem inadequate.[22]

Another approach views foreign aid primarily as an instrument for exercising political influence over foreign countries—largely as a means of intervening in the internal affairs
of other countries in support of, let us say, responsible, democratic, and civilized governments (or, perhaps a difficult distinction, governments friendly to the giver). The situation, it
may be argued,

. . . does justify a strong, conscious support of the forces for de-
cency and orderly progress at work in any developing society. As
a positive force engaged in building elements of democratic
strength in an environment of change, foreign aid can help offset
the destructive efforts of those who would submerge individual
freedom in a sea of turbulent ideology and totalitarian institu-
tions.[23]

If the long-run future of the world depends basically on political factors, on the development of a community of reasonable
governments, one may argue that a certain kind of foreign aid
program is justified entirely on political grounds, even though
it does not increase living standards and is not designed to do
so.

Although some critics might disapprove of this approach as
involving undesirable political intervention, others would oppose such policies on the basis of doubts as to the ability of the
aid granter to define policies that will have the desired effect.
As Domar puts it:

---

[22] *Ibid.*

[23] John D. Montgomery, *The Politics of Foreign Aid* (New York: Praeger, 1962),
p. 279. See also Hollis B. Chenery, "Objectives and Criteria of Foreign Assistance," in Gustav Ranis (ed.), *The United States and the Developing Economies* (New York: Norton, 1964), pp. 80–91.

I do not wish communism on any country, advanced or under-developed, but we must realize that the chances for our effective *interference are small. If we only knew how to save a country during those critical years some action might be recommended, but our performance . . . has revealed a striking degree of ignorance and ineptitude. Indeed, it is likely that in our anxiety to permit only an orderly change we may inhibit any change, and thus create the most favorable conditions for a communist victory.*[24]

Milton Friedman sees foreign aid yet more unfavorably, as acting contrary to United States political objectives in encouraging socialist economies, centralized rather than open political systems, and damaging economic development because of the inefficiency of these political systems. Thus such foreign aid is objectionable both on political grounds and in terms of economic effects, the latter because of the ineffectiveness of the promoted political institutions.[25]

Evaluation of these alternative approaches evidently depends on a number of aspects of political theory regarding which our knowledge is limited. Although it is widely postulated that rising living standards are the key to achieving political stability, peace, and democratic governments capable of resisting communist pressures, critics have pointed out that this interpretation may not be realistic. Perhaps it is not so much that rich societies become orderly as that orderly societies perform effectively and develop favorable living standards. Therefore, attempting to make disorderly societies affluent so that they will be orderly may be a hopeless game; such attempts may threaten peace by increasing the power of societies that will abuse their power. There are too many counterexamples to the proposition that wealthy societies behave in a civilized manner and pose no threat of war.

Even the spread of communism is not closely related to the degree of affluence of the societies involved, in some areas being almost entirely a matter of application of well-developed tactics of terror. The defense against communist

[24] Evsey D. Domar, "Reflections on Economic Development," *The American Economist,* 10 (Spring 1966), 13.

[25] See his "Foreign Economic Aid: Means and Objectives," *Yale Review* (Summer 1958); reprinted in Ranis, *op. cit.,* pp. 24–38.

expansion in Asia may not be so much affluence as effective police protection against terrorists and external pressure. Again, perhaps it is not so much that affluence fends off communism as that an effective local government that protects people both prevents communist terror and promotes economic progress.[26]

The limitations of our knowledge regarding the effects of alternative political systems and the primitivism of our thought as to broad international political strategy, as well as differences in political values, impede agreement on political terms of reference of foreign aid. However, evaluations of alternative foreign aid programs will be clarified by explicit definition of the political position on which a given approach rests.

FOREIGN AID AND INCENTIVE SYSTEMS

Interpretation of foreign aid primarily in terms of its influence on the incentive systems prevailing in the recipient nations, the approach emphasized in this study, has been suggested by a number of writers. Of course, this approach is a straightforward application of a basic idea of economics. A classic statement is that of Milton Friedman. In his view, "A free market without central planning has, at least to date, been not only the most effective route to economic development but the *only* effective route to a rising standard of life for the masses of the people."[27]

On this basis, he criticizes as destructive the granting of foreign aid on terms that encourage central planning.[28] Friedman notes that the United States itself would never have met these criteria, would have been denied aid as an insufficiently "planned" economy. This criticism applies to the emphasis of international agencies and of the United States Agency for International Development on "a national devel-

---

[26] For such an interpretation, and an independent interpretation of political factors relating to economic development, see Stephen Enke, *Economics for Development* (Englewood Cliffs, N.J.: Prentice-Hall, 1963), Chaps. 20, 28.

[27] Friedman, *op. cit.,* p. 33.

[28] *Ibid.,* p. 32.

opment plan" dealing with aggregates and thus associated with the central planning approach as against a "plan" relating to modification of the incentive system and the framework for the making of economic decisions.

Mikesell distinguishes two functions of foreign aid:

> *(1) to assist countries in implementing private and public measures which will mobilize and reallocate their human and material resources for maximum social and economic progress; and (2) to supplement a country's domestic resources for higher rates of growth and social progress. By and large, countries that are not making satisfactory progress, regardless of their per capita income, have failed to realize the potential returns from their own resources.*[29]

The essential function of "concessionary foreign aid," which is under discussion here, is the first one: "In the case of a country not making reasonably productive use of its resources, its primary need is not supplemental resources from the outside, but, rather, the organization and reallocation of its internal resources for productive employment."[30] Thus, if the economy is not structured for efficient use of its own resources, additional resources provided from outside may do little good. The crux of the matter, in the terminology used here, is the ruling incentive system and the efficiency-change system of the recipient economy.

On the other hand, once countries are using their resources effectively and showing sustained growth, their future progress is not contingent on foreign aid. External provision of resources may speed the growth process, but such external resources can be gained through ordinary international capital movements. What is required is only access to foreign capital on reasonable terms.

Mikesell characterizes the first, and essential, type of foreign aid as governed by microeconomic rather than macroeconomic criteria, its function being

---

[29] Mikesell, *op. cit.,* p. 258. See also pp. 156–157.
[30] *Ibid.,* p. 259.

. . . to facilitate economic and social transformation by overcoming temporary shortages in specific human and material resources, by promoting strategic activities, by inducing and facilitating critical governmental policies, and by providing a certain amount of working capital or margin of resources for carrying out programs involving a shift in the structure of the economy.[31]

IMPLICATIONS OF ALTERNATIVE APPROACHES TO FOREIGN AID

Different approaches to the interpretation of foreign aid imply different conclusions, not only as to whether foreign aid is desirable and the scale of the appropriate program but also as to the structural nature of the program and therefore to the incentive system that it presents to recipients. Moral or religious approaches to foreign aid lead to the granting of aid to all poor countries, perhaps in proportion to their poverty, with no strings attached and no quid pro quo.

Political approaches in which the political benefits arise from increased living standards must assess foreign aid in terms of a theory of living standards. Political approaches centering on the political effects of the aid lead to a quite different kind of foreign aid program, one guided by political theory and aimed at direct achievement of certain political goals.

Milton Friedman's criticisms of aid programs encouraging centralized planning and government investment might lead not to the rejection of aid but rather to a quite different kind of aid program, one designed to encourage private economic activity and decentralization of power. A foreign aid program set up to present recipient governments with an incentive system that encourages nongovernmental economic activity might be justified both on political grounds and on the basis that—according to some theories of economic development—it is the most hopeful path to economic development.

The theory developed here leads to evaluation of foreign aid programs mainly on the basis of their effects on the incentive system of the recipient societies with reference to population control, environmental preservation, and efficiency change.

[31] *Ibid.,* pp. 258–259.

This theory leads to programs in which foreign aid is conditional, the criteria relating to the required modifications of incentive systems and differing widely from criteria suggested by other approaches.

If the achievement of improved living standards depends on the political system and the incentive systems that it defines, an effort to bring about economic development through foreign aid while exerting no influence on the political system of the recipient nation is not promising. On the basis of this framework, a foreign aid program involving a general "tax" on advanced countries that is distributed to nations in relation to their poverty cannot be expected to have a favorable effect on world living standards.

POLICY TOWARD FOREIGN AID

Existing foreign aid programs reflect some of the ideas discussed earlier as well as the institutions and decision-making arrangements within which the policies were determined. Some observations are presented on the origins of existing aid programs and the kinds of programs that might result in increased living standards.

THE RATIONALE OF EXISTING FOREIGN AID PROGRAMS

There is no single well-defined and generally accepted rationale to which aid-granting and aid-administering agencies respond. As a recent review has stated:

> It is impossible to escape the impression that one of the very real problems that plague Western foreign aid policies is a deep uncertainty and confusion about the nature and purpose of foreign aid. . . . The very language of foreign aid is far too often likely to simplify to the point of distortion, to mislead and to create false expectations in donor and receiving countries alike, with all the attendant hazards of disenchantment and rejection.[32]

It is possible to distinguish several major themes that charac-

---

[32] Goran Ohlin, *op. cit.,* p. 13.

terize the thought of different agencies or different periods of time.

One distinctive point of view is shared by a number of international agencies:

> *There can be no doubt that the principal vehicle of the conception that rich and advanced countries should assist poor and under-developed ones as a matter of moral principle and international solidarity has been the United Nations and the international agencies and organisations affiliated with it. . . . The conception of international economic integration tends to imply a preference for assistance that is multilateral in the sense that it is administered by international organisations, and financed by assessments of the capacity to contribute on the part of the richer nations.*[33]

This approach is associated with an emphasis on the amount of foreign aid, with an effort to increase its amount, to reduce the political conditions attached to it, and to increase its control or planning through international agencies. This approach does not seem to emphasize critical thought over the effects and the effectiveness of aid programs. The crucial judgment seems to be that if the results of past foreign aid have been disappointing, leaving many recipient countries with no substantial improvement in their position, the answer must be to increase foreign aid: "In the face of the distressingly low level and slow rate of improvement of economic productivity in the less-developed countries, there can be no doubt that there is still a need to expand the contributions made by external assistance."[34]

The foreign aid programs of some nations have a more definite rationale and performance orientation. In the case of the United States, the Marshall Plan had a well-defined rationale of making good the war-caused losses of capital goods in societies with an established capacity for effective economic activity. The Point Four program of 1950 was justified in terms of the theory that lack of technical knowledge was the bottle-

---

[33] *Ibid.,* p. 14. See also *Development Assistance Efforts and Policies, 1966 Review* (Paris: Development Center of the Organization for Economic Cooperation and Development, 1966), Chap. 4.

[34] Ohlin, *op. cit.,* p. 11. See also pp. 13, 24–25.

neck preventing economic development. The broadening of aid programs to include military aid during the Korean War, growing experience that technical assistance had little effect in promoting economic development, and the adoption of increasingly ambitious foreign aid programs have led to a situation in which the rationale of the programs is no longer so clear, which has led to continuing reevaluation and discussion.[35]

The foreign aid programs of the United States and other nations, however, in comparison with the aid programs of the international agencies, are oriented more to the view that such programs *should* possess some defined rationale and should promise to produce measurable benefits, rather than to the concept that foreign aid is given as a moral obligation irrespective of its effects. The efficacy of existing foreign aid programs in promoting economic development has been questioned by a number of scholars.[36]

Political statements regarding foreign aid that are made in the donor country naturally tend to emphasize potential payoffs to that country, perhaps not accurately reflecting the factors actually governing the aid program. Thus United States policy statements on foreign aid stress national security, humanitarianism, and national economic benefit.[37] However, some aid-granting agencies have given great attention to the estimated effects of different kinds of aid and to the conditions that should be attached to aid to maximize its probable effectiveness in improving the economic performance of the recipient nation.[38]

A FOREIGN AID PROGRAM TO INCREASE LIVING STANDARDS

A foreign aid program responsive to the theory developed in this book can be outlined as follows. First, it is necessary

[35] *Ibid.,* pp. 16–18.

[36] *Ibid.,* pp. 23–26; on the United States aid program, see Ranis, *op. cit.;* David A. Baldwin, *Foreign Aid and American Foreign Policy* (New York: Praeger, 1966).

[37] Mikesell, *op. cit.,* p. 5.

[38] *Ibid.,* Chaps. 5–6.

clearly to distinguish foreign aid designed to increase living standards from foreign aid given for military or political reasons and that given for humanitarian reasons or as relief. Unless the pessimistic forecasts made in the late 1960s of growing famines within a decade prove to be very wide of the mark, international aid given for relief purposes will pose grave problems and involve demands for more resources than will be available.

A prerequisite for the foreign aid program aimed at increasing living standards is a defined political framework covering the granter or granters and the recipient nations. This framework would include a system of security such that success in raising the living standards of the recipient nations would not result in their being attacked by other countries.

Another element in the political framework is a set of rules of the game, or a basic political charter, accepted by the granting and recipient nations or by a community of nations participating in the program. On the part of the recipient nations, the rules would involve not only the meeting of certain standards of political institutions but political arrangements that, as viewed by the group of nations in question, would be consistent with high and increasing economic efficiency. Arrangements for stable rules of international trade and capital movements among the participating nations would be a part of this charter.

The next element in the program is an agreement among the participating nations to meet certain standards of population control and environmental preservation. During a transition phase, the nations of the group that were able to do so could offer conditional foreign aid tied to fulfillment of this aspect of the charter, which would permit nations otherwise incapable of doing so to accomplish the transition to a state of controlled population and environmental preservation.

It might also be appropriate to include certain arrangements for conditional foreign aid under defined circumstances in order to accelerate growth of economic efficiency in nations with initially lower living standards or greater opportunities for increasing efficiency. However, such appropriation would not be essential to the program. If the principles of the political charter are efficacious, the security of the participating nations is assured, their population behaves in a controlled manner (presumably being stable or declining), and their environment is preserved, the nations can expect an increase in economic efficiency and a rise in living standards. If these are open political and economic systems, and if exchange of ideas and trade among the participating nations is not restricted, some increase in economic efficiency is almost certain; forced-draft increase in efficiency is not required and may not be desirable.

This program is not primarily one of foreign aid. Its central element is the political charter, incorporating undertakings with regard to population control and environmental preservation. The foreign aid is incidental, to permit nations otherwise incapable of doing so to make the transition to meeting these standards. The advantages in security, political effectiveness, and trade from participation in a group of nations that are effectively carrying out such a program would confer on the participating nations benefits that would operate in the manner of conditional foreign aid. That is to say, nations in the program would have an incentive to stay in and, if the program were successful, nations not included would have an incentive to meet the required standards in order to gain participation.

Among ways in which this approach differs from the predominant one of recent decades are the following:

1. It gives priority to control of population and preservation of the environment rather than to an attempt to bring about a generalized economic development. There is no hazard of a population-income race, with attendant destruction of the environment.

2. This approach does not rest on any conception of unilinear evolution, progress, economic development. Rather, it involves the adoption of certain sets of policies judged efficacious in permitting societies to preserve a high standard of life by meeting nature's conditions for achieving such a standard.

3. Recognizing that success or failure turns on societal control systems, which are inherently a political matter, the

approach is explicitly political. It involves an undertaking by a group of nations to apply foresight, to fill the role of the lawgiver and provide a promising experiment. If it succeeded, the approach would provide the means also to save nations initially committed to experiments that will fail.

A necessary prerequisite for this program, of course, is that there be at least one nation that has an effective program of population control and environmental preservation and has the clarity and self-confidence to define a political charter and to welcome other nations to join it in a constructive effort to achieve a high quality of life.

CONCLUSIONS

Much of the discussion of foreign aid in recent decades, as well as a part of actual foreign aid policy, has rested on one or another of the anthropocentric approaches to man, nature, and living standards. The religious or moralistic approach, the concept of economic development within the framework of unilinear evolution as involving progress or modernization, exploitation theories of living standards—these have been the basis of much recent thought and practice. Policies based on these approaches commonly will have an adverse long-run effect on living standards by unfavorably altering the external environment or incentive system confronting individual societies. They may lead to unfavorable selection in two ways: they may reduce or delay penalties to societies for unfavorable performance, and they may prolong experiments with unfavorable policies that ultimately will fail. In some cases the particular conditions under which aid is granted provide the recipient nation a short-run incentive to adopt policies that in the long run will be damaging.

Foreign aid can promote an increase in living standards by providing incentives for recipient governments to adopt policies that will lead to population control, environmental preservation, and increased economic efficiency. The design of a foreign aid program having this effect, however, would require an accurate theory of the determinants of living standards and could not be apolitical.   Because of the important involvement of political and international factors, such a foreign aid program may be most useful as an element in an international charter among nations agreeing to pursue common policies to preserve a high quality of life.

CHAPTER 14 / Theories of Economic Development

This chapter applies the ideas developed in earlier chapters to an interpretation of several prominent approaches to the theory of economic development.

CLASSICAL ECONOMICS AND THE THEORY OF ECONOMIC DEVELOPMENT

Although some writers on economic development have noted that classical economics was primarily concerned with this subject, the relevance of this body of thought is not widely appreciated. Modern interpretations commonly emphasize the classical economists' ideas on topics stressed by modern theory. Adam Smith's interpretation of the efficiency of specialization and division of labor, a factor governed by the scale of the market and therefore by the scope of trade, is emphasized. Also pointed up is the classical emphasis on the accumulation of capital. This interpretation fits in with modern theory, with its emphasis on narrowly "economic" factors affecting production.

Actually, the thought of the classical economists was much more comprehensive. Indeed, their theory dealt with all three systems represented in this study as determining the standard of living. Perhaps because they view classical theory as representing an obsolete political philosophy, many current analysts fail to see that, according to this theory, the prime cause of improvement in economic efficiency is the creation of a political system that provides incentives to productive innovation. The lack of progressiveness of most societies and the subsequent stagnation and decline of societies that had once been progressive are seen as resulting from political systems that make productive innovation impossible or unrewarding. Since the preeminent stifler of improvement in economic efficiency is government, laissez faire—a misleading term that must be interpreted in a specific sense—is the key to economic progress.

This interpretation arises from an analytical framework in which alternative political and social institutions are evaluated not in terms of their direct effects, estimated in isolation, but rather in terms of their ultimate effects on the operation of the system as a whole. In terms of theory, this idea is a great step forward; it is an early version of systems analysis or an ecological approach to the determination of living standards.

Another basic idea of the classical economists is that, in the absence of population control, improvement in production methods will be only temporarily reflected in improvement in living standards. The final effect is on population. Without population control, therefore, the ultimate effects of economic development may be to make matters worse. "The final result of improvements, therefore, is to increase the equilibrium population, which is to increase the total sum of human misery."[1] For classical economics, the key to improvement in the quality of life and the real wage of workers was population control.

Finally, although classical economics did not emphasize environmental destruction as we are required to do by the developments of recent decades, man's relation to his environ-

[1] Kenneth E. Boulding, Foreword to Thomas Robert Malthus, *Population: The First Essay* (Ann Arbor: University of Michigan Press, 1959), p. xi.

ment was brought into the picture through the emphasis on the limited factor of production, land. It is this limited endowment of nature, of course, that makes population control essential, that precludes continued economic progress through capital accumulation accompanied by population growth. Thus, if the limitations of land are interpreted broadly as the limitations of nature, classical economics not only dealt with this factor but took it as a foundation on which the whole theory was built.

THE CLASSICAL THEORY AS SYSTEMS ANALYSIS

A primary theme of both Adam Smith and John Stuart Mill was that the legal and institutional framework of the economic system must be appraised in terms of the effects, realistically evaluated, of alternative institutions on the performance of the system, taken as a whole.[2] This approach contrasts with approaches in which government actions are evaluated in terms of their direct effects, or of their nominally intended direct effects, without consideration of their incentive effects. The neglect of such incentive effects in mercantilism, reflected in the extreme regulatory practices of the French government, provided a major point of reference for Adam Smith, following the thinking of the physiocrats. A central point of the classical economists was that such shortsighted exercise of power was destructive of economic achievement.

[2] See Nathan Rosenberg, "Some Institutional Aspects of *The Wealth of Nations,*" *Journal of Political Economy,* 68 (December 1960), 557–570; Warren J. Samuels, *The Classical Theory of Economic Policy* (Cleveland: World Publishing, 1966). The latter work gives numerous references to this recent literature. See also Jacob Viner, "Adam Smith and Laissez-Faire," in J. M. Clark *et al., Adam Smith, 1776–1926: Lectures to Commemorate the Sesquicentennial of the Publication of "The Wealth of Nations"* (Chicago: University of Chicago Press, 1928); W. W. Rostow, *The Process of Economic Growth,* 2nd ed. (New York: Norton, 1962), pp. 4–8, 248–249. Approaches similar to the one developed here are taken in J. M. Letiche, "Adam Smith and David Ricardo on Economic Growth," in Bert F. Hoselitz (ed.), *Theories of Economic Growth* (New York: Free Press, 1960), pp. 65–88, and Joseph J. Spengler, "John Stuart Mill on Economic Development," *ibid.,* pp. 113–154.

In their time the classical economists were successful in converting to their theory those who possessed political power. The result was an era of severe limitation of direct government controls over economic activities—unusual in history—that provided the political framework within which the industrialization of the West occurred.[3]

The classical economists explained improvements in economic efficiency by the elimination of power systems that had discouraged productive innovation. In explaining why some societies advanced while others did not, why some continued to advance while others became stagnant or retrogressed, the variable to which the classical economists turned was the power system, the political and institutional framework within which economic behavior occurred. The crucial factor was that people should be free to innovate, to exert themselves, and to enjoy the fruits of their labors.

Smith's interpretation as to why the towns progressed before agriculture after the collapse of the Roman Empire is in this vein. The inhabitants of cities and towns, although initially "they seem, indeed, to have been a very poor, mean set of people,"[4] for reasons that are spelled out in detail, "it appears evidently, that they arrived at liberty and independency much earlier than the occupiers of land in the country."[5] Thus

> . . . order and good government, and along with them the liberty and security of individuals, were, in this manner, established in cities, at a time when the occupiers of land in the country were exposed to every sort of violence. . . . That industry, therefore, which aims at something more than necessary subsistence, was established in cities long before it was commonly practiced by the occupiers of land in the country.[6]

Mill consistently emphasizes the role of institutions and

[3] John Stuart Mill, *Principles of Political Economy* (New York: Appleton-Century-Crofts, 1881), II, pp. 531–532.

[4] Adam Smith, *An Inquiry into the Nature and Causes of the Wealth of Nations* (New York: Random House, 1937), p. 373.

[5] *Ibid.*, p. 374.

[6] *Ibid.*, p. 379.

government actions in preventing people from innovating or depriving them of an incentive to do so. He observes that even turmoil and near anarchy do not have the influence in preventing development that attaches to unwise government policies:

> *The free societies of Italy, Flanders, and the Hanseatic league, were habitually in a state of such internal turbulence, varied by destructive external wars, that person and property enjoyed very imperfect protection; yet during several centuries they increased rapidly in wealth and prosperity, brought many of the industrial arts to a high degree of advancement . . . because in the midst of turmoil and violence, the citizens of those towns enjoyed a certain rude freedom, under conditions of union and cooperation, which, taken together made them a brave, energetic, and high-spirited people. . . . Nations have acquired some wealth, and made some progress in improvement, in states of social union so imperfect as to border on anarchy: but no countries in which the people were exposed without limit to arbitrary exactions from the officers of government, ever yet continued to have industry or wealth. A few generations of such government never failed to extinguish both. Some of the fairest, and once the most prosperous, regions of the earth, have, under the Roman and afterwards under the Turkish dominion, been reduced to a desert, solely by that cause. I say solely, because they would have recovered with the utmost rapidity, as countries always do, from the devastations of war, or any other temporary calamities. Difficulties and hardships are often but an incentive to exertion:* what is fatal to it, is the belief that it will not be suffered to produce its fruits.[7]

Mill quotes with approval the verdict of French writers that the *taille* was the main cause of the backward state of French agriculture.[8] The ending of economic growth in Holland he attributes to excessive taxation of profits, leading to diminution of the motive to save and to the flight of capital, and

> *. . . although I by no means join with those political economists who think no state of national existence desirable in which there*

[7] Mill, *op. cit.*, pp. 490–491. Emphasis added.
[8] *Ibid.*, p. 492.

is not a rapid increase of wealth, I cannot overlook the many disadvantages to an independent nation from being brought prematurely to a stationary state, while the neighboring countries continue advancing.[9]

It is in this context of an effort at realistic appraisal of the effects of alternative policies on economic progress that Mill reiterates the rule: *"Laissez-faire,* in short, should be the general practice: every departure from it, unless required by some great good, is a certain evil."[10]   In many modern interpretations, the classical "laissez faire" is depicted as an absolute ideological principle, but the leading classical economists attempted to be realistic in their appraisal of the way in which various institutional arrangements would perform particular functions.   Thus Smith's adverse comments on government economic activities derived in part from his unfavorable estimate of the efficiency of the English government of his time. He was ready to assign different functions to governments in relation to their capacity to perform them effectively.[11]   The lack of absolutism in Mill's espousal of laissez faire, even at this stage of his life, is indicated by his assertion that although the Continental nations had assigned government an excessive province, England by his time had made the opposite error.[12]

Mill assumed that the lesson of the destructive effects of direct government controls over economic activity had been learned for good: "The degree in which the maxim, even in the cases to which it is most manifestly applicable, has heretofore been infringed by governments, future ages will probably have difficulty in crediting."[13]   And, again: "The time has gone by, when such applications as these of the principle of 'paternal government' would be attempted, in even the least enlight-

---

[9] *Ibid.,* pp. 492–493.

[10] *Ibid.,* p. 569.

[11] See Rosenberg, *op. cit.,* pp. 565–567, for a number of relevant references.

[12] Mill, *op. cit.,* p. 386.

[13] *Ibid.,* p. 570.   The detailed regulations of the French government before the French Revolution, a major point of reference of the classical economists, are referred to in this connection.

ened country of the European commonwealth of nations."[14]
History reversed course after these words were written.

An attempt to account for the indirect effects of policy actions, or their interpretation on the basis of systems analysis, is a central theme of the classical approach. The seeming incommensurability of causes and effects in dynamic systems (a major idea in the recent cybernetics literature) is illustrated by Mill: "A limitation of competition, however partial, may have mischievous effects quite disproportioned to the apparent cause."[15]

The classical economists recognized the existence of economic retrogression, interpreting it in terms of the same theory. Thus Mill attributes the economic decline of Spain and Portugal to oppressive exercise of government power. Again, his optimism has not been well borne out:

> *The notion, for example, that a government should choose opinions for the people, and should not suffer any doctrines in politics, morals, law, or religion, but such as it approves, to be printed or publicly professed, may be said to be altogether abandoned as a general thesis. It is now well understood that a regime of this kind is fatal to all prosperity, even of an economical kind: that the human mind, when prevented either by fear of the law or by fear of opinion from exercising its faculties freely on the most important subjects, acquires a general torpidity and imbecility, by which, when they reach a certain point, it is disqualified from making any considerable advance even in the common affairs of life, and which, when greater still, make it gradually lose even its previous attainments. There cannot be a more decisive example than Spain and Portugal, for two centuries after the Reformation. The decline of those countries in national greatness and even in material civilization, while almost all the other nations of Europe were uninterruptedly advancing, has been ascribed to various causes, but there is one which lies at the foundation of all: the Holy Inquisition, and the system of mental slavery of which it is the symbol.*[16]

[14] *Ibid.*, p. 572.

[15] *Ibid.*, p. 547. The unprogressiveness of the English silk industry, so long as foreign fabrics were prohibited, is offered as a specific example.

[16] *Ibid.*, pp. 555–556.

The Enlightenment, Smith's contemporary history and the era to which Mill looked back, was uniquely productive of "experiments" in changing political institutions and their effects on economic advancement. It was the era of the enlightened monarchs, when drastically new policies could be introduced overnight on the accession of a new king or the elevation of a new adviser. The common interpretation of these experiences was that the release of economic activity from the constraints of private and government power, plus such stimulative measures as could be conceived of and carried out by the governments of those times, indeed caused abrupt and rapid economic progress. The period includes many such episodes: Milan under Count Karl Joseph von Firmian, Tuscany under Hapsburg Grand Dukes who applied liberal policies, Austria under Joseph II, Spain under Charles III.

The means to economic progress, it appeared, although politically difficult to achieve, were not difficult to define. Effective government and removal of economic restrictions seemed to do the job. The end of progress, equally well defined and often abrupt, was associated with the decay of government or the retreat from economic openness as the offended political interests, commonly the nobility and the Church, reasserted themselves.[17]

The classical theory represents living standards as depending on economic behavior and population growth. These depend on the set of rules or incentive system to which people respond, which depends on political and institutional factors. Population growth, in conjunction with the limited endowment of nature, will bring the standard of living of the lowest orders of society to the subsistence level unless mechanisms exist to hold down the birth rate. Different societies are not at different stages of a single, one-directional development. Living standards can fall as well as rise. The conditions under which favorable living standards could be indefinitely sustained are defined by nature and are not easily attained.

---

[17] See Will and Ariel Durant, *Rousseau and Revolution* (New York: Simon and Schuster, 1967).

ROSTOW'S STAGES OF ECONOMIC GROWTH

The Rostow theory of economic growth[18] involves five stages: (1) the traditional society, (2) societies in the process of transition or those that have developed the preconditions for take-off, (3) the take-off, (4) the drive to maturity, and (5) the age of high mass consumption. Implicit in the idea of such a system of stages is that the process is normally irreversible. The take-off is a take-off into *sustained* economic growth: "The forces making for economic progress, which yielded limited bursts and enclaves of modern activity, expand and come to dominate the society. Growth becomes its normal condition. Compound interest becomes built, as it were, into its habits and institutional structure."[19]

A basic question is what this characterization pretends to be. Is this a general theory of economic growth or development, a theory that captures its essential features and therefore applies to all cases? Or is it only a picture drawn from a limited set of cases, illustrative of these but having no asserted relevance to other cases? Is it a hypothetical picture designed to *dramatize* certain symptoms of the growth process but not to define causal relations, nor to be a basis for realistic interpretation or policy prescriptions?

The author's position is equivocal. On the one hand, he says of his set of stages: "They constitute, in the end, both a theory about economic growth and a more general, if still highly partial, theory about modern history as a whole."[20] But, on the other hand:

> *I cannot emphasize too strongly at the outset that the stages-of-growth are an arbitrary and limited way of looking at the sequence of modern history: and they are, in no absolute sense, a correct way. They are designed, in fact, to dramatize not merely the uniformi-*

---

[18] W. W. Rostow, *The Stages of Economic Growth: A Non-Communist Manifesto* (Cambridge, England: Cambridge University Press, 1960), and *The Process of Economic Growth,* 2nd ed. (New York: Norton, 1962).

[19] *The Stages of Economic Growth,* p. 7.

[20] *Ibid.,* p. 1.

*ties in the sequence of modernization but also—and equally—the
uniqueness of each nation's experience.*[21]

The anomalous methodological position of Rostow's theory
does not seem to be a matter only of his verbal characterization but truly to reflect the way the author sees his propositions. In short, he seems willing to use them as a basis for
generalization without accepting the burden of establishing
their general validity. After "having accepted and emphasized the limited nature of the enterprise," the author affirms
that "the stages-of-growth are designed to grapple with quite
a substantial range of issues."[22]

EVALUATIVE COMMENTS

In interpreting Rostow's stages-of-growth framework as a
general theory of economic development, we can say that it
defines a set of five models (or submodels of a general model)
asserted to apply sequentially, defining a path of unilinear
evolution. Societies are asserted to fall into two groups, those
that have passed the take-off stage and thereafter continue to
progress indefinitely, and those that have not yet surmounted
this hurdle. The substantive content of the theory lies in its
specification of the set of stages that define the growth path
and determine whether or not, and if so, how rapidly, an economy will move up the path from one stage to the next.

Four problems with this approach can be summarized as
follows. First, the author does not seem to justify the specification of discrete stages. What are called stages may not in-

---

[21] *Ibid.*

[22] *Ibid.*, pp. 1–2. Habakkuk criticizes this methodological position. Rostow had
offered the characterization: "These stages are not merely descriptive. . . .
They have an analytic bone structure, rooted in a dynamic theory of production." Habakkuk observes, "This is a mistaken view. The book contains some
ideas on how one stage proceeds to the next, but they do not cohere into
anything which could reasonably be dignified as a theory of production. The
work is essentially an essay in classification." H. J. Habakkuk, "Review of
Rostow's Stages of Economic Growth," *Economic Journal,* 71 (September
1961), 601. For a critical discussion of this and other "stages" approaches, see
also Stephen Enke, *Economics for Development* (Englewood Cliffs, N.J.: Prentice-Hall, 1963), Chap. 10.

volve structural changes in the economy that have significance for causal analysis, but may merely involve description of what things look like at different points in a continuous process.

Second, the Rostow framework does not seem accurate even as a description of symptoms. The inadequacy of efforts to fit broad historical processes into a set of stages has often been noted.[23] The vagueness of specification of Rostow's stages has been criticized: "The take-off can only be confidently identified retrospectively; one can only tell if growth is going to be self-sustaining if in fact it has been sustained for a long period."[24] Counterexamples to the theory abound—cases of societies seemingly at the "take-off stage" but somehow not taking off,[25] of societies seemingly having achieved self-feeding development, which then proved abortive.[26]

Third, in the Rostow characterization of economic development, special importance is given to the distinction between pre-take-off and post-take-off societies. Thus the approach might have been represented as basically a two-stage or dualistic theory. The most important distinction between these two stages is that once a society advances to the second, it not only remains in it but automatically, it seems, enjoys something like a standard rate of economic progress. This idea receives great emphasis from Rostow's repeated references to

[23] See Gerald M. Meier and Robert E. Baldwin, *Economic Development: Theory, History, Policy* (New York: Wiley, 1957), pp. 143–147; see also Daryll Forde, *Habitat, Economy and Society* (New York: Dutton, 1963), pp. 460–464. A review of earlier versions of the stages approach that illustrates their shortcomings is Bert F. Hoselitz, "Theories of Stages of Economic Growth," in Bert F. Hoselitz (ed.), *Theories of Economic Growth* (New York: Free Press, 1960), pp. 191–238. See also Gunnar Myrdal, *Asian Drama* (New York: Twentieth Century Fund, 1968), pp. 1847–1851.

[24] Habakkuk, *op. cit.,* p. 603.

[25] Lauchlin Currie, *Accelerating Development: The Necessity and the Means* (New York: McGraw-Hill, 1966), Chap. 6.

[26] "The problem in important areas of Latin America . . . is not how to get the process of economic development started, but rather how to regain the momentum of economic advance, which looked so promising many years ago and has since been frustrated. Argentina, Chile, and Uruguay make strange studies in the theory of frustrated development." Andrew Shonfield, *The Attack on World Poverty* (New York: Random House, 1962), p. 13.

the implications of growth occurring like compound interest in the post-take-off society.[27]

The proposition that economic development, once attained, is not only irreversible but inevitable is readily testable, and we are immediately struck by the extent to which such a proposition is inconsistent with experience. Many societies can look back on a phase of rapid progress that proved temporary or abortive. Explaining why economic progress was arrested or reversed in some cases—most cases—seems as important as explaining how it ever began it all.

Finally, Rostow's definition of the conditions required for the focal act of take-off involves some difficulties. Considerable emphasis has been placed on his specification of criteria with reference to the aggregate saving ratio, but his own discussion emphasizes other factors that would make this aggregate meaningless in such a way that one wonders why Rostow offers this criterion, equivocally as he does:

> *The use of aggregative national-income terms evidently reveals little of the process which is occurring. It is nevertheless useful to regard as a necessary but not sufficient condition for the take-off the fact that the proportion of net investment to national income . . . rises from, say, 5 percent to over 10 percent.*[28]

Rostow's detailed characterization of preconditions for take-off seems to involve not aggregative constraints but structural conditions of many types.[29] Whence, then, the seemingly rather offhand assertion regarding the movement from, say, 5 percent to over 10 percent saving rate? No basis seems to

---

[27] *The Stages of Economic Growth*, pp. 2, 7, 10, 36.

[28] *Ibid.*, p. 37. Cameron argues that this asserted condition is inconsistent with the facts: "Research indicates that almost every developed country of today entered a phase of sustained growth with investment ratios substantially below the magic figure of 10 per cent; and that the rise in that ratio followed rather than preceded the adoption of new technologies." Rondo Cameron, "Economic Development: Some Lessons of History for Developing Nations," *American Economic Review Papers and Proceedings*, 57 (May 1967), 313.

[29] *Ibid.*, Chaps. 3, 4.

be created for believing that this is, in truth, a necessary condition for self-feeding economic progress. What is the meaning of the assertion, "It is nevertheless useful to regard as a necessary but not sufficient condition . . ."? If the assertion is not *true*—and the author does not seem to claim that it is true—in what connection is it *useful?*[30]

We end, as we began, on a methodological note. There is a Rostow who does not seem to assume the responsibility involved in a procedure of inductive inference in deriving valid causal or general propositions. His discussion of the past is anecdotal, illustrative, descriptive. On this basis, it would seem unfair to characterize his product as a theory, a framework for discussing economic development in general terms. But there is another Rostow who treats his description as if it were a theory, who applies it to explanation and implies that it has important implications for policy.

The two Rostows taken together cannot be accepted. If this is theory, it must be validated by showing that it has definite meaning and applies in all cases or in some defined set of cases. If it is not theory, it cannot be used validly as a framework for the historical interpretation of policy evaluation.[31]

THE ROSTOW APPROACH AS AN EXAMPLE OF UNILINEAR EVOLUTION

The Rostow theory is a specific version of the model of unilinear evolution. Its basic proposition is that all societies are traveling down the same road. The theory is patterned after

[30] The failure to distinguish true prerequisites from consequences of economic growth, as well as the limitations of a generalized model neglecting differences among actual cases, is discussed by Alexander Gerschenkron, "Reflections on the Concept of 'Prerequisites' of Modern Industrialization," in his *Economic Backwardness in Historical Perspective* (New York: Praeger, 1965), especially pp. 32–33, 41–42.

[31] Myrdal makes the point with some vigor: "When challenged . . . the doctrines tend to withdraw into qualifications and reservations that render them tautological and hence, though then foolproof against criticism, empty of empirical meaning. It is, however, precisely this continual shift from a specious set of propositions to an empty tautology that may strengthen the survival value of this approach. The tautology lends it an air of scientific truth, the speciousness an impression of significance." *Op. cit.,* p. 1855.

the Marxian model of unilinear evolution and is represented as an alternative to the Marxian view of inexorable historical development.[32] The assertion of discontinuous stages of growth is important, as is the specification of the conditions that must be met in order to move from one stage to the next, but the basic content of the theory attaches to its assertion of single-track development.

The theory derives appeal from the certainty of evolution to a predetermined and happy outcome—that is, from its embodiment of the idea of progress. It is an anthropocentric or humanistic interpretation of man's position and prospects.

As interpreted on the basis of a scientific or naturalistic approach, the theory thus presents an erroneous picture of man's relation to nature, the conditions under which his civilization will survive, and the consequences of alternative policies. Although it has been criticized by many economists, the Rostow approach—taken together with related theories derived from it and the vocabulary and set of concepts to which it gave rise—remained the major influence on academic theory and policy discussion relating to economic development in the 1960s. As such, it is an important contribution and a useful point of departure for comparison of naturalistic and anthropocentric approaches to the determination of the standard of living.

THEORIES OF ECONOMIC DUALISM

An approach to the theory of economic development that received great attention in the 1960s involved the concept of a dual economy, a two-sector economy, the behavior of which is importantly affected by interaction among its parts. The dual economy is "an economy with an advanced or modern sector and a backward sector as well."[33] These two sectors are asserted to have definable differences in economic structure that explain differences in their behavior and that contribute

---

[32] *The Stages of Economic Growth,* Chaps. 1, 10.

[33] Dale W. Jorgenson, "The Development of a Dual Economy," *Economic Journal* (June 1961), 310. References to earlier contributions to this approach are given by Jorgenson.

to explaining the behavior of an economy that includes both kinds of sector—the dual economy. In some cases, the concept of "economic and social 'dualism' " is extended to include any important relations of backward national economies or sectors of national economies with advanced or modern economies or "enclaves."[34]

What specification of theory is involved in this conceptualization? The basic assertion is the existence of two classes of situation calling for models of different structure. How are the two domains defined? What are their boundaries? We are given not a defined boundary so much as descriptions of two illustrative cases, similar to Rostow's description of his stages of economic growth. Fei and Ranis spell out at length a description of an idealized case, the backward agrarian economy, the central feature of which "is the overwhelming preponderance of traditional agricultural pursuits."[35] Other characteristics of this idealized agrarian economy are that "the agrarian economy is essentially stagnant, with nature and population pressure vying for supremacy over long periods of recorded history. Moreover, the prognosis for the future is likely to be 'more of the same.' "[36] Any existing nonagricultural pursuits are characterized by modest use of capital. In earlier versions of the Fei-Ranis theory, the agrarian economy was also asserted to have a labor surplus, to be characterized by "widespread disguised unemployment."[37] As a result of criticism from Jorgenson and others, this characteristic of the agrarian economy seems to have been defined more cautiously.[38]

Attributes are assigned to the "agrarian economy" quite

[34] Dale W. Jorgenson, "Testing Alternative Theories of the Development of a Dual Economy," in Irma Adelman and Erik Thorbecke (eds.), *The Theory and Design of Economic Development* (Baltimore: Johns Hopkins Press, 1966), p. 45.

[35] John C. H. Fei and Gustav Ranis, "Agrarianism, Dualism, and Economic Development," in Adelman and Thorbecke, *op. cit.,* p. 4.

[36] *Ibid.*

[37] John C. Fei and Gustav Ranis, "A Theory of Economic Development," *American Economic Review,* 51 (September 1961), 535.

[38] Fei and Ranis, "Agrarianism, Dualism, and Economic Development," *op. cit.,* p. 19.

freely: "But it is almost typical of the agrarian economy that the owning classes do not have a clear vision of the future and do not associate productivity increases with current allocation decisions about the work and leisure of their resources."[39] We also have an accompanying "agrarian thinking," or "agrarianism": "The agrarian view is one of resignation and fatalistic acceptance of the restraining hand of 'natural law' while dualistic writers wish to attain a better future through a fuller understanding of the growth process and the application of relevant growth promotion policies."[40]

This picture, then, is asserted to apply to many historical and present-day societies: "The agrarian pattern should by no means be viewed simply as a historical curiosity; in fact, much of the present-day underdeveloped world, particularly in Africa, finds itself in an essentially agrarian condition."[41]

The other ideal case is the "mature industrial economy." The theory of economic development is to be built on these two concepts, the crux of development being the transformation from agrarianism to dualism to maturity: "A relevant theory of development must be able to analyze not only the workings of the dualistic economy and the conditions for a successful transition from dualism to maturity, but also the workings of the agrarian economy and the transition from agrarian stagnation to rigorous growth under dualism."[42]

This theory is closely related to Rostow's. Fei and Ranis note that Rostow's concept of the take-off was their point of departure.[43] Their more recent work continues to rely on this concept. The "agrarian society" can be associated with Rostow's pre-take-off stages of growth; the "mature industrial society" is comparable with his post-take-off society that is able "to enjoy the blessings and choices opened up by the march of compound interest."[44] The stage of dualism, then, can be

[39] *Ibid.,* p. 17.
[40] *Ibid.,* p. 7.
[41] *Ibid.*
[42] *Ibid.*
[43] Fei and Ranis, "A Theory of Economic Development," *op. cit.,* p. 534.
[44] Rostow, *The Stages of Economic Growth,* p. 6.

interpreted as a different, or more detailed, conceptualization of what is involved in the take-off, the transition to automatic growth. The transition is depicted as involving a historical stage in which a given society encompasses one sector of activities that has taken off and another that has not. In place of Rostow's two basic stages, we have a three-stage picture of the historical growth process. All the difficulties inherent in Rostow's approach attach also to this extension or elaboration of the Rostow theory.

The earlier discussion of the Rostow approach and the treatment of economic dualism in Chapter 10 provide a basis for criticism of dualistic theories of economic development. Well-defined and discrete dual sectors in an economy seem to exist in the mind of the observer, the actual situation involving a complex continuity of economic activities. Insofar as differences in wage rates, yields on capital, and factor productivity in different kinds of activities exist, they seem better explained in terms of specific impediments to factor mobility, including the exercise of power by privileged groups, than by any metaphysical principle of dualism. As a substantive theory of economic change, the view of a dual economy comprised of a pre- and a post-take-off sector (like Neanderthal man and modern man having dinner together) is subject to all the suspicions that apply to other theories of unilinear evolution.

REDUNDANT LABOR IN THE AGRARIAN SECTOR

In the earlier works of Fei and Ranis, the dualistic approach was associated with the asserted existence of redundant labor in the agrarian or backward sector of the economy. These two ideas do not necessarily go together. One could assert the existence of redundant labor in some industries or regions without invoking a generalized dualism, and Jorgenson adopts dualism while rejecting redundant labor. However, dualistic theories in some cases have posited redundant labor in the agrarian sector, the extreme assertion being that removal of labor from this sector to employment in the advanced sector would have no adverse effect on agricultural output.[45]

The condition of redundant labor in the agrarian sector offers an opportunity for economic progress perhaps even more attractive and encouraging than that of Rostow's idea of helping an economy through the take-off by providing it with additional capital. What is needed is only to shift labor from the agrarian sector, where its departure will cause no decline in output, to the advanced sector, where the labor will have high productivity and can receive high wages.

Jorgenson argues persuasively that empirical studies seemingly supporting the existence of a large labor surplus failed to take account of the seasonality of agricultural labor requirements, the peak-load problem. In his interpretation, simply allowing for these factors reduces the estimated labor redundancy to nominal proportions.[46] The observation that agricultural workers do not seem to be working very hard or effectively does not imply that some workers could be removed without a loss of output unless it can be shown that such removal would cause the remaining workers to work harder or with more efficiency—and the peak-load constraint is still relevant.

The concept of "disguised unemployment" seems to have involved implicit theorizing that was widely accepted without examination. The implication was that the reason why workers did not work harder or more effectively is that there was only a fixed amount of work to be done, which they had to share among themselves. This idea is a "lump-of-labor" approach, viewed from the supply side. Acceptance of this persuasive concept, therefore, implies that if some workers are

[45] Fei and Ranis find that the agrarian sector is characterized by "workers whose contribution to output may have been zero or negligible." "A Theory of Economic Development," *op. cit.,* pp. 533–534. The idea is taken from the earlier influential statement of W. Arthur Lewis in "Economic Development with Unlimited Supplies of Labour," *The Manchester School,* 22 (May 1954), 139–192; see also, W. Arthur Lewis, "Unlimited Labour: Further Notes," *The Manchester School,* 26 (January 1958), 1–32.

[46] Dale W. Jorgenson, "Testing Alternative Theories of the Development of a Dual Economy," in Adelman and Thorbecke, *op. cit.,* pp. 48–59.

removed, the others will thereby be freed from the constraints that prevented them from working more effectively, and the same amount of labor will be performed by a smaller number of people.[47]

But unenergetic and ineffectual labor seems sufficiently prevalent to require an explanation other than that there is absolutely nothing further to be done—as in societies where the men characteristically do very little work at all, the work that is done being imposed on the women. If the constraint on the intensity and effectiveness of labor is anything other than the nothing-to-do constraint, however, "disguised unemployment" is a misleading concept. Removal of workers will not cause the remaining laborers to work harder. Indeed, by permitting the remaining workers to maintain an accustomed standard of living with less work, such removal may cause a reduction in labor per worker. Output per worker depends not only on the intensity of labor but also on factors affecting efficiency of production. The discussion of efficiency change in earlier chapters disclosed no basis for believing that removal of some workers would increase the efficiency of production sufficiently to prevent a decline in total output.

To shift labor from agriculture while bringing about an increase in per capita agricultural output involves several sets of problems: (1) modifying the incentive system applying to agriculture in order to motivate increases in efficiency, (2) providing opportunities in other pursuits by creating additional money demand for output, and (3) preventing an increase in demand from being nullified by increases in wage rates and profit margins of a protected ingroup. Basic issues in three major policy areas are involved: incentive systems and economic efficiency, control of total demand, and the area of wage-price push and exercise of economic power. A defect of the redundant-labor approach is that it does not sufficiently emphasize the dependence of a favorable outcome on policy in these three areas.

---

[47] Lewis, "Economic Development with Unlimited Supplies of Labour," *op. cit.*, pp. 215–216. See also the criticisms of Myrdal, *op. cit.*, pp. 2041–2061.

INTERPRETATIONS OF ECONOMIC DUALISM

In the theory of economic development, economic dualism is a stage in the development process, a zone on the track of economic progress as this progress is represented within the framework of unilinear evolution. This theory offers a variant or an elaboration of Rostow's interpretation of the take-off.

Application of the mainstream of economic theory, or of approaches not utilizing the framework of unilinear evolution, presents a different picture. Dualism is not a clear-cut phenomenon but rather represents an oversimplification of situations in which different sets of rules apply to different areas, industries, or groups of workers. The existence of high-wage and low-interest-rate sectors is explained by restraints on the movement of workers and capital, reflecting a combination of government policies and exercise of power by private groups that is permitted or supported by government. It is not a distinctive stage in single-track economic development, but is rather the outcome of a particular set of politically defined rules of the economic game, a situation that exists to some degree in many economies.

THE CRITICAL-MINIMUM-EFFORT THESIS

The critical-minimum-effort thesis as developed by Leibenstein represents economic development as requiring a discontinuous stimulant to the economy.[48] If the disturbing stimulant is sufficiently great, economic development will occur, and will continue thereafter without limit. The emphasis is not on the structure of the economy or the political system but on the amount of the initial stimulating factor.

This thesis provides the ideal rationalization for emphasis on foreign aid as the key to economic development. Foreign aid can provide the required external stimulus to real income in the recipient nation. Since the lack of economic progress does not reflect deficiencies of a structural nature but only the historical absence of a sufficiently great external stimulus,

---

[48] Harvey Leibenstein, *Economic Backwardness and Economic Growth* (New York: Science Editions, 1963), Chap. 8.

foreign aid can meet the need. If foreign aid has been granted but has not worked, the diagnosis is simply that the amount was not large enough. It was below the critical minimum effort, which is definable only *ex post*. The remedy, therefore, is more foreign aid.

THE THESIS

The basic thesis is that "in order to achieve sustained secular growth, in the general case, it is necessary that the initial stimulant or stimulants to development be of a certain critical minimum size."[49] Involved are the ideas that (1) an external stimulant is required, (2) the crucial factor is the size of this stimulant rather than the structure of the economic and political system, and (3) once thus begun, the process can be expected to lead to "endless expansion."[50]

This theory belongs to the unilinear-evolution class; it explains differences in performance among societies by assigning them to a nongrowth or a growth evolutionary track, which depends on the existence or nonexistence of the take-off. Essentially, this theory is a variant of the Rostow approach, differing in its specification of the causes of the take-off.

The condition of the take-off, in this theory, is that a stimulant or shock must raise per capita income above the equilibrium level sufficiently to overcome income-depressing factors that otherwise would maintain income at a low equilibrium level or return it to that level after a lag. This theory is represented as an explication of the idea of a stable, vicious circle of poverty. Examples of income-depressing factors to be overcome by a quantitatively sufficient rise of income per capita are (1) induced increase in consumption that prevents or limits an induced rise in saving and investment, (2) induced increase in population that prevents or limits lasting growth in income per capita, and (3) induced soil depletion to the same effect.[51] However, these income-depressing factors are

[49] *Ibid.*, p. 94.
[50] *Ibid.*, p. 99.
[51] *Ibid.*, p. 97.

assumed to be subject to some maximum limit, such as the "biologically determined maximum rate of population growth between 3 and 4 per cent. . . . Thus, persistent capital accumulation above a certain minimum rate would permit development."[52] But also interpreted as determinants of the critical minimum effort are internal and external economies of scale and such noneconomic factors as unfavorable attitudes.[53] In any case, the key to achieving a take-off is the quantitative size of the stimulant, which must be large enough to raise per capita income to a critical minimum level.[54]

CRITICAL COMMENTS

Leibenstein's theory, like that of Rostow and others of the unilinear-evolution class, is inconsistent with the facts in depicting performance apart from the issue of take-off as being basically standardized, on a one-track line. We have referred to the cases of abortive and arrested economic development, of societies seemingly at the take-off stage but not advancing, as well as to the view that the discontinuity of the take-off exists largely in the eye of the beholder and can be detected only retrospectively.

Leibenstein represents all economies as being either on the standard growth track or on the standard stagnation track, depending on whether or not they happen to have been affected by a sufficiently large stimulant. In support of this approach, he states that "we know, generally speaking, that the broad characteristics of backward economies today are not different from what they were in advanced economies in a former period,"[55] and that "since human beings are basically similar, we should expect that the same theory should explain the existence of both the advanced and the underdeveloped countries."[56] Yet, speaking a bit less *generally*, even though "human beings are basically similar," eighteenth-century Europe differed radically from twentieth-century Asia in its

[52] *Ibid.,* p. 98.
[53] *Ibid.,* pp. 106–110.
[54] *Ibid.,* p. 254.
[55] *Ibid.,* p. 102.
[56] *Ibid.,* p. 104.

population-limitation system[57] and in the political framework of economic activity, characteristics that presumably are relevant. To neglect these differences in the governing systems, and to attribute the difference in performance to a purely hypothetical and unexplained difference in exogenous disturbances, does not seem satisfactory.

Leibenstein ridicules theories that explain differential economic progress by "institutional or extraeconomic factors": "The burden of such arguments usually appears to be the visualization of a devil of some sort whose removal would permit the natural progress inherent in the economy."[58] Yet later, when not defending the critical-minimum-effort thesis, he observes that noneconomic factors "may be very important,"[59] and he develops a conceptualization of the economic system as either a zero-sum or positive-sum game. Here he represents this consideration as crucially relevant and dependent on political and other noneconomic factors.[60]

In support of the critical-minimum-effort thesis, he argues that the extraeconomic factors must be shown to affect per capita output and that "once this is admitted we are led back to a consideration of the relationships between the economic variables, which, in turn, leads us to the familiar questions of equilibrium, stability, and the possibilities for change that we have already considered."[61]

This argument does not seem acceptable. The distinctive characteristic of Leibenstein's interpretation of *stability* is

[57] Thus Habakkuk argues that, in the case of European economic development, particular factors implied the absence of induced population growth such as would support the need for a discontinuous take-off, so that "we cannot deduce from the behavior of population the universal necessity for a take-off." H. J. Habakkuk, "Historical Experience of Economic Development," in E. A. G. Robinson (ed.), *Problems in Economic Development* (London: Macmillan, 1965), p. 114. See also p. 127.

[58] Leibenstein, *op. cit.,* p. 103.

[59] *Ibid.,* p. 109.

[60] *Ibid.,* Chap. 9. In a later article, Leibenstein also emphasizes the importance of differences in efficiency reflecting differences in the context in which economic decisions are made as explaining differences in performance among national economies. See his "Allocative Efficiency Vs. 'X-Efficiency,' " *American Economic Review,* 61 (June 1966), 392–415.

[61] *Ibid.,* p. 103.

that it depends on a single factor, real income per capita. But if what is preventing self-feeding improvement in economic efficiency is an inappropriate set of politically determined rules of the economic game, then correction of the situation requires political action, not exogenous increase in income per capita. To admit this possibility quite destroys the critical-minimum-effort thesis. For then economic progress can begin through revisions of the political framework with no economic discontinuity and no abrupt increase in income per capita.

One crucial respect in which actual societies violate the standardization postulate of the theories of unilinear evolution is with respect to their population-limitation systems. Leibenstein emphasizes the importance of desired family size as a determinant of the birth rate,[62] but then goes on to imply that the factors governing the birth rate are standard among societies at the same stage of development, and even that they cannot be affected except by altering per capita income.[63] His population theory is that an increase in income automatically reduces the birth rate,[64] seemingly according to a behavioral function that is standard among all societies. This is unilinear evolution with a vengeance.

The critical-minimum-effort thesis is stated at an aggregative level. But if economic improvements begin in certain industries and localities, the increases in income of people involved in this process, as well as their motivation and ability to finance additional innovation, would appear to be in no way indicated by data on national aggregates. As Habakkuk sees it, economic growth in Great Britain "took the form of the gradual linking together of a smaller number of points of growth which were initially widely dispersed—dynamic regions surrounded by wide areas which remained for a long time poor and stagnant."[65]

[62] *Ibid.,* p. 159.

[63] *Ibid.,* p. 151.

[64] *Ibid.,* pp. 167 ff.

[65] Habakkuk, *op. cit.,* p. 115. The author also observes (p. 130): "My impression is that, in these early stages the influences which may be broadly defined as social were of greater importance than the strictly economic factors."

The critical-minimum-effort thesis is subject to all the objections attaching to theories that treat economic development within the framework of unilinear evolution. This theory is peculiarly suited to justifying foreign aid, as it specifically defines an independent increase in aggregate income as what is required to get a nation past the take-off. The theory is peculiarly resistant to refutation by experience because the amount of the critical minimum effort for any particular nation can be stated only in retrospect, and failure to achieve the take-off by foreign aid can always be interpreted as indicating only that the amount of aid was not large enough.

CAPITAL AS THE KEY TO ECONOMIC DEVELOPMENT

As Kindleberger has stated, "In the view of many economists, capital occupies the central position in the theory of economic development . . . capital is regarded as not only central to the process of development but also as strategic."[66] According to some interpretations, a shortage of capital is the marginally binding constraint on economic development, and thus external provision of capital will accelerate economic development or move a society past the take-off.

The crucial question is whether capital is the decisive determinant of the rate of growth of output or whether it is rather an intervening variable, the ultimate cause being a more basic factor. The approach taken in this book represents capital formation as an effect of the existence of conditions favoring increase in economic efficiency, rather than as a prime cause of economic efficiency. As the point is made by Friedman, "The availability of capital while an important problem is a subsidiary one—if other conditions for economic development are ripe, capital will be readily available; if they are not, capital made available is very likely to be wasted."[67]

[66] Charles P. Kindleberger, *Economic Development*, 2nd ed. (New York: McGraw-Hill, 1965), p. 83.
[67] Milton Friedman, "Foreign Economic Aid: Means and Objectives," *Yale Review* (Summer 1958); reprinted in Gustav Ranis (ed.), *The United States and the Developing Economies* (New York: Norton, 1964), p. 30. The classical theory of Adam Smith depicted capital formation as a factor immediately

In the following paragraphs we briefly review three lines of thought commonly used to support emphasis on capital as the key to economic development.

CAPITAL AND THE VICIOUS CYCLE OF POVERTY

One approach emphasizing the crucial role of capital in economic development depicts the impediment to take-off as a vicious cycle of poverty. People are too poor to save. Therefore, they cannot invest. Therefore, they cannot adopt the new production methods that are more efficient and that embody the results of advances in knowledge. Therefore, they cannot escape from their condition of poverty. The key to economic progress, then, is investment, which breaks this vicious circle. Where this circle of poverty exists, the resources to provide the investment needed to break out of it must come from outside.

Critics have pointed out that these ideas do not fit the facts in several respects. Even very poor societies may produce substantial volumes of savings. In such societies the income distribution often is unequal, so that poverty coexists with high incomes. These societies thus have the capacity to save, and in some cases they have a substantial saving rate. Even where current savings are not large, holdings of wealth exist that could be invested in productive capital.

A distinctive feature of such societies, however, is that wealth is invested not in factories or productive capital but in other things. So far as there is a problem of wealth, it is not one of absence of wealth so much as failure to use wealth productively. This fact seems largely explainable in terms of the prevailing incentive system. A striking illustration of the significance of this point are those situations in which the inflow of capital from foreign aid is offset to a substantial extent by the outflow of local capital.

Moreover, people who are poor in some cases do save and

---

determining economic growth, but represented both economic growth and capital formation as depending on the rules of the economic game. See Irma Adelman, *Theories of Economic Growth and Development* (Palo Alto, Calif.: Stanford University Press, 1961), p. 41.

hold wealth in substantial aggregate volume. Again, what is distinctive about the society in which efficiency does not increase is that the wealth is not held in forms that make it available for productive investment.[68]

The fact that wealth is not more widely invested in business and in the financing of productive innovation in low-income societies is not, of course, an accident. It arises from the complex network of factors that prevents a self-feeding process of productive innovation and economic development from occurring. In the existing environment, the holding of wealth in nonbusiness forms may not be quaint or archaic but rather an intelligent adaptation to the existing incentive system. Where this situation exists, or is believed by wealth owners to exist, the presumption is that if income is increased by external injection of capital, the additional savings generated will not flow mainly into the financing of business but will flow into the same channels as other savings.

In this view, the existence of poverty does not in itself preclude such saving and investment as is necessary to institute a self-feeding process of economic development. Critics of the vicious-circle interpretation have pointed out that because all societies had low incomes at some point, this interpretation rather overexplains the problem. The crux of the matter, it seems, is the environment, the system, the framework within which the decisions of people, including their savings and investment decisions, are made.[69]

[68] Hirschman emphasizes as the primary factor holding back development in many societies not the shortage of resources potentially available for investment but a set of structural factors limiting the society's "ability to invest" effectively. In contrast to an initial deficiency of capital, these structural factors may continue to exist and result in abortive development if external capital is provided. Albert O. Hirschman, *The Strategy of Economic Development* (New Haven, Conn.: Yale University Press, 1958), pp. 35–36, 44–45.

[69] This view is consistent with Cameron's interpretation that the rise in the investment ratio "is a consequence rather than a cause of economic growth," and that "the key development in getting the growth process under way was a more intensive and efficient use of both the existing stock of capital and of normal increments to that stock." Cameron, *op. cit.,* p. 314.

CAPITAL AS AN INDEX IN THEORIES OF
UNILINEAR EVOLUTION

As noted earlier, Rostow takes the aggregative savings rate as an index of a society's readiness for the take-off into sustained growth. Such use of the savings ratio as an index for a set of development-determining factors is acceptable in terms of a theory of unilinear evolution. If, indeed, the development process is a standardized one, if all societies go down the same track, then the process of finding an index is not a difficult one. But if societies are not on the same track (for example, if the institutions governing the form in which wealth is held differ among the societies in question), then the savings rate does not have the same meaning in different societies. Consequently, it cannot be used as a one-dimensional index of the set of factors determining development.

The objection to Rostow's emphasis on the savings rate, therefore, is simply one aspect of the objection to his framework of unilinear evolution. There are subsidiary objections. If the developmental discontinuity of the take-off is not accepted as meaningful, then the assertion of a corresponding critical value of the savings rate is also not meaningful. Finally, it is not obvious that such a constraint can be stated meaningfully in terms of a national aggregate. If improvement in efficiency occurs in certain producing units, industries, or regions, it is not clear that an aggregate savings rate defines any meaningful constraint on the process.

The localistic and potentially self-financing nature of improvement in efficiency is emphasized by Zimmerman, who illustrates the point with reference to English and Japanese economic progress. He notes that improvement in efficiency does not necessarily require additional capital: "This is possible as a result of better organization of production, management (entrepreneurship) can substitute for capital. If the energies and ingenuity of the people are mobilized, more can be produced with the given resources." This fact is

of paramount importance for the theory of economic development, because it demonstrates that the individual plant as well as a country does not need to have a high average rate of savings and investment in order to start *economic development. The combination of managerial ability and a high* marginal *propensity to save is, even in a very low-income country, a sufficient condition to start economic progress.*[70]

CAPITAL AND THE PRODUCTION FUNCTION

If a conventional production function accurately represents the constraints on output, then, given full employment of labor, only through external provision of capital can there be an increase in output, which might then be interpreted as leading to further increases in output by increasing saving and investment. Thus conceptualization of the determination of output in terms of a production function can lead to the conclusion that only through externally provided capital can an economy rapidly get to the take-off—or at least that such provision of capital assuredly will result in an increase in output. But interpreting the set of cases in question in terms of *a* production function is subject to criticism. If efficiency in utilizing resources is not standardized but depends on political and institutional factors, the important question is which production function from a large set of potentially relevant ones is to prevail. The key to economic improvement then is to make the institutional changes required to bring into play a production function involving greater efficiency, rather than providing more capital within a framework that would lead to inefficient use of resources.

Theories emphasizing capital as the key to economic development have influenced governmental policies. "Under the influence of outmoded economic theories, policy-makers in many developing nations have developed a naïve faith that a rise in the investment ratio is a necessary if not a sufficient condition for economic development." As Cameron puts it: "The emphasis in development planning should shift, I suggest, from attempts to raise the investment ratio at whatever cost, to attempts to ensure a more rational, efficient, and intensive use of existing capital."[71]

[70] L. J. Zimmerman, *Poor Lands, Rich Lands: The Widening Gap* (New York: Random House, 1965), pp. 104, 105. The author notes that "in the eighteenth century Western countries were certainly not richer than the rest of the world" and "not much richer at that time than the poor countries are today." See also pp. 105–108.

[71] Cameron, *op. cit.,* p. 316. See also Myrdal, *op. cit.,* pp. 1968–2004.

SOCIOLOGICAL AND PSYCHOLOGICAL
THEORIES OF ECONOMIC DEVELOPMENT

At an opposite pole, in one sense, from theories depending on fixed relations among aggregative economic variables are recent contributions that emphasize the individual personality as the central factor explaining the rate of economic growth.[72] As McClelland states his theme, "The hypothesis that gave rise to the present study is that achievement motivation is in part responsible for economic growth."[73] He adds that developing his thesis "involves an explanation of how the modern psychologist looks at human motivation and, more particularly, of how he measures it."[74] Hagen's goal is more ambitious:

The following chapters then evolve, piece by piece, a fully defined model of society, a model which stresses the chain of causation from social structure through parental behavior to childhood environment and then from childhood environment through personality to social change. The model is applied first to traditional society and then to the process of transition from a traditional state to economic growth.[75]

He also observes, "the conclusion is drawn that economic theory has rather little to offer toward an explanation of economic growth, and that broader social and psychological considerations are pertinent."[76]

ALTERNATIVE PSYCHOLOGICAL THEORIES

Hagen's psychological interpretation of economic development involves an application of a psychoanalytic theory of

---

[72] David C. McClelland, *The Achieving Society* (Princeton, N.J.: Van Nostrand, 1961); Everett E. Hagen, *On the Theory of Social Change* (Homewood, Ill.: Dorsey Press, 1962).

[73] McClelland, *op. cit.*, p. 36.

[74] *Ibid.*

[75] Hagen, *op. cit.*, pp. 8–9.

[76] *Ibid.*, p. 8.

personality, which depicts personality as shaped by the experiences of early childhood and as resistant to change thereafter. On the basis of this theory, it may be entirely rational, although somewhat at odds with economists' usual approach, to argue that the road to economic development is through such things as toilet training. His contribution is constructive in that it broadens the range of discussion of the subject.

Interpretation of economic behavior, however, is highly sensitive to the particular psychological theory applied. The psychoanalytic approach is extreme in representing behavior as shaped by early experiences and limited in its response to later experiences. The mainstream of psychological thought represents the individual as a more open system, subject to learning and behavior modification as an adult. Indeed, a theory in which individuals lose their adaptive capacity at an early age is difficult to reconcile with natural selection and cultural control of individual behavior, which require a continued capacity to adapt to adult life to fit changing societal roles.

Psychological theories representing individual behavior as responsive to the cues, payoffs, or reinforcement of actions defined by man's environment seem consistent with orthodox economic theory and with the approach taken in this book. People respond to the payoffs of the game into which they are thrown. The way to bring about behavior leading to favorable living standards is to establish rules of the game that provide an inducement to the required behavior. What is distinctive about Hagen's approach is his application of a particular psychological theory. Both the current weight of psychological opinion and the logic of natural selection seem at present to argue for using rather the approach taken here.[77]

ACHIEVEMENT NEEDS: CAUSE OR EFFECT?

Within the framework of this study, we should not deny the relevance of achievement needs and related attitudes and so-

---

[77] See Albert Bandura, *Principles of Behavior Modification* (New York: Holt, Rinehart and Winston, 1970).

cial values to the determination of living standards.[78] The question is the extent to which these attitudes emerge from experience in the society, and thus from the rules that determine the extent to which "achievement" does or does not pay off. Achievement need and other social values and attitudes perhaps should not be viewed as ultimate explanations of differences in societal improvement in efficiency, for the differences in attitudes themselves must be explained. Such societal norms appear to reflect the lessons of past experience and thus reflect the set of societal rules that determine the rewards and punishments attaching to various kinds of actions.

Another way to arrive at this conclusion is to question the conventional definition of "achievement." The differences among societies may be not so much in the degree to which achievement is sought as in what is perceived as achievement. That is, achievement may be defined functionally as "what pays off in this society." If hard work and cleverness pay off in one society, while in another society the rewards are to obedience and political orthodoxy, the "achievers" who rise to the top will behave differently in the two cases. Therefore, perhaps the basic point is that in some societies what is regarded as an achievement is not the kind of behavior that leads to improvements in efficiency, or what is conventionally labeled "achievement" in the West.

This approach argues for a broadening of McClelland's approach in three respects:

1. If "achievement" is to mean "contributing to improvement in societal efficiency," it must be defined with reference to a theory of efficiency change incorporating the control aspects and political aspects of this subject. An emphasis on individual achievement with inadequate controls against negative-sum or socially destructive interaction was the curse of ancient Athens and many subsequent societies.

2. Improvement in societal economic efficiency does not re-

<hr />

[78] For a discussion of ambiguities in the concept of achievement motivation and the state of the evidence, see Roger Brown, *Social Psychology* (New York: Free Press, 1965), pp. 460–474.

quire a universal willingness to innovate but only the existence of some innovators, or achievers, plus a situation in
which others are not motivated to or lack the power to prevent innovation or to deprive the innovators of their rewards. This condition is largely political.

3. Societal attitudes are continually revised in response to
experience, and thus the key to producing attitudes favorable to efficiency and innovation is to introduce laws and a
power system within which these qualities are rewarded.
A direct attempt to change the attitudes of certain individuals in a society in which the new attitudes will lead to behavior that is unrewarded or punished is not promising.

PERSONALITY DIFFERENCES AND THE POLITICAL FACTOR

What is required for economic improvement is only that
some persons be moved to innovate, with the mass of people
learning from demonstration effects and following along at
some reasonable interval behind. To follow along behind, of
course, no longer involves innovation nor outstanding
achievement. The new ways become the norm.

The innovators in a number of actual cases have been members of an alien culture, or of a societal subgroup that developed its own social system.[79] Rapid efficiency change appears
to require conditions much less restrictive than a universal

---

[79] An interesting case is the special role of former serfs and their sons as entrepreneurs in a Russia where "the dominant system of values . . . remained
determined by the traditional agrarian pattern" and was such that "throughout most of the nineteenth century a grave opprobrium attached to entre-
preneurial activities in Russia." Alexander Gerschenkron, "Social Attitudes,
Entrepreneurship, and Economic Development," in his *Economic Backwardness in Historical Perspective* (New York: Praeger, 1965), pp. 59–60. In this
case, the hostile general culture "did not prevent the brilliant period of rapid
industrialization in the 1890's, when the annual rate of industrial growth was
in the vicinity of 9 percent" (p. 62).

Gerschenkron's conclusion is quite consistent with the approach taken here:
"Perhaps the generalization may be ventured that adverse social attitudes
toward entrepreneurs do not significantly affect the processes of industrialization unless they are allowed to become crystallized in governmental action"
(p. 71). He notes that such government intervention may be more common
in present-day countries than it was in prerevolutionary Russia.

enthusiasm for innovation or achievement. The crucial factor seems to be that such innovation should not be prevented by others or deprived of its rewards. As we have noted, this factor depends basically on the political system.

Thus it may be unrealistic and misleading to argue that the means to economic development is an attempt to adjust the psychology of the individuals making up the society. The performance of any society can be revolutionized without changing the psychology of individuals. It requires only a recasting of roles, a revision of the rules within which power is gained and exercised. The drastic change in the behavior of the German nation from the 1920s to the 1930s presumably did not reflect a reconstruction of the psychology of individual Germans so much as a shifting of roles—a new group began running the show. It may be reasonable to believe that in every society of substantial size there exists a " 'reserve army' of entrepreneurs that are as achievement-motivated as any Puritan ever was."[80] Following this line of thought the occurrence of innovation in some societies but not others can be explained by Mill's words: "What is fatal to it, is the belief that it will not be suffered to produce its fruits."

CONCLUSIONS

The Rostow theory of economic development is an application of the framework of unilinear evolution and is basically anthropocentric. The dualistic and the critical-minimum-effort theories are variants of the Rostow approach that share its weaknesses. The classical theory of a century and more ago approached determination of living standards in a naturalistic way, emphasizing the dependence of innovation and economic efficiency on the institutional and political factors that define the incentive system applying to economic activity. This theory also dealt with the crucial role of population change and its responsiveness to institutional and political

---

[80] Albert O. Hirschman, *op. cit.*, p. 4. Hirschman offers additional examples and supports the view that the individual qualities required for economic development exist in latent form in all societies.

factors. The constraints imposed on man by the limited endowments of nature were taken into account in the theory; it was not a theory of predetermined human progress.

"Economic development" in the sense of single-track human progress was not influential in earlier economic theory. It was created by the concepts and the viewpoints of the 1950s and 1960s. Detailed consideration of the theories of economic development discloses no persuasive scientific support for such theories. Their prevalence seems to be explained, rather, by the appeal of their optimistic view of man's position and prospects and by their consistency with the political ideas of the times.

CHAPTER 15 / Beyond Economic Development

The concept of "economic development" derives from an optimistic view of man's position and prospects. For economic development clearly is advancement, modernization, the overcoming of backwardness; it is progress. What is wrong is only that some nations have been short-changed in economic development. They are underdeveloped. But economic development is not only desirable but universally attainable.

Indeed, each nation has a *right* to receive its free dividend of progress. The task of speeding the development of underdeveloped countries and narrowing the gap between them and the more fortunate nations is simplified by the fact that economic development involves movement down a single path of progress. The underdeveloped nations differ only in that they are behind schedule. Whatever pushes them ahead along the path confers on them the blessings of progress. Happily, after a certain point, after the take-off into sustained growth, future progress is automatic. Then the fate of man and his civilization, one may infer, is secure.

ECONOMIC DEVELOPMENT AS PROGRESS:
SOME DIFFICULTIES

Although it has dominated thought and policy in the past decade, this view involves some difficulties. To begin with, we note that the posited law of irreversible progress seems not to have applied to earlier societies. On the contrary, the usual pattern has been one of rise and fall. Economic development was followed by economic deterioration. Indeed, this whole conception of human societies in terms of "economic development" is a creation of the past two decades. "Economic development" in the modern sense did not exist in the earlier economic literature. It came into being when the concept was created, mainly during the 1950s.

The recent origin of the idea of economic development might strengthen our belief in it if the idea had stemmed from new scientific knowledge. Such, however, is not the case. On the contrary, the source of Rostow's important formulation of this approach is the Marxian version of unilinear evolution. The theory of economic development appears to be only another version of a basic theme of Judeo-Christian belief, the idea that the universe was built to serve man, as a means to his ultimate exaltation. Thus the theory of economic development presents an anthropocentric picture of the universe similar to those of earlier prophets of progress like Condorcet, Godwin, and—in his own way—Marx. Rather than stemming from recent scientific discoveries, the theory of economic development rests on foundations that are basically antiscientific.

As natural scientists in the 1960s became aware of the accelerating destruction of the environment, they warned that this "economic development" could not be extrapolated into the future. The finite space and matter of the earth could not accommodate continued growth of human population, continued exploitation of natural resources, and accelerating pollution and destruction of ecosystems. Such recognition of the finite and fragile endowment of nature—a theme emphasized by the classical economists and Malthus—seems to undercut the idea of economic development, for this idea implies that "progress" such as has occurred in the West in the past two centuries can be indefinitely extrapolated into the future and extended to all nations and all areas of the world. If this kind of progress is destroying the earth and is an evolutionary dead end, the position and prospects of man are radically different from the picture depicted by the theory of economic development.

It might be argued that the very process of development holds the answers to these problems, that shortly we shall turn a corner and find the problems of population growth and environmental destruction being automatically solved as a part of the process of progress. Unfortunately, the theory of economic development provides no identification of the mechanisms that would bring this progress about. We note again that in past experience with economic development, societies never turned this corner. Overpopulation and environmental destruction seem to have figured in the decline of past civilizations.

In a scientific view of man's position and prospects, the fall of existing civilization not only is possible but could be close at hand. Basic elements in the deterioration of societies presumably would be the adverse effects of overpopulation and crowding, the reduction in the standard of living and the quality of life from crowding and environmental destruction, and the loss of societal coherency and effectiveness because of group conflicts, dissension, and disorder. In some societies, such adverse developments in recent years have raised the possibility that within a matter of decades, decay and decline could be under way. Indeed, within the naturalistic interpretation this is the expected outcome unless some major changes occur in the institutions and performance of national societies.

ECONOMIC DEVELOPMENT AS A DELUSION

The influence of the theory of economic development is indicated by the prevalence of its concepts—economic development, less-developed nations, developing nations—and by the active effort that is required to think about the position and prospects of present-day civilization without these concepts.

If these concepts do not correspond to reality, they give rise to a misinterpretation so coherent and pervasive as to effect a great delusion.

That an era should be dominated by such a delusion would be nothing new. History is full of examples: the early Christians awaiting the Second Coming and the millennium, the Marxist view of a world on the verge of a utopia achieved by nationalizing capital goods, the "new era" of the 1920s, the Third Reich as it was seen by its proponents. The question raised is whether "economic development" in fifty years—or even in ten—will not join the list of great delusions that moved an era or a generation and then were lost, undermined by reality. Looking backward, economic development may seem a short-lived delusion, born in the optimism of the 1950s, reaching a symbolic high-water mark in the United Nations declaration (made on the suggestion of President Kennedy) of the 1960s as "the decade of development," and beginning to die by the late 1960s.

THE SCIENTIFIC VIEW OF MAN'S POSITION AND PROSPECTS

The scientific or naturalistic theory of living standards and of man's relation to nature depicts as sheer presumption the story of economic development, of inexorable progress down a single path toward human exaltation. The scientific model is not one of unilinear evolution but of open evolution, of natural selection to an outcome that is neither predetermined nor influenced by human pretensions. In the scientific view of the universe, man is not the reason for the game, but only a player in it. His fate, like that of other forms of life, depends on his performance, his ability to adapt to conditions defined by the external world.

Natural selection is wondrously efficient in achieving adaptation and in building complex systems of living things. It does this, however, not by avoiding failures, but by extinguishing those who fail. It is not a system of perfect planning, but a system of trial and error. The logic of natural selection thus in no way precludes the possibility that existing civilization should fall. What natural selection ensures is that this civilization will fail unless it somehow begins to meet survival criteria defined by the laws of matter of the universe. To meet these criteria would require of human societies an abrupt change—a performance that was not accomplished by earlier advanced civilizations and that does not seem possible under existing institutions and political systems. Basic conditions for the survival of civilization and maintenance of living standards appear to be rigorous population control and environmental preservation and the maintenance of societal rules leading to constructive rather than destructive interaction among individuals and groups. The crux of the matter, for man as for other animals, is societal control over individuals, to produce individual behavior that will produce group performance that will meet nature's criteria for survival.

The ancient role of the lawgiver could be fulfilled in our time, for we have now deciphered the code; we have defined the great game of natural selection in which man plays a part and by which his fate will be determined. The knowledge now exists to permit an enlightened group of nations to put into play a strategy that might continue to raise living standards and the quality of life. We can prescribe what system of games within games will create incentive systems, or principles of selection, that might bring forth behavior of individuals, groups, and nations that will control population, preserve the environment, and build mutually rewarding interchange and economic efficiency—thus staving off defeat in the big game.

Such success would show for now that civilized man is, after all, a viable evolutionary experiment. It seemed that civilized man's susceptibility to anthropocentric delusions—his insistence upon shaping his image of the universe to fit his emotionally pleasing dramas—would lead him to self-destruction. But at the last moment he put aside his beguiling myths, looked honestly at himself and his universe, reasoned subtly and profoundly, and disciplined himself to make a future for his children. This is one way the story could go.

Index

A NOTE ON THE TYPE

The text of this book was set in Videocomp. The type face is Primer, originally designed by Rudolph Ruzicka for Linotype, who was earlier responsible for the design of Fairfield and Fairfield Medium, Linotype faces whose virtues have for some time now been accorded wide recognition.

The complete range of sizes of Primer was first made available in 1954, although the pilot size of 12 point was ready as early as 1951. The design of the face makes general reference to Linotype Century (long a serviceable type, totally lacking in manner or frills of any kind) but brilliantly corrects the characterless quality of that face.

DESIGN *by J. M. Wall*

Cover photo by George W. Gardner
Cover design by Hermann Strohbach